R

Welcome!

Building your own website is cheap and easy these days. If you're simply planning to set up a blog, you won't have to pay a penny, since sites such as WordPress (see Chapter 6) are free to use. You'll even get a unique website name, such as davidludlow.wordpress.com.

If you have your heart set on a more professional-looking web address, such as www.davidludlow.com, you'll be pleased to hear that it won't break the bank. Domain names cost from as little as £3 per year; find out how to buy one on page 14.

WordPress and other websites such as Jimdo (see page 18) are great for getting your site online in just a few minutes, but they may be limiting if you have grander ambitions. Whether you run a club and want a place for members to interact or you have a small business and need to set up an online shop to boost sales, you'll find guides on how to build the perfect site inside this book.

If you want complete control over the way your site looks and works, you'll find step-by-step guides to the latest web technologies, such as HTML5 and CSS. You'll also learn how to add dynamic features such as interactive Google maps, videos and photo galleries.

Whatever your level of experience, this book will teach you how to build a website the right way.

David Ludlow, Editor
david_ludlow@dennis.co.uk

Contents

CHAPTER 1
Getting started

Find out about web hosting and site-creation tools, plus how to make a site in 30 minutes

Understanding web hosting	8
Free web-hosting packages	10
Web-hosting packages	12
Buying a domain name	14
Web-design software	16
Build a website in 30 minutes	18

CHAPTER 2
Planning and design

Planning is an essential part of web design, to ensure your site is easy for visitors to use

Planning your site	22
Perfecting your site's navigation	26
Creating a unified look	28

CHAPTER 3
Anatomy of a web page

Understanding HTML is key if you want to create the best possible site

How to begin	32
Basic HTML tags	36
Formatting tags	38
Preparing images	40
Adding links	42
Layouts with tables and lists	44
Uploading your website	46

CHAPTER 4
Using CSS

Our step-by-step guide to mastering Cascading Style Sheets will enable you to produce a richer design for your website and take precise control over all its elements

Understanding CSS	50
Applying the basics	52
Putting CSS into practice	56
Developing your layout further	60
Creating a navigation bar	62

CHAPTER 5
Looking good

The latest versions of HTML and CSS provide even more tools to make your site stand out from the competition, and with our help you'll find them easy to get to grips with

Introducing HTML5	68
Building HTML5 pages	70
Introducing CSS3	73
Create stylish text with CSS3	76
Animation with CSS3	79

CHAPTER 6
Content management

If your website has a lot of pages, you'll need some way of organising them all. Find out how WordPress helps you keep track of things

Using WordPress to build your site	84

CHAPTER 7
Adding sparkle

There are many ways to make your site more exciting, including adding video, weather forecasts or even a community forum

YouTube video 94
Driving directions 95
Weather forecasts 96
Photo slideshows 97
RSS feeds 98
Internet forums 100

CHAPTER 8
Finishing touches

Catch any legal problems, host adverts to earn cash and find out how popular your site is

Legal considerations 104
Bringing visitors back 106
Understanding Google Analytics 107
Making money from your site 108

CHAPTER 9
Business websites

Getting an online presence for your business is crucial if you want to attract more custom

Identifying your needs 112
Getting your business online 113
Creating an online shop 116
Google Webmaster Tools 120
Making your website local 126

CHAPTER 10
Advanced projects

These projects will improve your site further still, from random photos to Google Maps

Improving your search ranking 132
Displaying random photos on your site 135
Making a slideshow for your website 138
Hosting your own videos 142
Make your site work on mobile devices 144
Google charts and graphs 147
Embedding Google Maps on your site 150
Hosting with Google Apps 153

Glossary 156

Which type of website?

A quick and easy site

If you want to build a good-looking website in just a few minutes, see our guide to the easy-to-use and highly customisable online website builder, Jimdo.

Page 18

A custom-built site

The best way to create a site is to code it yourself. For an introduction to HTML and CSS, see chapters 3 and 4. The latest web standards are covered in chapter 5.

Page 30, 48 & 66

A large, multipage site

If you're creating a site with lots of pages, you need a content management system. Wordpress is traditionally associated with blogs, but is ideal for a standard site too.

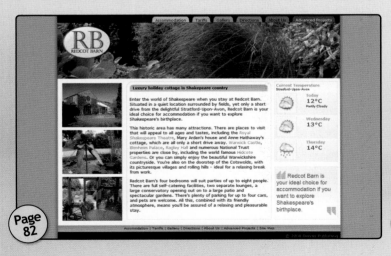

Page 82

An informative site

Whether you run a club and want to promote it or you need to provide information for wedding guests, adding driving directions and an interactive map is simple.

Page 95 & 150

A forum

Forums are great places for groups of like-minded people to chat, offer advice and arrange gatherings, and adding a forum to your website is easy.

Page 100

A business website

Getting your business online is sure to bring in extra customers, and our step-by-step guide will help you create a professional-looking site in no time.

Page 113

An online shop

If your business involves selling goods, an online shop is essential. On page 116 you'll find a detailed walkthrough on how to build yourself an online storefront.

Page 116

A photography portfolio

When showing off your photos, you need a way to display them as large as possible. Turn to page 138 for a guide on using the excellent TripTracker slideshow.

Page 138

CHAPTER 1

IN THIS CHAPTER

Understanding web hosting 8

Free web-hosting packages 10

Web-hosting packages 12

Buying a domain name 14

Web-design software 16

Build a website in 30 minutes 18

Getting started

You've decided to create your own website, and your head is buzzing with ideas about what will be on it and how it will look. However, first you need to decide where to host it. You can't host it on your home PC, as it will be unavailable when you switch off the computer. Instead, you need a web-hosting provider. In this chapter, we'll compare the most popular options.

You'll want your site to have a memorable address such as www.bradpitt.com rather than http://bradpitt.geocities.com, so we'll show you how to register a domain name. We'll also compare a variety of web-creation programs and design software. And if you're really pushed for time, we'll even show you how to create a website in just 30 minutes.

Understanding web hosting

When choosing a web-hosting provider, you need to make sure you get the right email options, as well as support for existing domain names

Whether you want to promote a local karate club, flaunt your photography skills or raise the profile of your business, you'll need a place to store your website online so visitors can access it. A web-hosting provider can give you this, plus email facilities and a unique domain name. It doesn't have to be expensive or difficult to set up an account, either.

Opting for a package that includes a domain name (as we discuss on page 14) means that you can get your own personalised email address, such as jim@jimmartin.com. This is often preferable to the generic email addresses that you get from your internet service provider (ISP) and it also means that, if you change your provider, your email address won't change.

One option for email is to buy just the domain name with no web hosting. You'll usually get free email forwarding where, for example, you could have all email that's sent to jim@jimmartin.com forwarded to jim@myisp.com. Should you swap ISPs, you can change the email address to which mail is forwarded, such as to jim@mynewisp.com. This way, all your contacts email

Below: Paid-for hosting, such as that from Hetzner Online, gives the best range of features

the same address regardless of your internet provider. However, it will look as though the email you send is coming from your ISP email address. You can change this by altering the settings in your email program, but this doesn't always work, and some ISPs block email sent through them that isn't from one of their email addresses.

Another option is to upgrade your domain name to a web-hosting package that provides email but no web hosting. For around £15 a year, you'll get enough email addresses for you and your family, and storage space for emails. If you change ISP, you won't have to make any changes to your email account. You'll also get these more advanced email services when you sign up for a paid-for web-hosting account (see page 12 for details).

WHAT'S IN A NAME?

If you've already registered a domain name but want a web-hosting package, don't panic: you can usually transfer your domain to a new provider for free. In general, when you log on to your web host account, there'll be an option to transfer a domain name. You'll need to have already created an account with your new web host, so it can be instructed to receive your domain name. Your new web host will provide instructions on how to transfer a domain name into your account.

How the domain is transferred will depend on the type of domain. For .co.uk domains, you need to provide the IPS tag of your new web host; there's a full list at www.nic.uk/registrars/becomeregistrar/taglist. For .com addresses, you usually have to unlock your domain and make a note of the unique transfer code. This code has to be given to your new web host.

Domain transfers take a few days to complete. Bear in mind that transferring a domain does not transfer your content or your current web hosting. All content must be transferred manually. Also, cancel your existing web-hosting account, or you'll still be charged every month.

HETZNER DEDICATED ROOT SERVERS

HETZNER ONLINE

PRICES FREE FALL

HETZNER DEDICATED ROOT SERVER EX 4
£110 £**39**
SETUP FEE

HETZNER DEDICATED ROOT SERVER EX 4S
£110 £**45**
SETUP FEE

HETZNER DEDICATED ROOT SERVER EX 5
£39 £**0**
SETUP FEE

HETZNER DEDICATED ROOT SERVER EX 6
£110 £**55**
SETUP FEE

HETZNER DEDICATED ROOT SERVER EX 4

- Intel®Core™ i7-2600 Quadcore incl. Hyper-Threading Technology
- 16 GB DDR3 RAM
- 2 x 3 TB SATA 6 Gb/s HDD 7200 rpm (Software RAID 1)
- Linux operating system
- Unlimited Traffic*
- IPv6 subnet (/64)
- Domain Registration Robot
- No minimum contract
- Setup Fee £39

monthly £ **39**

HETZNER DEDICATED ROOT SERVER EX 5

- Intel®Core™ i7-920 Quadcore incl. Hyper-Threading Technology
- 24 GB DDR3 RAM
- 2 x 750 GB SATA 3 Gb/s HDD (Software RAID 1)
- Linux operating system
- Unlimited Traffic*
- IPv6 subnet (/64)
- Domain Registration Robot
- No minimum contract
- Setup Fee £0

monthly £ **45**

TÜV SÜD
Energieeffizientes Unternehmen
Standard geprüft 2011

eco INTERNET AWARD 2011 WINNER
Verband der deutschen Internetwirtschaft e.V.

GreenIT
Best Practice Award
2011

Hetzner Online actively supports the protection of the environment by using 100% renewable energy. Take the step with us towards a cleaner future.

WWW.HETZNER.INFO

* Traffic usage is free. We will restrict the connection speed to 10 Mbit/s if more than 10.000 GB/month is exceeded. Optional, a permanent 100 Mbit/s bandwidth will be charged at £6 per additional TB.

All prices exclude VAT and are subject to the terms and conditions of Hetzner Online AG. Prices are subject to change. All rights reserved by the respective manufacturers.

Free web hosting

Before you can start on your website, you need a good web-hosting service. We look at those that will serve your site for free

Running a complex and popular website usually comes with financial burdens, but creating and maintaining an internet presence needn't be a bank-breaking endeavour. One of the best ways to keep initial costs down is to opt for a free hosting service. These services provide web space for you to store your site, although they often impose some restrictions.

The most significant of these is the domain name. Free web-hosting services don't provide you with your own domain name. This means that, while you may be after www.ritzbakery.co.uk, you may have to make do with http://sites.google.com/site/ritzbakery or www.ritz-bakery.freehost.co.uk.

This isn't necessarily a problem if you're building a website as a hobby, but it's not ideal if you want to appear more professional. Some free web-hosting services allow you to use your own domain name, but you'll have to buy this separately, often for a yearly fee. This can then redirect users to your free hosting package, so a visitor typing www.ritzbakery.co.uk into their browser actually ends up at a different website, such as www.freehost.co.uk/ritzbakery. You can find more on buying and managing domain names on page 14.

Free web-hosting services tend to have tight bandwidth restrictions and come with a small amount of web space. This limits what you can put on your website

Free web-hosting packages

Package name	URL	Space	Monthly bandwidth limit	Email accounts	Adverts
Jimdo Free	www.jimdo.com	500MB	Unlimited	0	Yes
One.com Free	www.one.com	5GB	Unlimited	Unlimited	No
Free-space	www.free-space.net	200MB	2GB	5	No
350 Pages	www.350.com	20MB	1GB	No	Yes
Free Virtual Servers	www.freevirtualservers.com	100MB	100MB	Unlimited	No
Google Sites	http://sites.google.com	100MB	Not stated	Free Gmail account	Yes
Webs	www.webs.com	40MB	100MB	0	Yes
WebEden Free	www.webeden.co.uk	20MB	1GB	0	Yes

Please note: Details correct at time of going to press

and how many people can visit. One way to reduce the effect of these limits is to store disk-hungry content such as photos and videos elsewhere. YouTube can host your videos, while a photo service such as Flickr (www.flickr. com) can store images. Find out how to embed YouTube videos in your web pages on page 94.

While some hosting providers offer generous bandwidth limits and plentiful web space, they may lack advanced features such as MySQL databases and support for scripting languages such as PHP and Perl. This may not matter at first, but as your ambitions grow and your website expands, you may wish to add a blog or keep a customer database. Turn to Chapter 10 for examples of what these technologies can offer. Another disadvantage of a free service is that File Transfer Protocol (FTP) access to your site may be limited. This means you must upload files using a proprietary web interface, perhaps one file at a time, which can be a real aggravation if you have a large website with lots of files.

You will probably also have to put up with some form of external advertising on your website if you choose free hosting. Adverts are usually placed at the side or bottom of each web page. Often the only way to avoid them is to pay a fee for your account.

TWO APPROACHES TO FREEDOM

Google Sites is an example of a completely free service. All you need is a Google account, which is also free. Google Sites allows you to create a basic website using templates you can modify. You get 100MB of dedicated storage to play with, and a limited range of tools. You can also add gadgets such as clocks, search bars and games.

Left: WebEden offers a wide range of hosting services and allows you to create a website in minutes

It's a fast way to get a personal website, but it's not suitable for a small business and it won't be easy to reuse the content or expand your site beyond the initial format if you want to make it bigger and better later.

One.com's free hosting package provides a more traditional and complete hosting service. You get 3GB of storage space for your web pages, images and other content, and (amazingly) unlimited bandwidth. This is coupled with an unlimited number of email accounts, FTP access and support for MySQL databases, and a handful of scripting languages such as PHP and ASP. It's also easier to scale up from this kind of website simply by upgrading your account. It's not strictly free – you pay a setup fee of £9 – but it's still excellent value. The package includes your own domain name, which you can use for a year, after which you must pay to keep it. This option is more suitable for burgeoning business websites.

Operating system	Example domain name	Use your own domain name	Website-creation tools	Extra notes
Not stated	ritzbakery.jimdo.com	No	Yes	Template based. Editable HTML. Online shop. Unintrusive ads
Linux	www.ritzbakry.com	Yes	Yes	Free domain name and hosting for first year, £9 setup fee
Linux	ritzbakery. freesitespace.net	Yes	Yes	Supports PHP, CGI, Perl and MySQL
Not stated	www.ritzbakery.350. com	Yes	Yes	Limit of 15 web pages. Template based. Can't edit HTML
Linux	www.ritzbakery.com	Yes	Yes	Domain name required. Unlimited MYSQL databases. Unlimited bandwidth for 80p per month
Not stated	http://sites.google. com/site/ritzbakery	No	Yes	Basic template editing. Can't edit HTML
Not stated	www.ritzbakery.webs. com	Yes	Yes	Some ads
Linux	http://ritzbakery. webeden.com	Yes	Yes	Template based. Can't edit HTML. Some ads, limit of 15 pages.

Web-hosting packages

There's a dizzying choice of hosting providers out there. Here we look at the most popular paid-for packages to make choosing a host easier

If you've tried to create a website using the free web space that came with your broadband package – or you've tried out some of the free hosting services we mentioned on page 10 – you'll already know the main drawbacks. Quite apart from the fact that your website's address isn't particularly personal or memorable, you may also want faster server speeds, more space and extras such as database access and scripting services that let you create a more dynamic site.

Hosting packages offer a set amount of storage and a bandwidth limit – the amount of data that can be downloaded from your site – for a monthly fee. You should work out how much space and bandwidth you'll need. Most hosting companies will slow down your connection or charge you extra if you exceed your monthly bandwidth, rather than shutting your site down.

Some packages include a domain name, so you can choose something short and memorable such as

Web-hosting packages

Package name	URL	Monthly price inc VAT	Extra costs	Space
1&1 Starter	www.1and1.co.uk	£2.49	£9.99 setup fee	5GB
1&1 Standard	www.1and1.co.uk	£4.99	None	50GB
JimdoPro	www.jimdo.com	£5.00	None	5GB
Fasthosts Personal Standard	www.fasthosts.co.uk	£5.99	None	15GB
Fasthosts Business Premium	www.fasthosts.co.uk	£10.79	None	100GB
Hetzner Online Level 1	www.hetzner.de	€1.90 (around £1.50)	None	2GB
Streamline Personal	www.streamline.net	£3.99	None	3GB
Mr Site Takeaway Website Standard	www.mrsite.co.uk	£3.40	None	150MB
One.com 10GB	www.one.com	£1.90	£9 setup fee	10GB
Heart Internet Starter Pro	www.heartinternet.co.uk	£2.49	None	5GB
DreamHost	www.dreamhost.com	$8.95 (around £5.60)	None	Unlimited

Details correct at time of going to press. Check websites for current deals

www.ritzbakery.co.uk. If you want a package that doesn't come with a domain, there are several in the table below, or you can turn to page 14 to find out how and where to buy one. Email accounts are usually included with the package, along with tools to help you manage your site. Some packages come with complete website-creation tools, but others don't. Some support Microsoft FrontPage extensions, which means you can design a website in FrontPage and publish it directly to your hosting package from your desktop.

DECISIONS, DECISIONS

One important decision you will need to make is whether to opt for Linux- or Windows-based servers. This will be influenced by your choice of web-design application or scripting language, and the advanced features you want. If you want a dynamic site that creates web pages on demand, you need a combination of a scripting language and a database. The most popular combination is MySQL for the database, which holds the content, and the PHP scripting language, which extracts content from the database. You can use a database for many things, such as a chat forum (see page 100) or a content management system (see chapter 6). Each function usually needs its own database, so plan your needs from the outset and choose a package with sufficient databases.

Reliability is also important, as you don't want your site to disappear for days on end. Look for a provider's

Left: One.com's Cloud Drive is included with all its hosting packages and lets you access your files from any device, synchronise files, plus back them up

'guaranteed uptime', which tells you the percentage of time the server remains accessible online. Even an uptime of 99.9 per cent could mean your site is inaccessible for 40 minutes every month. It may be worth paying for this level of uptime if you earn money from your website. You can also check forums to see how other users rate a particular company for technical support.

The table below provides a summary of some of the most popular and best-value web-hosting packages, along with their key features. For the latest prices, visit the web addresses shown in the table.

Monthly bandwidth limit	Email accounts	Operating system	Domain name included	Website-creation tools	Programming	MYSQL slots
Unlimited	1,000	Windows or Linux	No	Yes (8 pages)	PHP	1
Unlimited	3,000	Windows or Linux	No	Yes (12 pages)	PHP, Zend Framework, Perl, Python, Ruby, SSI	10
Unlimited	1	Not stated	Yes	Yes	JavaScript	0
Unlimited	500	Windows or Linux	No	Yes	PHP, CGI, Perl and Python (Linux); ASP.NET, PHP and ASP (Windows)	1 slot £25 extra per year
Unlimited	1,000	Windows or Linux	Yes (plus 300 subdomains)	Yes	PHP, CGI, Perl and Python (Linux); ASP.NET, PHP and ASP (Windows)	5
10GB	100	Not stated	Yes	Yes	PHP	0
Unlimited	500	Windows or Linux	Yes	Yes	PHP, Perl, Python, ASP, (ASP.NET £30 per year)	0
2GB	20	Not stated	Yes	Yes	JavaScript	0
Unlimited	Unlimited	Linux	Yes	Yes	PHP	1
30GB	1,000	Linux	No	No	PHP, CGI, Perl, Python, ASP, Ruby	0
Unlimited	Unlimited	Linux	Yes	Yes	PHP, CGI, Perl, Python, Ruby on Rails	Unlimited

Buying a domain name

For a professional appearance, your website needs its own unique web address, or domain name. Here's how to get one

A domain name is a unique name for your website. It's more than just an address that enables people to find your site, though. It's a brand, and something to be remembered by. It's important to choose the right domain name for your website if you want to entice people to visit and then keep coming back.

There are two important things to consider when choosing a domain name. First, your chosen name should be both memorable and relevant to the content of your site. There's little point in choosing www.jimsphotos.com if your name isn't Jim and you haven't got any photos to show. Your choice of domain name should also make it easier for people to find you. If you run a book club in Oxford, for example, people might guess at www.oxfordbookclub.com if they're not sure of the exact address, so it makes sense to register this domain.

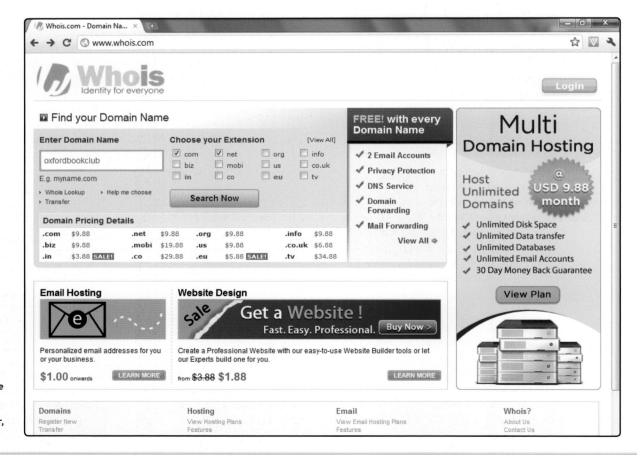

Right: To see if a domain name is available to register, visit www.whois.com and type in the name you want to register, excluding the 'www.' part

Access denied

Some domain names can turn out to be more trouble than they're worth. An example is a UK family that decided to register www.narnia.mobi in 2006 for their son, who is a huge fan of the CS Lewis books. However, now that more people are accessing websites from mobile devices, companies are beginning to register .mobi domains, which they see as theirs. Sure enough, the administrators of the estate of CS Lewis took the family to court and successfully won the right to the domain name.

Similarly, it's inadvisable to register a domain that sounds like another successful site. A few years ago, a student named Mike Rowe registered the domain www.mikerowesoft.com but ended up having to hand it over to Microsoft. Companies want to protect their trademarks, and you may find yourself the subject of legal proceedings if you do anything that might infringe them.

Domain names come in various types dictated by their endings. The most common ending for UK-based sites is .co.uk, but there is nothing to stop you registering a .org or .net extension, or even a more exotic .info, .me or .tv.

All .co.uk domain names are managed by Nominet, a not-for-profit company established to oversee the .uk top-level domain (TLD). You can buy a domain name directly from Nominet, but the company recommends that you use a licensed registrar. When you consider that buying a domain from Nominet costs around £80 for two years, it makes sense to follow this advice: buying the same domain through a registrar should cost under £10.

Most web-hosting providers also act as registrars and, although you are not obliged to buy the domain from your chosen host, it's far more convenient to do so. Prices vary between registrar services, though, so it could be worth shopping around before you buy.

Plenty of companies on the internet will register a domain name on your behalf, and you can also use these services to find out whether or not your desired domain name is available. Bear in mind that there's little chance of general, popular names being available, such as www.johnsmith.co.uk or www.karateclub.com. However, more descriptive names such as www.swaffham-karate.com or www.martinaccountants.co.uk may well be.

A NAME YOU CAN TRUST

If the particular domain name you want is unavailable, you have a number of options. You don't necessarily have to think of another name. Instead, you could find out if the same domain name is available with a different ending, such as .info or .biz. Of course, this means that another website will have a similar domain to your own, which could cause confusion. An alternative for those

who simply must have a certain name is to find out who currently owns the domain name and try to buy it. Enter the URL into a browser's address bar and look at the website that appears. If it's related to the domain name, you may have an uphill struggle, but if you are directed to a holding page with contact information, there's a good chance you will be able to negotiate a purchase.

Once you have bought your domain name, you must link it to your website. These are two entirely separate entities. A website is a collection of pages about a particular subject that's stored on a server, while the domain name is the information used to find those pages – a bit like a postcode. When www.ritzbakery.co.uk is entered in a web browser, it's crucial that the visitor arrives at the Ritz Bakery website.

When you sign up for a web-hosting package, you'll usually be given the option to search for a new domain to buy, or to associate the web space with a domain you already own. This is a straightforward process, and you'll simply need to follow the step-by-step instructions provided by your host.

Some hosting packages (free ones in particular) offer the chance to create a subdomain under the host's name, such as ritzbakery.freehost.co.uk. This can be useful for creating multiple websites. For example, we could establish http://bookings.ritzbakery.co.uk for the booking system.

FORWARD THINKING

Even if your website is hosted by a free service that doesn't allow personal domain names, you can use a domain forwarding service to associate your own domain with your website. This means that even if the Ritz Bakery website's URL is www.ritzbakery.freehost.co.uk, you could buy the domain www.ritzbakery.co.uk and automatically forward visitors who type in this URL to the one at the free host. This service is usually provided for free or for a nominal fee. Again, if you require this service, shop around before you buy your domain name.

TIP
Don't rush into buying a domain name that isn't what you really want. Plan the purchase of a domain name at the earliest possible stage, and make sure the specific name you want is available before creating things such as logos for your site.

Anatomy of a web address (URL)

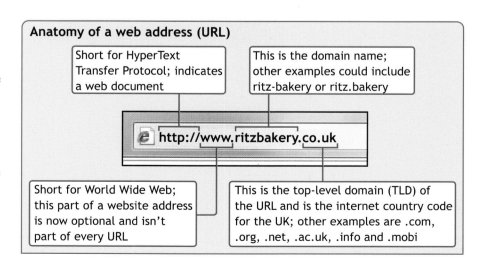

Short for HyperText Transfer Protocol; indicates a web document

This is the domain name; other examples could include ritz-bakery or ritz.bakery

http://www.ritzbakery.co.uk

Short for World Wide Web; this part of a website address is now optional and isn't part of every URL

This is the top-level domain (TLD) of the URL and is the internet country code for the UK; other examples are .com, .org, .net, .ac.uk, .info and .mobi

Web-design software

Whatever your ambitions, there's a web-design program to suit you, from those that build a site to others that let you create dynamic pages

The internet has been part of our lives for more than 10 years. Time enough, you'd think, for someone to create a web-design package that wasn't frustrating to use. All too often, though, web-design software feels arcane and impenetrable to all but the initiated. We don't generally recommend using software to create a site visually, but we also appreciate that some people don't have time to code an entire website using HTML and Cascading Style Sheets (CSS).

Before you spend any money, bear in mind that there are plenty of good online website creation tools. While these mean you can work on your site only when you have internet connectivity, they also save you from having to upload your site from your computer. They can also be upgraded from time to time and some – such as www.jimdo.com – provide an entirely 'what you see is what you get', or WYSIWYG, environment to work in.

Right: From novices to experts, there's a web-design tool to cater for all skill levels

The first thing to consider when choosing a package is the quality of its output. By this we don't just mean whether or not the code conforms to W3C standards (W3C is the non-profit organisation responsible for web standards). Given that most web-design programs are intended for non-technical users, the quality of the website depends largely on the quality of the templates, its default settings and the advice it provides in its manual or help file.

Some programs have a clumsy or imprecise design environment. Few things are more frustrating, particularly for users who don't want to tweak HTML code to correct problems with alignment and so on. As well as working with HTML, web-design programs should support other web technologies. At the very least, this means being able to create or link to CSS, so that you can customise the look of an entire site, applying styles to many pages at once. This is one of the cornerstones of modern web design. You should also look for a program that enables you to use scripting technologies and other dynamic web-design elements. This will mean that you can add photo slideshows, videos, forms and other widgets to your pages.

EASY DOES IT

Ease of use is one of the most important aspects. Key tools and features should be clearly labelled and easy to find, objects on your page should behave logically and predictably and help files should be comprehensive and well written. A good package should also allow you to publish your website to a web server without difficulty.

Even if you consider yourself a novice, you may find that you want to progress beyond the basics later without having to upgrade to a new program. The software should allow you to move from using the visual workspace (usually referred to as WYSIWYG) to working directly with the code.

CoffeeCup HTML Editor 12.7

Price: $69 (around £44)
Details: www.coffeecup.com

As it name suggests, CoffeeCup HTML Editor 12.7 requires you to have at least some knowledge of HTML. However, you shouldn't let this put you off, as there are plenty of wizards, tools and menus to help you at every turn.

As we'll reiterate throughout this book, building a website with HTML and CSS code gives you precise control over the look and feel of your site. HTML Editor 12.7 builds on the success of previous versions and provides even more tools, making it a far superior alternative to Windows Notepad. For a start, the code is coloured so it's easy to locate the elements. Auto-complete and tag libraries (including brand HTML5 tags) help you build pages quickly, and it's easier than ever to work with linked HTML and CSS files. The tabbed interface makes it easy to work on multiple files, and integrated FTP enables you to upload files directly to your web space.

The new My Websites tool helps you to create a well-structured website, encouraging those good file-keeping habits that we talk about in 'How to begin' on page 32. Pre-made code helps you to add common elements to pages, while updated markup means that code will meet current standards for validation with W3C, so pages should be compatible with all browsers. It's easy to check how pages look in

different browsers – you can link the program with as many as 10 installed browsers. The live preview allows you to keep track of basic formatting, and making sure that text and photos are where you want them. The entire time you can make changes in the code editor.

All this, combined with other new features such as the CSS menu designer and website templates to get you started, makes CoffeeCup HTML Editor 12.7 an essential tool for anyone who wants to get involved with the code behind their website.

CoffeeCup Web Form Builder 2.1

Price: $69 (around £44)
Details: www.coffeecup.com

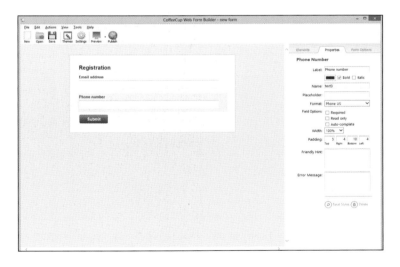

Web forms are one of the most useful ways of getting visitors to your site to interact with you, letting them enter information that's sent back to you. The main problem is that forms can be tricky to design and layout, and even harder to control the submission method.

With its Web Form Builder, CoffeeCup makes the job incredibly easy. This simple bit of software lets you drag and drop form components onto a page. You can customise each data entry field, so it works the way you want it to, such as making sure than an email address is entered correctly.

Once you're happy with the bare basics, there's a large template library to choose from so you can customise the design of your form and make sure that it fits in with your site's design. While you can take your form and add it to your website, Web Form Builder makes it even easier with built-in support for CoffeeCup's S-Drive.

S-Drive is simple fast web hosting that you can automatically upload your forms to. Copy and paste the code the software generates into your website and your form appears as you designed it with the minimum amount of fuss and hassle.

Web Form Builder gives you a choice of what to do with the data that you capture. As well as saving to S-Drive you can choose to have it

emailed to you or added to a SQL database, letting Web Form Builder fit in with what ever system you've got in place.

With forms an important part of any website, Web Form Builder takes the pain out of making them, the annoyance of integrating them and difficulty of knowing what to do with the collected data.

Build a website in 30 minutes

Need a web presence fast? Here we take you through the process of creating a functioning site for free in just half an hour

ESSENTIALS

SKILL LEVEL
Beginner
Intermediate
Expert

HOW LONG
30 minutes

Bottom: Jimdo lets you creat a professional-looking website in no time

One way of creating a basic but good-looking website is to sign up for a free Jimdo account and use its excellent web builder tool. It's free to use, although you'll have to put up with a few adverts. You can pay £5 per month for JimdoPro if you want to remove the ads and gain extra features such as a domain name, email account and better online shop facilities.

Go to www.jimdo.com. In the box, type in your chosen website name and an existing email address. Tick the box to agree to the terms and conditions, then click the Create my site! button. If you see a message that says the address is already in use, keep trying until you find one that hasn't been taken. You'll now be sent your username and password via email. Copy your password, then click the link in the message to go to your new website. You'll see the default site with a pre-made menu and a home page with a large arrow pointing to the Login button.

Although the site looks pretty good, there's plenty of room for improvement. For a start, your website name's visibility on the banner image is poor and, while the quality of the text is good, you'll almost certainly want to personalise it.

Click Login and enter your password. A small control panel will appear in the top right corner of the page. You can follow the simple instructions and use the online help to create a professional-looking website in no time.

There are lots of templates to choose from, so you'll easily be able to find something that matches the look and feel you want for your website.

While Jimdo is free, most of the big website hosts provide similar tools for their paid-for hosting. These will let you create a simple, yet attractive website in just a few clicks and have the site automatically saved to your web hosting.

Tools like this are useful for creating simple websites or for generating some starter pages that you can edit later using the skills you'll learn in this book. However, if you stick to these tools you'll end up with quite a basic website that doesn't do everything you want it to do. As such, we recommend using them only for very basic sites or as a place-holder while you work on something more complicated.

CHAPTER 2

IN THIS CHAPTER

Planning your site.........................22

Perfecting your site's
   navigation 26

Creating a unified look...............28

Planning and designing

Once you've signed up to a hosting package, it's easy to plough ahead with your first web page. However, it's essential to spend some time planning your site, paying particular attention to the focus of your site, what to say on each page and how it looks.

Only you can decide on the first two, but entire books are dedicated to the third. In this chapter, we'll show you how to do

MacBook Air

the groundwork, covering navigation principles, creating a unified look, colour schemes and font choices. You'll also be shown how to make your site accessible to disabled visitors, who may be using software to convert web pages into spoken English. Follow our tips from the start, and you won't have to go back and change the code later.

Planning your website

A little time spent on planning your site now will save you hours of frustration later. Follow these easy guidelines for a better-quality site

Once you've arranged your hosting package and domain name, it can be tempting to plunge in and design your site as you go, but you'd be asking for trouble. If you attack website development this way, you'll quickly create a sprawling mess of pages, riddled with repetition and annoying navigation quirks – all of which can be avoided with some careful planning.

First, consider the focus of your site. Do you want to sell things to people, or get them to read as many articles as possible? Are you trying to attract advertisers to your site, or simply provide information about a club? You also need to consider your readers. Are they computer-savvy, at home with the latest web technology, or could they be older 'silver surfers' who might be put off by quirky, hard-to-see navigation bars?

Our advice is to start with pen and paper, and write a mission statement for your website. It might sound over the top, but it's worth the effort. Make sure your website is going to give people what they want, whether you're creating a small site for family to keep up to date with a growing baby, or a much bigger site for which you must attract the widest possible audience. If you do want to attract a big audience, aim to give visitors something they can't easily get from another website. There are millions of websites out there; if yours repeats the content of too many others, you'll struggle to get your voice heard above the established players.

MAPPING YOUR WEBSITE

It helps to create a 'map' of your site. Draw a box on the left-hand side of a piece of paper: this is the home page. Decide, in broad strokes, what information will be on it and work your way right. Connect other pages to the home page with lines, and you'll have the beginnings of your navigation structure. At the very least, you'll need an About page or a Contact Us page; these are standard pages that you'll find on virtually every website.

Once you have a list of pages, you'll also have a preliminary version of the file structure of your site. If you're using a content management system (CMS) application such as Wordpress (see chapter 6), this isn't something you need worry about. However, if you intend to upload pages manually, you must use a logical folder structure. For instance, you'll need an Images folder for any pictures on your site. It's important that you stick to your own rules; don't store images anywhere else in the name of convenience. Finding files using an FTP client is much harder than it is in Windows, and if you have random files sprinkled all over your web space, you'll be left with a confusing, unmanageable mess.

KEEPING UP APPEARANCES

Borrowing ideas from your competitors might sound like the fast-track to unoriginality and, worse, potential legal issues. However, one of the best ways to prepare is to spend a few hours online looking for sites you like. Work out what you like about them, and find out if they have anything in common. If they have features you dislike, or if anything slows you down while you're browsing, make a note, and ensure that you don't repeat those mistakes. The most important thing to bear in mind is that the average internet user's attention span is ferociously short. If your site is even remotely frustrating to use, hard to navigate or boring, your visitor will leave and probably never return. Turn to page 106 if you need a little inspiration on this subject.

At this point, it's worth going back to your notepad and sketching out a few page designs, bearing in mind the traits of your favourite sites. Chances are they'll have a logo in the top-left corner that also acts as a link to take you back to the home page, plus either a vertical or horizontal navigation bar. There may also be a separate list of pages available on the left-hand side. At the very bottom of the page, you might want some small links to your site map, contact pages and other major sections. These are standard design trends and your visitors will expect to find links in these common areas.

HOME IMPROVEMENTS

Assuming first impressions last, you'll want to spend a lot of time on your home page. This is the first thing most visitors will see, unless they're arriving via a Google search that takes them to another page on your site. If your home page doesn't look spectacular, visitors may not get past it.

Think about the images you can use. You could use a different image every few days to keep things fresh; news sites, in particular, benefit from being constantly updated.

You should also think about logos, and whether you want something exciting such as a video on the front page (see page 94 to find out how to add video to your site).

CREATION THEORY

Finally, decide how you're going to create your website. Although it's easier to opt for a template-based web-design package, there's more chance of you getting the desired results if you start with a blank canvas and simply use HTML (outlined in chapter 3) and CSS (chapter 4). Using HTML and CSS isn't difficult. Even if you start by using a template from a package such as Jimdo (see page 16), you can take the code it generates and tweak it manually afterwards.

Best laid plans Mapping out your site

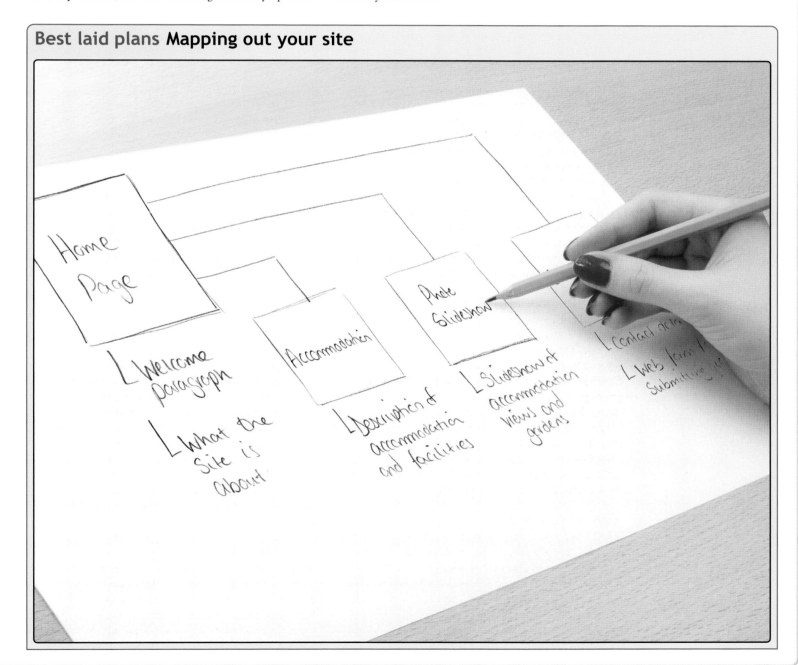

1&1 BUSINESS HOSTING

UNLIMITED FEATURES FOR YOUR PROFESSIONAL WEB PROJECTS

Do you need more from your hosting? Then choose a solution that's all-inclusive! The 1&1 Business package features innovative tools and technology, plus many unlimited features. With more than 11 million customer contracts, £2 billion in annual turnover, 5000 employees and 5 high-performance data centres in Europe and the USA, 1&1 is one of the world's leading web hosts. With 20 years' hosting experience and 1500 developers, we continue to be a reliable partner. 1&1 takes pride in offering you reliability, security and top performance.

 ### UNLIMITED

Unlimited webspace, unlimited traffic, unlimited IMAP/POP3 e-mail accounts, unlimited MySQL5 Databases (1 GB each)

 ### WINDOWS OR LINUX HOSTING

Choose the operating system that best suits your business

 ### FAIL-SAFE SECURITY

Geo-redundant 1&1 Data Centres host your website in two secure locations

 ### WORDPRESS, JOOMLA!® DRUPAL™...

...and other popular open source applications. Benefit from unlimited access to 65 1&1 Click & Build Applications

 ### DEDICATED SSL CERTIFICATE

1 Dedicated SSL Certificate is included with 1&1 Business

MEMBER OF
united internet

DOMAINS | E-MAIL | WEB HOSTING | eCOMMERCE | SERVERS

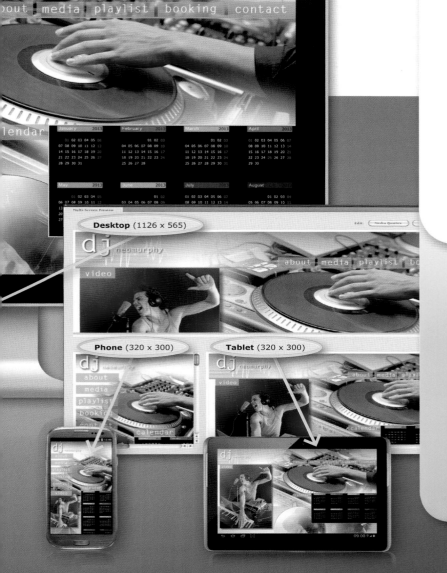

Perfecting your site's navigation

Clear navigation is essential if you want a popular, usable website. Here's how to help your visitors find everything quickly and smoothly

Below left: Wikipedia makes its hyperlinks obvious by using a standard shade of blue

Below right: Amazon's navigation bar on the left-hand side is big, bold and easy to spot and use

Virtually all websites have a navigational structure, yet it's so easy to get it wrong when making your own site. Navigation is crucial: a frustrated visitor will almost certainly leave and look elsewhere if they can't find what they want on your website. The components of a website that make up its navigation structure are known as navigational elements. These elements should be consistent and easy to understand, and follow internet conventions.

The first thing to consider is your website's name. This isn't normally considered a navigational element, but some visitors will type it to get to your site, and possibly tell others about it as well. For this reason, keep it short and avoid punctuation and unconventional spelling. Keep subfolder names short, too, so users only type www.ritzbakery.co.uk/directions, for example, rather than something unwieldy such as www.ritzbakery.co.uk/resources/widgets/drivingdirections.html.

When people are browsing your site, they're likely to want to return to the home page. This is partly because some visitors will arrive on your site via other pages, thanks to search engine results, and partly because some visitors like to jump back to the home page before using the navigation bar to go to a different page. It's conventional to have a hyperlink to the home page on every single page of your site: this is usually a logo in the top-left corner. It should be the same logo each time and, to avoid confusion, it shouldn't act as a link when the user is already on the home page.

HYPER ACTIVE

Without hyperlinks, or links for short, the internet as we know it simply wouldn't exist. When you're using a web browser, every mouse click takes you to a new page or website. You almost never think about it, and that's how it should be.

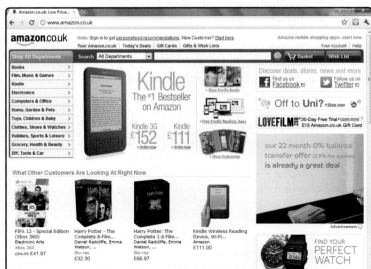

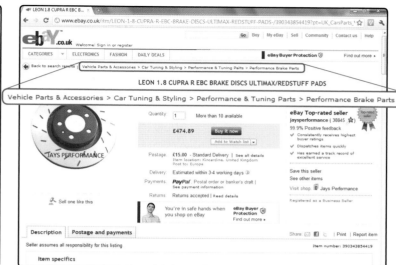

Clicking on a hyperlink is now second nature to almost all internet users. Ask someone to describe a link on a website, and he or she will probably say it's blue, underlined text. Because so many people are familiar with this format, you should think carefully before changing it. If you decide that, for your website to look really great, you simply have to change the appearance of your links, make sure they are distinct from normal text. The easiest way to do this is to make them a different colour, one that really stands out.

If anyone looks at your site and can't immediately tell where all the links are, they won't like it. This becomes even more important if you want people to spend a decent amount of time on your site, reading all that you have to offer. If using the most basic navigational element is too difficult, people won't stay. In his book *Homepage Usability: 50 Websites Deconstructed*, web-usability expert Jakob Nielsen says, "People spend most of their time on other sites than yours". Making your site look distinctive, compared to others, is half the battle. The other half is making sure it still conforms to expected web standards.

The way that links on your site behave is also important. It's usually bad practice to make links open new windows (or tabs) when clicked. Multiple windows are annoying to visitors, who have to wade back through the open windows when they want to return to their first step. However, it's acceptable – if not expected – that links to sites besides your own will open a new tab or window. If you do this, there's a good chance the user will see your site and browse it again when they finish reading the linked-to site and close that window or tab.

RAISING THE BAR

Navigation bars are a common way of getting around a website, and most run horizontally across the top of every page (see page 62). Ideally, navigation bars should be text-based; they're usually narrow, so there isn't room for images. Images can often be mistaken for advertising content, so people are unlikely to click on them.

ON THE BREADCRUMB TRAIL

The term 'breadcrumb trail' has its roots in the fairytale Hansel and Gretel, in which the protagonists ensure they can retrace their steps by leaving a trail of breadcrumbs. A digital breadcrumb trail works in the same way: it is an onscreen representation of every step someone has taken on a website to bring them to their current location. This means that it's possible for them to return to the home page, go back a single step (which the browser's Back button also permits) and, more importantly, go back to any step in between.

So, for example, if a visitor to a website started at the Home page, went to an About page, then on to a Pictures page and then a Holiday page, the breadcrumb trail would look like this:

Home > About > Pictures > Holiday

A breadcrumb trail is hierarchical, and really only works if your website's pages are laid out in a linear way. If your site is a sprawling mass of random pages with no logical path through them, a breadcrumb trail won't add much usability. This gives you another great reason to plan your site carefully and think about the structure of your pages before you start uploading anything.

AND FINALLY…

Perhaps the most important thing to remember when designing your site's navigation is to keep it simple. Animated, drop-down navigation bars and breadcrumb trails are navigational niceties, and there's certainly room for them. But if your site is illogically laid out or flouts navigational norms, these tools will add nothing.

Above left: The First Post doesn't have a breadcrumb trail, but it uses a standard three-column layout

Above right: eBay uses a navigation bar and a breadcrumb trail so users can retrace their steps

Creating a unified look

To make life as easy as possible for your visitors, you should apply the same design elements, colours and fonts throughout your website

BENEFITS

Consistent page design and a familiar look that will help your visitors navigate your site

Learn which colours and fonts work best

We've already seen that if the navigational elements on a website are all over the place, and the link that takes visitors back to the homepage is constantly moving and changing size, then navigating your site will become a chore and, ultimately, it will cost you readers.

You should approach the visual style of your website by following the maxim of less is more. The best way to bring a unified look to your website is to use CSS; this will be covered in detail in chapter 4. CSS ensures that all the elements on your site have exactly the same look throughout. If you change a design element or a font in

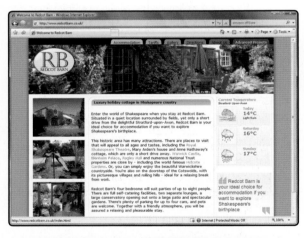

Right: It's easy to see the consistent look across these four pages of our website

CSS, every instance of that element or font will change across your entire site.

IT'S HUE YOU KNOW

Choosing your website's colour scheme can be tricky. Using a few colours on a website can be effective, as it will emphasise certain parts of your site and draw attention to different elements. However, you need to think like a professional designer and become familiar with the concept of complementary colours: these are pairs of colours that are opposite each other on the colour wheel, such as blue and orange, for example. Two such colours provide harmonious contrast.

Along with this, it's worth bearing in mind that shades of the same colour – such as the shades of green in the website shown opposite – can help to create a sense of consistency and familiarity.

Rather than trying to pick colours manually, we recommend Adobe's Kuler (http://kuler.adobe.com). We've included an in-depth guide on how to use this tool on the next page. Kuler will pick five colours according to the rules you select, and you can then copy their hexadecimal (Hex) values, which are shown underneath them. You'll need these, since HTML and CSS both use Hex values for defining colours.

WHAT'S YOUR TYPE?

Think carefully about your choice of font. The rule that applies to printed material such as this book applies on websites, too: don't use more fonts than you need. In fact, you should try to limit your choice to two fonts, and use only these throughout your site.

It's true that there are some striking-looking typefaces out there, but unless you're using your website to make a specific statement about design, you should stick to the classics. Times New Roman is a safe, easy-to-read font that works in most web browsers, while Georgia is a good alternative when it comes to serif fonts (the typeface you're reading now is a serif font). Sans serif fonts – such as those used for the title and standfirst on the opposite page – should be used as your second font. Arial or Tahoma are good choices. It's really up to you to decide whether you choose serif or sans serif for the titles

and heading; just make sure that you use the other type for the body copy.

Consistency is as important as the fonts that you finally settle on. You need to make sure that the font you use is not only the same throughout your site, but also the same size, and you must use styles such as bold and italics consistently.

Even humble links needs thinking about. There are various ways of styling a link, such as underlined, underlined only when you hover the mouse over it and so on. However, the web standard is to underline the link and colour it in a standard shade of blue. Whatever you choose to do, avoid making your links blend into the page. If people can't instantly identify a link, they won't know to click it.

SNAP DECISIONS

To maintain your unified look, try to make sure that any images you use appear in roughly the same places on each page. An image-editing program such as Adobe Photoshop Elements will allow you to change the dimensions of an image before you upload it. This is doubly important for pages that contain multiple images.

Furthermore, text should flow around the images in the same way throughout your website. If the pictures have captions, those captions should have the same font at the same size.

IS IT COMPATIBLE?

There's no point having a consistently applied design if it doesn't display properly in certain browsers. Different browsers support different web standards, which is something you'll need to bear in mind if you have hopes of reaching a wide audience. To find out about testing the compatibility of your website without having to install every version of every browser, see page 49.

You'll also need to think about the resolution of your site. You might have a 24in monitor with a resolution of 1,920x1,200, but few of your potential visitors will. If you design your site to a width of 1,920 pixels, most people will quickly leave it. Instead, work to a width of 1,024 pixels, which should make your site compatible with just about everyone's monitor.

Above left: Apple's website is an excellent example of unified design. New visitors should be able to navigate with ease

Above middle: Sip Hawaii might be great if you love coffee, but its heavy-handed design is likely to put buyers off particularly because it uses lots of different fonts

Above right: Your computer may have hundreds of fonts installed, but you should stick to using just two of them

CHAPTER 3

IN THIS CHAPTER

How to begin......................................32

Basic HTML tags...............................36

Formatting tags...............................38

Preparing images............................40

Adding links 42

Layouts with tables
    and lists 44

Uploading your website..............46

Anatomy of a web page

In order to create the best website possible, you need to understand the HTML code that browsers use to display web pages. This may sound daunting, but HTML is written in plain English and is actually easy to learn.

Whether you plan to create all your pages from scratch in HTML or use an HTML editor, it's vital that you are able to edit

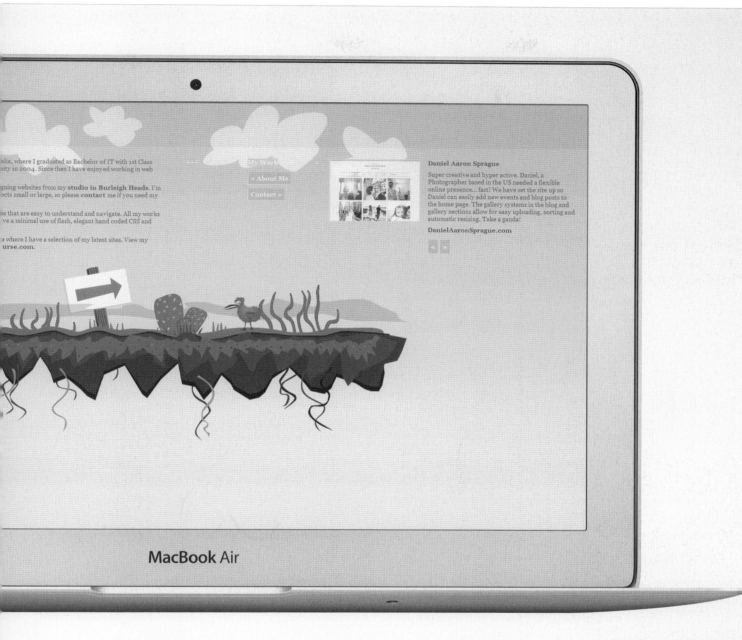

MacBook Air

and fine-tune the code to get your pages looking exactly the way you want them. In this chapter, we'll explain how to use HTML tags to create a web page by formatting text, including images, creating lists and tables, and adding links. You'll also learn how to make your pages work in different browsers, and how to upload your finished pages to your web space.

How to begin

You may be itching to start your first web page, but first you need to be familiar with all the various page elements and how to manage them

Below: These two pages are different, but appear to have the same filename. This is because filenames are case-sensitive

One of the real secrets to effective web design is careful planning and organisation. This works on two levels. First, you need to ensure that your site is focused, well laid out and easy to navigate, as we explained in the last chapter. Second, you should manage it in such a way that it is easy to find your way around and locate those pages that require a tweak, an update or a wholesale revamp.

GETTING ORGANISED

Before you do anything else, then, you should create a folder on your computer that will store your site, and make sure that you only ever work in this directory. It's tempting to put this on the desktop to make it easy to find, but this is rarely a good way to work. Using the desktop as anything other than a temporary resting place

for files in transit is a sure-fire way to clutter things up, and it will lead to the kind of situation that ultimately slows you down.

Instead, head for your My Documents folder and create a new folder. Over the next few chapters, we'll be developing a basic website to demonstrate how the whole process works. Our site is devoted to a ficticious holiday cottage called Redcot Barn, so we'll simply call our folder Redcot Barn. Inside it, we'll create another folder called 'images' where we'll store all the graphics, and additional folders for each major section of the site.

Careful planning here will make all the difference when you put your site online. Organising all your images in one place makes them easy to find when you want to re-use them on more than one page, and creating new folders for every section will help you to keep your

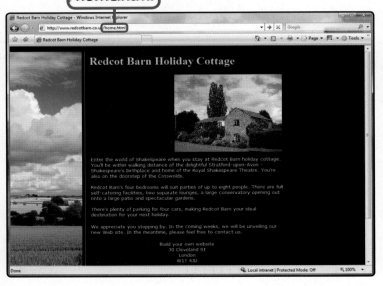

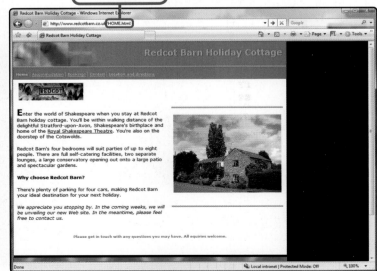

page addresses short and easy to remember. It might even improve your chances of coming out closer to the top in a Google search.

CASE SENSITIVITY

Windows doesn't make any distinction between upper- and lower-case characters, but many web servers do. The most common web server operating system is Linux, which, having its roots in Unix, sees no greater similarity between 'a' and 'A' than it does between 'X' and 'Y'.

This only holds true for the filename of a web page, not the domain name. While WWW. REDCOTBARN.CO.UK and www.redcotbarn.co.uk would both get you to the same place, you could conceivably store three different pages at www. redcotbarn.co.uk/HOME.html, www.redcotbarn.co.uk/home.html and www.redcotbarn.co.uk/Home.html. There are times when this could be useful but, generally speaking, using anything other than lower-case characters introduces an extra level of complexity to your address. It means you have to spell out every part in detail and rely on your visitor to type it in exactly. By sticking with lower case throughout, you can tell people verbally to go to 'redcot barn dot co dot uk slash home dot html', rather than 'redcot barn dot co dot uk slash capital h, lower-case o-m-e, dot lower-case h-t-m-l'.

Any page whose filename can be put directly after your domain, such as the home.html in the example above, appears directly inside the folder you created on your hard disk and not in any subfolders held within it. When you transfer it to your domain – that is, your online web space – it will also appear in the top level there, This, conversely, is called the 'root'. We will use this naming convention throughout this section.

USING FOLDERS ONLINE

As your site grows, organisation becomes ever more important, and subdirectories become key to effective organisation. These form the words between the slashes on your site. So, if we wanted to create a series of local information pages for our holiday home business's website, we could create /cotswolds-attractions.html, /stratford-attractions.html and /london-attractions.html, but this would add three more pages to the root directory of our website. This can get confusing and cluttered, just as your Windows desktop does when you drop files there.

It is better to create a separate folder into which you can save all pages with a similar theme. In our example, then, we would create a folder called /attractions/ into which we would save three pages: cotswolds.html, stratford.html and london.html.

The other advantage of creating folders is that you can create extremely logical filenames that get your readers to your pages more quickly and with less effort. You cannot rely on repeat visitors to remember the exact filename of every page on your site. There's a chance

they'll try /attractions/cotswolds.htm, cotswolds.shtm and cotswolds.php, before giving up and looking elsewhere for the information they need.

Creating a new folder inside /attractions/ called cotswolds, and saving the Cotswolds page inside this folder using the name index.html, means it will load automatically whenever someone visits redcotbarn.co.uk/attractions/cotswolds. You can see for yourself how much easier this is to remember than the cumbersome redcotbarn.co.uk/attractions/cotswolds.html.

CHOOSING THE RIGHT FILENAMES

Carefully thought-out and logically named folders and pages don't only help your readers, but they also help Google. Optimising your directory and filenames in this way and giving them addresses that relate to their contents ensures that they are indexed more effectively, increasing your chances of showing up on the first page of any set of search results. For a business, this means increased traffic and the potential for a commensurate boost in income. For more information on how to make your site Google-friendly, you should follow the project on page 132.

You should use a small number of hyphens to break your page addresses into logical sections, so folders are called brewing-winemaking, local-transport and walking-tours rather than 'brewing and winemaking', 'local transport' and 'walking tours'.

Although web browsers can now handle character spaces, the result in the browser's address bar is ugly, as each space is replaced by '%20'. Potentially, this will render a site about the Twenty 20 cricket league as Twenty%2020.htm and can introduce untold confusion. Other characters outside of a specific subset are likewise swapped out for their ASCII code equivalents.

Above: When you're creating your website, you should store the pages on a local hard disk and not on your web space

Knowing the rules will help you. Internet regulation RFC 1734 specifies how addresses should be encoded when used in a browser. It permits the numbers 0 to 9, the letters a to z in their lower- and upper-case variations, and the characters $-_.,+!*'(and). This gives plenty of scope for creating unique and memorable addresses for every page on your site, with dashes, underscores or dots used in place of spaces. However, we recommend that you avoid $!*'(and) because they are confusing to spell out when you read an address aloud; $ could be called string or dollar, while (and) aren't actually brackets – which are [and] – but parentheses. Incidentally, { and } are braces and as they render as %7B and %7D, they should also be avoided in any page or folder names.

Below: Use services such as Browsershots to preview how images will look in different browsers without having to install them on your system

MAPPING THINGS OUT
You may find it helps to draw out a sketch of the directory structure of your proposed site at this stage, and use this as a map for when it comes to building the pages. This will help you to ensure that you have included all relevant information and linked all your pages appropriately. In particular, it will show you the relationship between related pages gathered together in a folder, so you can link cotswolds.html, stratford.html and london.html both to each other and to the top-level /attractions/ folder, in which you should create an introductory page called index.html; this will introduce the local area in broad strokes, before presenting a menu of links to the pages mentioned above for a more detailed exploration of each area.

Work logically through this map, starting with your homepage, which should appear at the top of a tree, whose branches fan out like a family tree. Ensure that there is an easy way back to the top of the structure for anyone who needs to return to your homepage (most commonly implemented through a logo, graphic or text link, such as Home, in the top-left of the page) and resist the temptation to publish any pages that are incomplete.

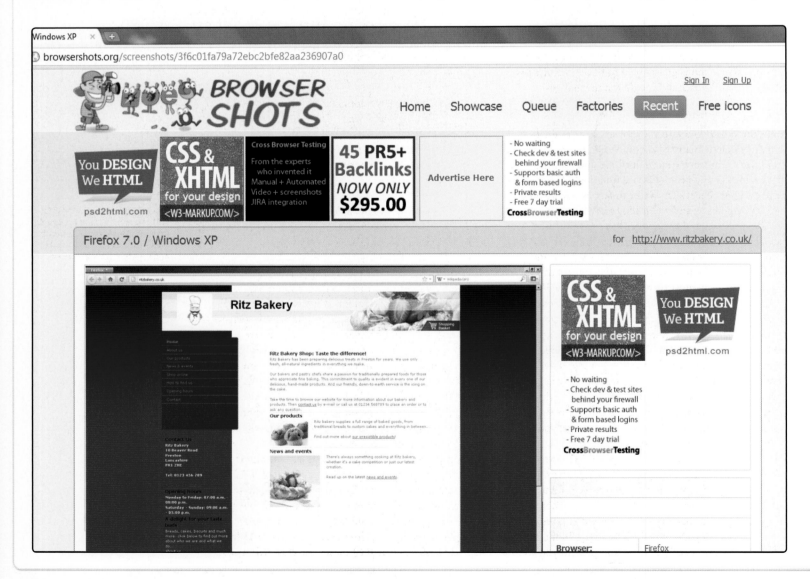

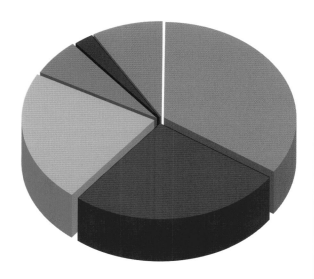

- Internet Explorer (34.3%)
- Safari (6.2%)
- Firefox (26.2%)
- Opera (2.4%)
- Chrome (22.2%)
- Others (8.7%)

Five steps to methodical web design

1 Gather together related pages in parent folders that allow your readers to type the shortest possible web address every time. This makes them easier to remember, and easier to pass on by word of mouth.

2 Use logical file and folder names to give yourself the best chance of coming top in search engine results lists.

3 Avoid obscure characters in file and folder names, and use logical punctuation such as dashes, underscores and dots rather than spaces.

4 Test, test and re-test your pages at every stage of construction. Don't be tempted to cater only for Internet Explorer or screen sizes above 1,024x768 pixels, or you risk losing a sizable chunk of your potential audience.

5 Never publish your pages until they are complete and ready for public consumption. Pages that are still 'under construction' look unprofessional, and may even discourage visitors from returning to your site.

UNDER CONSTRUCTION

Even if you mark pages as works in progress, it looks unprofessional and is guaranteed to have your visitors heading straight back to Google for alternatives.

TESTING, TESTING

You should test your site at every stage of production. As you may include many common elements on every page, you should not leave testing until the end (or ignore it altogether), as any problems you find could affect every page on your site. It's far better to test as you go, and tackle problems as and when they arise.

Don't be tempted to assume that everyone uses the same browser as you. Most visitors to your site will use Internet Explorer (see the pie chart above), but its market share is being eroded with the growth of serious competitors. The most recent figures from W3Counter (www.w3counter.com) put Internet Explorer's combined market share at 34.3 per cent, Firefox at 26.2 per cent, Google's Chrome at 22.2 per cent, Safari at 6.2 per cent and Opera at 2.4 per cent. Other browsers, make up the remaining 8.7 per cent. To put this in perspective, Internet Explorer's market share has virtually halved in the past three years. If you only test your site with Microsoft's browser, thereby disregarding the significant number of people using alternative browsers, you'll be doing your site a massive disservice.

You don't have to install every possible browser on your PC to test your pages. Just upload them to a development directory on your web server and use a service such as Browsershots (http://browsershots.org) to test pages on your behalf. Tell it where the pages can be found and which pages you'd like it to use in the test, and it will visit them in each browser and present you with a screenshot of the results in Windows, Linux and Mac OS X, so you can check if there are any problems, or if certain elements are displayed differently.

REMEMBER...

If you're still in the process of developing pages, do not link the development folder to the root of your web space, where they will be easy to find and confuse with a finished site. Develop everything on your hard disk, and upload pages to the web space only when you need to test them or when they're ready for public consumption.

Pages will work in almost the exact same way on a hard disk as they would when published on the internet. Double-clicking a page on your drive will open it in your browser; clicking any links that it contains will take you to the pages to which they refer.

You're bound to spend many hours developing your site, so it makes sense to create a backup of the folder you've created in your My Documents folder. You shouldn't need to buy an expensive external hard disk for this, since your site is unlikely to occupy more than a couple of gigabytes. A low-capacity USB flash drive should suffice; even 4GB models cost as little as £5.

Top left: Internet Explorer is still the most widely used web browser. However, you should make sure that your website appears correctly on other browsers, too

Basic HTML tags

Even a basic understanding of the way HTML tags work will help enhance the way your web pages look and make them more appealing to visitors

A web page can be as simple or complex as you want it to be. Typing the word 'hello' into a file called index.htm, saving that to your computer's hard disk and then opening it in your browser will display the simplest yet least engaging web page you could ever hope to encounter. However, by surrounding your content with tags that describe what it is and how it should look, you can produce something that will be more pleasant to read and is likely to hold your visitors' attention for much longer.

HAPPY COUPLES

Web pages are programmed in plain English. Because many tags use words that could also be used in your content – such as 'head', 'body' and 'align' – they are always encased in angled brackets. Tags are used in pairs, where one half of the pair switches on an effect or opens a particular section, such as a paragraph, and the other half of the pair, which uses the same tag name preceded by a forward slash (/), switches it off.

For example, the line of HTML that is shown in Figure 1 would be rendered as shown in Figure 2. This is a paragraph using bold, bold italic, plain italic and underlined text.

Notice how the bold italic text is rendered that way because the bold tag <b> was already in use when we applied the italic tag <i>. We also switched off the italic tag </i> before switching off the bold tag </b>, and then opened the italic tag again for the words 'plain italic'. We could have left the italic tag open throughout and just closed off the bold tag after the words 'bold italic', but it's good practice not to have your tags overlapping. Any tag that opens within another tag should be closed off before you close the container tag. You can re-open it again immediately outside of that container if necessary.

The tag <u>, which we used to underline our text, is no longer widely used, and you should avoid underlining text because it makes the words look like a link to another page. For emphasis, you can make text

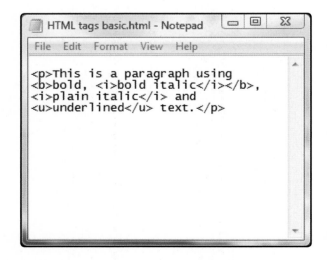

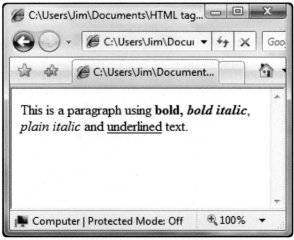

Left: Figure 1
Right: Figure 2

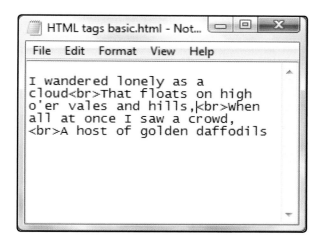

Left: Figure 3
Right: Figure 4
Below: Figure 5

bold, apply italics or change its colour. There's also an `<em>` tag, which defaults to italics. However, you can change its behaviour (as with any tag) using CSS. This is useful when you want two emphasis styles.

Having said that, browsers are perhaps the best example of how backwards-compatibility should work in software. Because they must still be able to render pages produced 10 or more years ago, even deprecated tags such as `<u>` still work, which means the pages you produce today should keep working well into the future.

The `<p>` and `</p>` tags in the example define the start and end of a paragraph. A web browser inserts a blank line after the `</p>` tag automatically. If you just want to move the cursor to the next line on the page so you can begin a fresh line without inserting a blank one between that and the text before it, use the tag `<br>` to insert a break.

As an example, to lay out Wordsworth's poem *Daffodils* correctly using the `<br>` tag, write the HTML shown in Figure 3. The result, when viewed in Internet Explorer, is shown in Figure 4 and correctly places each sentence of the poem on a new line.

PAGE OF REASON
Some tags apply not to specific sections of text but to a whole page, and they define where various structural sections begin and end. Again, they are always contained within angled brackets, opened and closed off using the same name in each instance but with a leading / before the closing tag, and never overlap.

The main page-wide tags, presented in the order in which they are applied, are shown in Figure 4, and must be used in every page you create. Most HTML editors provide these barebones of a web page for you.

As you can see, the `<html>` tag, which defines the very top and end of the file, surrounds all other tags. Within this, you have two main sections called `<head>` and `<body>`. Between `<body>` and `</body>`, as you can imagine, is where the main, visible content of your page will go.

The `<head>` tag is used for mainly administrative purposes. It tells the browser which character set to use when it renders the page. It tells search engines how they should index the page, and it tells any device that is capable of outputting the content (computer screen, smartphone, printer or screen reader for the visually impaired) how that content should be styled.

The `<head>` section also contains the `<title>` tag. Anything you enter between that and `</title>` will be displayed in the bar at the top of a browser, on the tab in any browser that is capable of opening more than one page at a time, in browser history lists and in the list of results returned by a search engine.

Give careful thought to what you include here. It's good practice to include your site name at the beginning so it is visible even if your visitor has several tabs open at once. It's also worth including a number of key phrases that relate specifically to the individual page to which it is attached, to make it stand out in search results. So, in our holiday cottage example, you could use the code:

```
<title>Redcot Barn | memorable family
breaks in Shakespeare country</title>
```

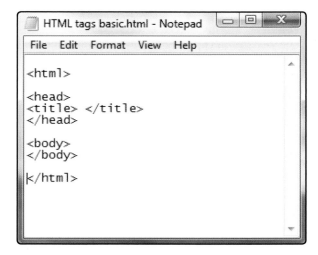

Formatting tags

It's vital that you format the words on your web pages correctly, or else visitors will struggle to navigate the site and may look elsewhere

BENEFITS

Use formatting tags to guide visitors around web pages and define their hierarchy

Modify a font's appearance to suit your needs

As we've already explained, the simplest web page can consist of nothing more than a line of text tapped out on a blank page. Although this is the fastest way to convey a limited amount of information, it lacks structure, which is essential for guiding your visitor around the page and defining a hierarchy of importance. HTML is well suited to this task.

On page 36 we covered the tags <b>, <i> and <u>, which deal with bolding, italicising and underlining text, and we showed you how these tags can be combined to build up a range of effects.

HTML also has a range of pre-defined header styles, which use the tags <h1> to <h7>. Any text that is wrapped inside one of these tags (such as <h1>) and closed off with a matching tag with a leading / (such as </h1>) will be treated as a separate paragraph, and will have a blank line added beneath it. You can see from the

Below: Basic HTML tags for headline formatting and adding emphasis should render identically in any browser, as seen here in IE7 and Firefox

images below how these headings look in their default state in Internet Explorer (left) and Mozilla Firefox (right). In Chapter 4, we'll show you how headings can be tailored to your specific needs.

HAPPY FAMILIES

Every browser has a default font setting. This can be defined by the user through the browser preferences. Unless you override it in your code, the setting will be used to display any unstyled text on your pages. You can specify your own font settings using the font tag. This can have a range of variables attached to it – including font face, size and colour – to tailor the style of the text to which it has been applied. It works like this:

```
<font face="Arial" size="-1"
 color="red">
```

American spellings are common in HTML; notice how the word 'colour' is spelt without a 'u'. The face command specifies the name of the font that should be used. In the example above we've used Arial, but this will rely on the visitor's computer having that font installed. There is no way you can guarantee this, so it is usual to specify a range of similar fonts separated by commas, such as 'Arial, Helvetica, sans serif'. When your visitor's browser loads the page, it will read through this list and use the first one it comes to that is installed on its system.

Say your preference is for Helvetica, with Arial as a fallback for people who don't have Helvetica installed. In this case, reverse the order so the tag starts:

```
<font face="Helvetica, Arial,
 sans-serif"...
```

Other commonly used families are as follows:

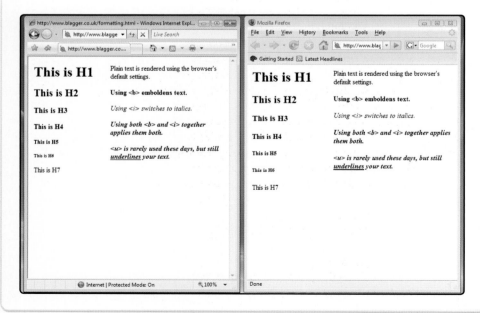

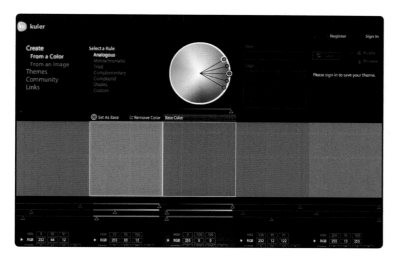

Red colors

HTML name	Hex code R G B	Decimal code R G B
IndianRed	CD 5C 5C	205 92 92
LightCoral	F0 80 80	240 128 128
Salmon	FA 80 72	250 128 114
DarkSalmon	E9 96 7A	233 150 122
LightSalmon	FF A0 7A	255 160 122
Crimson	DC 14 3C	220 20 60
Red	FF 00 00	255 0 0
FireBrick	B2 22 22	178 34 34
DarkRed	8B 00 00	139 0 0

Pink colors

HTML name	Hex code R G B	Decimal code R G B
Pink	FF C0 CB	255 192 203
LightPink	FF B6 C1	255 182 193
HotPink	FF 69 B4	255 105 180
DeepPink	FF 14 93	255 20 147
MediumVioletRed	C7 15 85	199 21 133
PaleVioletRed	DB 70 93	219 112 147

Orange colors

HTML name	Hex code R G B	Decimal code R G B
LightSalmon	FF A0 7A	255 160 122
Coral	FF 7F 50	255 127 80
Tomato	FF 63 47	255 99 71

Green colors

HTML name	Hex code R G B	Decimal code R G B
GreenYellow	AD FF 2F	173 255 47
Chartreuse	7F FF 00	127 255 0
LawnGreen	7C FC 00	124 252 0
Lime	00 FF 00	0 255 0
LimeGreen	32 CD 32	50 205 50
PaleGreen	98 FB 98	152 251 152
LightGreen	90 EE 90	144 238 144
MediumSpringGreen	00 FA 9A	0 250 154
SpringGreen	00 FF 7F	0 255 127
MediumSeaGreen	3C B3 71	60 179 113
SeaGreen	2E 8B 57	46 139 87
ForestGreen	22 8B 22	34 139 34
Green	00 80 00	0 128 0
DarkGreen	00 64 00	0 100 0
YellowGreen	9A CD 32	154 205 50
OliveDrab	6B 8E 23	107 142 35
Olive	80 80 00	128 128 0
DarkOliveGreen	55 6B 2F	85 107 47
MediumAquamarine	66 CD AA	102 205 170
DarkSeaGreen	8F BC 8F	143 188 143

Brown colors

HTML name	Hex code R G B	Decimal code R G B
Cornsilk	FF F8 DC	255 248 220
BlanchedAlmond	FF EB CD	255 235 205
Bisque	FF E4 C4	255 228 196
NavajoWhite	FF DE AD	255 222 173
Wheat	F5 DE B3	245 222 179
BurlyWood	DE B8 87	222 184 135
Tan	D2 B4 8C	210 180 140
RosyBrown	BC 8F 8F	188 143 143
SandyBrown	F4 A4 60	244 164 96
Goldenrod	DA A5 20	218 165 32
DarkGoldenrod	B8 86 0B	184 134 11
Peru	CD 85 3F	205 133 63
Chocolate	D2 69 1E	210 105 30
SaddleBrown	8B 45 13	139 69 19
Sienna	A0 52 2D	160 82 45
Brown	A5 2A 2A	165 42 42
Maroon	80 00 00	128 0 0

White colors

HTML name	Hex code R G B	Decimal code R G B
White	FF FF FF	255 255 255
Snow	FF FA FA	255 250 250

Serif
Times New Roman
Times
Georgia

Sans-serif
Verdana
Arial
Helvetica
Geneva

Monospace
`Courier New`
`Courier`

SIZE ISN'T EVERYTHING
The `size=` attribute can be specified in several ways. In our example, we've said that the font should be one size smaller than the default on the visitor's browser. We could easily have stated '-2' for much smaller text, or '+2' to make it larger. However, this doesn't give you complete control over your page, and because you don't know how your visitor's browser is set up you can't be sure how the text will look on their screen.

For this reason, you may want to use pixel sizes for greater control. Just be careful when doing so. Ideally, you should apply pixel sizes only to items that absolutely must be styled in a specific way, such as entries in a menu that have to line up with one another. Your visitors may have set up their browser in a certain way because they have a visual impairment. If that's the case, they will not thank you for reducing the size of the main body of words on your page, thereby rendering it illegible for them. Remember, anything that makes your pages hard to read will send your visitors straight back to Google and on to your competitors.

If you do choose to use pixel sizes, you should structure your code as follows, replacing the size attribute with whatever you consider appropriate:

```
<font face="Arial, Helvetica,
 sans-serif" size="10px"...
```

COLOURFUL LANGUAGE
In our font setting example, we used a plain-English name for the font colour (`color="red"`). It is one of 147 colours to have been blessed with a name as well as the hexadecimal code used for other colours. You can find a list of colours at http://en.wikipedia.org/wiki/Web_colors#X11_color_names.

If the colour you want doesn't have a name, you must use the hexadecimal code. This specifies the quantity of red, green and blue that should be mixed to create that colour using the standard hexadecimal base. The base runs from 0 to 9 and also adds the letters A to F. The brightest possible colour on a computer screen is white, while the darkest is black, produced by turning off all colour. Black is represented using the code 000000.

All codes are six digits long, although it is sometimes possible to use a three-digit shorthand. The first two digits define the amount of red, the second pair defines the amount of green and the third pair the amount of blue used to make up the colour. The code 000000 tells the browser to use no red, no green and no blue when formatting the text to which it is applied. Knowing that the hexadecimal scale runs from 0 to F, and that white is at the opposite end of the scale to black, we can work out that white must be maximum red, maximum green and maximum blue – or, to use hexadecimal code, FFFFFF.

When used in the font tag, these colours are preceded by a hash (#). If we want a mid-grey rather than red and use a hexadecimal rather than a named colour, we write:

```
<font face="Arial, Helvetica, sans-
 serif" size="10px" color="#CCCCCC">
```

Adobe's Kuler application at http://kuler.adobe.com helps you choose colours that work well together, and specifies hexadecimal equivalents.

Left: Adobe's Kuler application helps you pick harmonious colours, and provides the hexadecimal codes used to render them correctly in a browser

Right: Many 'web-safe' colours have been given names that are easy to remember, so you don't have to resort to codes

Preparing images

As well as knowing which images are right for your website, you need to understand compression, cropping, sharpening and watermarking

Without images, a website would be dull, uninspiring and quickly passed by. However, while newspapers and magazines need the best possible picture quality, websites are a different matter. Large images take up lots of server space, and take a long time to download on the visitor's computer.

SAVING GRACES

Photos should be saved in the JPEG format, which compresses images by merging areas of similar colour. Flat graphics, such as logos with solid colours, should be saved in GIF or PNG formats, from which compression tools will remove colours and use dithering to fool the eye into thinking they are still there.

Most graphics software has a dedicated web-saving mode, previewing the results of any compression. It's essential that you use this rather than just using a Save As option from the File menu, as heavy compression can have a detrimental effect on your images.

Generally, the more complex an image, the less it can be compressed. The two right-hand images below are

sections of a JPEG, saved using Photoshop's Save for Web feature with quality settings of 0 and 100 per cent. The middle image will download quickly, but has artefacts and blocking. The image saved at 100 per cent looks great, but will take a long time to download. A quality setting of 50 per cent is usually the best compromise.

Likewise, the three images on the page opposite show a graphic saved in GIF format with eight, 32 and 256 colours. Because we have applied dithering, there's little difference between the 32- and 256-colour versions, yet the file size is smaller: 92KB as opposed to 144KB. Clearly, the most appropriate compression here is to reduce the number of colours to 32 and apply dithering. The eight-colour image, as you can see, is unusable.

CLEAR AND SIMPLE

Images on the web are rarely more than 500 pixels wide when embedded in text, but many are even smaller. It's important to resize images before uploading them to your web space rather than allowing them to be downloaded at their full size and shrunk by the visitor's browser.

Below: JPEG is a highly efficient compression method. When the photo below is examined up close, you can see the compression in action. The one in the middle has been heavily compressed and the one on the right lightly compressed

8 colours

32 colours

256 colours

When resizing, ensure that you maintain the image's aspect ratio to avoid it looking squashed or stretched. Smaller graphics can be harder to see clearly, so increasing contrast, saturation and sharpening in an image editor can pay dividends.

PUBLISHING YOUR PHOTOS

Once you've gathered your resized and compressed pictures into the images folder of your site, you can put them on to your pages (we'll show you how to upload files on page 46). The <img> tag that places images on a page takes several variables. However, unlike other tags, it isn't closed off by a matching </img> tag. The tag used to include a picture stored in the images folder of your site might look like this:

```
<img src="/images/kitchen.jpg"
 alt="Self-catering kitchen" width="450"
 height="337" border="0" align="left"
 hspace="5" vspace="10">
```

The top line is the only essential part of the image tag. The rest gives greater control over the use of the image, but if it is left out the image is still displayed. The opening tag tells the browser it's working with an image, while src tells it that what follows is the source of the file. It's called kitchen.jpg and is stored in the images folder. The images part is preceded by a forward slash (/), which tells the browser to look in the root of the website's space on the server. It's advisable to use this method – rather than the full address of the image's location, such as www.redcotbarn.co.uk/images/kitchen.jpg – as it allows you to move the page to another folder on the site or re-use this line of code on another page.

The alt="Self-catering kitchen" part defines a tooltip that pops up when the visitor moves their mouse over the image, and is displayed within the image space before the image loads. If the image cannot be loaded, this line gives your visitors a clue as to what they are missing, so make it descriptive and helpful.

EXTRA DIMENSIONS

The width= and height= parameters define the image dimensions. Without them, the browser will use the image's size as it was saved from your camera or image editor. Specifying dimensions gives you more control, and tells the browser how much space to leave for the image on the page if it starts laying out your words before the image has finished loading.

Specifying border="0" determines the thickness of the border around the image. The amount will depend on how well you want the picture to blend into the page. If your pages have white backgrounds and your image features a cloudy or burnt-out sky, you may specify a border of 2 or 3. Specifying 0 means that if you use the image as a link by wrapping it in <a> tags (see page 56), it won't be surrounded by the default blue and purple borders used to denote new and visited links respectively.

The last three variables in the tag define how the image interacts with other elements on the page. Here we have set it to align with the left-hand margin; we could have set it to 'right' or 'center' (American spelling). We have also set a gap of five pixels left and right of the image, and 10 pixels above and below the image. This gives the image breathing space, and prevents words and other images on the page overlapping it.

Above: Reducing the number of colours in the image to eight degrades the left-hand image. The remaining images are almost impossible to tell apart, but the one on the right is over 50KB larger than the one in the middle, which has only 32 colours and 100 per cent compression. The image on the right has 256 colours and 100 per cent compression

Below: Using photo-editing software to save web-friendly versions of images will reduce the amount of disk space and bandwidth they consume, and will lead to pages loading faster

Adding links

Any web page you create is only as effective as its links to the rest of the internet, so make sure you define your links correctly

BENEFITS

Learn how to add hyperlinks to your page

Use text and images as links

Make linked pages open in the same or different windows

If words and pictures are the flesh of your site, the links you use between pages on your site and those of others are the bones that hold things together and the joints that connect your site to the rest of the web.

The tag used to define a link is <a>, which stands for anchor. It is closed off by a matching tag that is preceded by a leading slash, </a>. Variables included as part of the opening <a> define the destination of the link, how it should be opened and to what it relates, while text or images used between this and the closing </a> become the elements on which visitors click to follow the link.

DROPPING ANCHOR

A typical link to another page on your site looks like this:

```
<a href="about.html" title="More
information about Redcot Barn">
About</a>
```

A link to an external site may look like this:

```
<a href="http://www.bbc.co.uk/news/"
title="BBC Homepage" target="_blank">
BBC homepage</a>
```

There are some subtle differences between the two. The first is in the address: while we are able to specify just the filename of the page that we want in our local site, we have to use the complete web address when pointing to external sites, and include the http:// at the beginning. If you were to just use www.bbc.co.uk, for example, the visitor's browser would look for a directory or file using that name on your own site and it would throw up an error when it couldn't find one.

The link on our local site assumes that the file about.html is stored in the same folder as the page from which we are linking to it. If it isn't, we need to include the folder where it can be found. Ideally, you should specify this in relation to the root of your web space, using the site map you drew in your planning stages. So, if we were coding a page to be saved at www.redcotbarn.

Below left: The link to the Directions page opens in the same tab in the browser

Below right: This link opens the page in a new tab

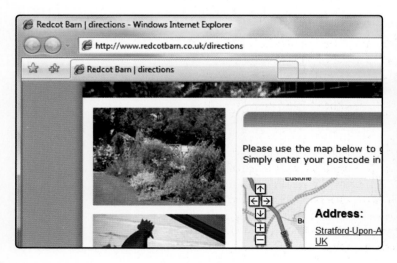

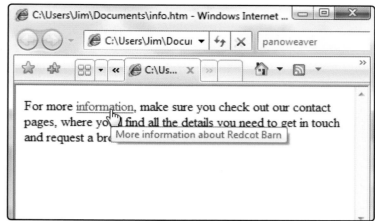

co.uk/contact/index.html and wanted to link to a file called index.html located at www.redcotbarn.co.uk/about/index.html, we could use any of the following:

```
<a href="http://www.redcotbarn.co.uk/
  about/index.html"…
<a href="/about/index.html"…
<a href="/about/"…
<a href="../about/index.html"…
```

The first is self-explanatory; the second works because the forward-slash that opens the address tells the browser to go to the root of your website, dig down to the 'about' folder and from there open the file index.html. The third variant works because most web servers are programmed to open files with certain names whenever they find them in a folder and index.html is one such name (index.htm, index.shtml, index.php and default.html are others).

The final option will be familiar to anyone who uses the Linux command line or used DOS before switching to Windows. The '..' tells the browser to move one level up the folder tree to the root and from there go into the folder called 'about' and then load the file index.html.

In the example links on the opposite page, we included a title variable. This works like a tooltip, with most browsers displaying it as your visitor hovers their mouse over the link. It helps search engines index your site and the places to which it links. Well-written titles will improve your standing in the search results.

MEETING TARGETS
In the link to the remote site, we've included a 'target' variable. This tells the browser how to open the link. If you leave this out, the browser opens the link in place of the current page. Generally, this is what you should let happen, but there may be times when you want your own site to remain open in one browser window while opening the link in another. Some modern browsers open the site you reference with a target="_blank" tag in a new tab of the same window.

The _blank tells the browser to start a new, blank workspace for the link. Other targets that can be included here are _self, _top or _parent, but these usually relate to handling links in sites that use frames. As few sites use frames, and we recommend avoiding them where possible, they're not covered in detail here.

PUTTING THINGS IN CONTEXT
Once you've defined the destination of your link, you need to decide what the visitor has to click on to reach the destination page. In the examples opposite we used text ('About' and 'BBC homepage'), but it could just as easily be a link to an image. In this case, you'll probably want to set your image's border variable to 0.

Here's a line of HTML code including a link (from another website to Redcot Barn) using text:

```
<p>Click <a href="http://www.redcotbarn.
  co.uk">here</a> to visit the Redcot
  Barn website.</p>
```

The word 'here' becomes a link, while the rest of the sentence is displayed as normal text. If you had an image of Redcot Barn and wanted to allow visitors to click on it to go to the website, your code would look like this:

```
<p>Click on the image on the right to
  visit the Redcot Barn website</p>
<a href="http://www.redcotbarn.co.
  uk"><img src="/images/redcot.jpg"
  width="250" height="150" border="0"
  align="right"></a>
```

Wrap the <a> tag around the element you want to make the link. Links can be positioned within other tags, such as the H1 to H7 headline tags, or around any complete element on the page, such as a CSS layer. Careful use of links, combined with the CSS techniques we'll explain in the next chapter, will allow you to create some impressive and truly interactive web design with very little effort.

Above left: A 'tool tip' caption tells your visitors where the link will take them if they click on the image

Above right: A 'tool tip' link, with a carefully written title, can help search engines to index your site properly

Layouts with tables and lists

Tables and lists give your web pages definition, so it's important to get a good grasp of how they can help as layout tools

By now you should understand the fundamentals of web design and you should have a clear grasp of formatting text, placing images and creating links between various pages on your site, and to sites beyond your own domain. Now it's time to start thinking about how it should all sit on the page.

A decade ago, web designers used frames to split the visitor's browser windows into discrete sections and load a separate page into each. Times have moved on, and frames are now frowned upon. These days, most layouts are created using cascading style sheets, which we will cover in detail in the next chapter. Before we have a look at those, though, we need to understand another key layout tool: the table.

TURNING THE TABLES
You can use a table to structure your whole page, positioning images and text in its cells to keep them properly arranged. The cells can have coloured backgrounds, their contents can be set to align left, right or centre, their boundaries set to have borders and padding, and cells that should span more than one column or row can be merged to form wider or taller spaces.

The three key tags used to define a table are `<table>`, `<tr>` (table row) and `<td>` (table data cell). These are used in turn to describe the layout, working from the top down. Each one must be properly closed off with a matching tag that is preceded by a slash. While you can get away with missing the `</p>` off the end of a paragraph, forgetting the `</tr>` at the end of a table row or the `</td>` at the end of a cell will have disastrous consequences.

To explain how it works, we're going to use code to create the table in the screen here. The table has three rows and two columns, with the cells of the top row merged to create a header cell. As you can see from the

Right: A simple HTML table, with two cells in the top row merged into one

code on the page opposite, the whole table is formed between the `<table>` and `</table>` tags. Each row of cells comes between `<tr>` and `</tr>`, and the contents of each cell are between `<td>` and `</td>`. We have centred the text inside each cell by attaching the variable `align="center"` to the `<td>` tags and stretched the only cell in the top row across both columns using the variable `colspan="2"`. If we hadn't done this then the browser would have been unable to render the table correctly, as all rows must contain the same number of cells, and we would have defined just one in the top row.

However, merged cells do not need to cross the whole of a table from one side to the other. If the rows below our top row had each been made up of three cells rather than two, we could have merged two cells into one on the top row and included another cell either before or after the two merged cells, so the total still added up to three – the number of cells in the rows below.

THE HARD CELL
We've applied some formatting to the whole table in the opening `<table>` tag. A one-pixel border will be drawn

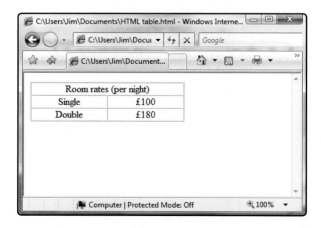

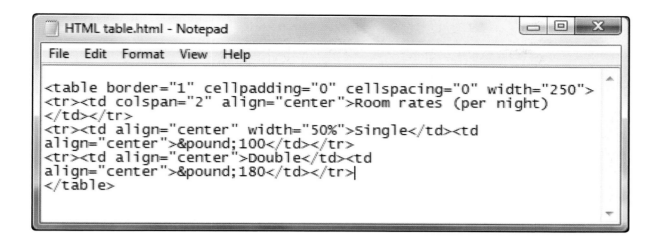

```
HTML table.html - Notepad
File  Edit  Format  View  Help

<table border="1" cellpadding="0" cellspacing="0" width="250">
<tr><td colspan="2" align="center">Room rates (per night)
</td></tr>
<tr><td align="center" width="50%">Single</td><td
align="center">&pound;100</td></tr>
<tr><td align="center">Double</td><td
align="center">&pound;180</td></tr>
</table>
```

around each cell, plus the table perimeter. We've chosen to remove all padding between the contents of the cells and their borders, and all the spacing that would, by default, appear between each cell in the table. Finally, we've fixed the table's width at 250 pixels.

Each of the individual table cells, apart from those at the top that have been set to span both columns, take up half the width of the table. We've specified that the first individual cell, which appears in the left-hand column of the second row, is 50 per cent in width, or half the width of the full table. All remaining cells in that column must be the same width. As there are only two columns, the cells in the second column must balance out the width and so use the other half of the width.

Instead of using the £ symbol on our table, we are using the code £. This ensures greater compatibility with the widest range of browsers and language settings, as you cannot know for sure that your visitors' browsers will correctly display the pound sterling symbol if used as a character. Similar codes can be used to define a non-breaking space ( ), copyright (©), a quarter (¼), a half (½) and three-quarters (¾).

MAKING LISTS

Lists work in a similar way to tables. It's easiest to think of them as a single-column table. Each entry in a list can be preceded by a bullet or a number. Bulleted lists are termed unordered and are initiated using the tag <ul>, while lists with leading numbers are termed ordered and initiated using <ol>. Each entry in a list is marked out using the tag <li> for list item, whether you're working with ordered or unordered lists. To see how this works, enter the following code and preview the results in your browser, then replace the <ol> and </ol> with <ul> and </ul> to swap the numbers for bullets:

```
<b>Redcot Barn house rules</b>
<ol>
<li>No pets</li>
<li>No smoking inside the building</li>
<li>No loud music after 11pm</li>
<li>Please tidy up after yourself</li>
</ol>
```

We've arranged the two lists side by side, as you can see in the screen below.

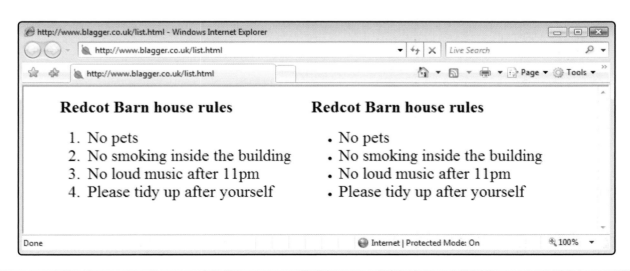

Top: The HTML code for our simple table

Bottom: Bulleted and numbered lists are almost identical in coding, but differ greatly when rendered on screen

Uploading your site

Once you've got to grips with all the main page elements and how they fit together, you're ready to prepare your website for publishing

BENEFITS

Learn how to transfer your website from your local hard disk to your live web space

Before you upload anything to your server, you'll need some details from your web host: your username and password, the address of the server and the directory into which you must upload files.

1 Download, install and launch CoffeeCup Free FTP from www.coffeecup.com/free-ftp and click the Servers button. Click the plus symbol on the dialog box that appears. Fill in the details and a memorable nickname. Leave the Passive box unticked unless your host has told you to use Passive FTP. Click the More Options button and enter the folder on your hard disk in which you have saved your files in the Local Folder box, and the folder on the server into which your host told you to upload them in the Remote Folder box.

2 Save your settings and click the drop-down arrow beside the Servers button. Choose the one you've just specified and CoffeeCup will connect to the server and display a list of your locally saved pages and files in the upper-left window of its interface, and the files on your server in the upper-right window. Delete any folders with names such as index.html, index.php or default.html in the right-hand window. Leaving them

where they are may mean they load instead of your own site if your new files don't overwrite them.

3 If you didn't specify a local folder when setting up the server connection, click in the address box above the left-hand window and type it, or click through the directory structure in the window itself to navigate to your files. Select all your files then click the Upload button on the toolbar. CoffeeCup will send your files to the server where they will be made live. Ensure that you have uploaded all the files that your site needs, including any that may be stored in subfolders, such as images.

Visit your site in a web browser. If you've uploaded the files to the root of your server space rather than to a hidden development folder that casual visitors will never find, they are now online for all to see, and you should check that they appear as expected. If you spot any problems, go back and take remedial action. Don't leave them online with the intention of doing it later; you have no way of knowing how many people may see them in the meantime, and if your pages are designed to promote your business they will have precisely the opposite effect if they are littered with spelling mistakes, have empty image boxes or don't render correctly in every browser.

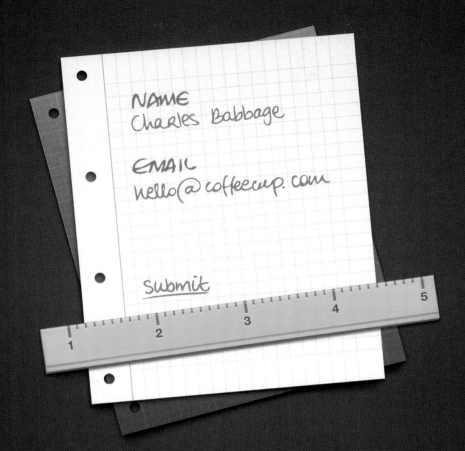

CHAPTER 4

IN THIS CHAPTER

Understanding CSS 50

Applying the basics......................52

Putting CSS into practice............56

Developing your layout
   further..60

Creating a navigation bar............62

Using CSS

While you can use HTML exclusively on your website, it's far better to use Cascading Style Sheets, or CSS. This sounds impressive, but it simply defines the way your website looks. CSS is distinct from HTML, and a simple change to one file can completely transform the way your site looks. CSS also allows you far more precision and control over page layout, and provides some clever tricks to make your site look great.

MacBook Air

In this chapter, we'll explain how CSS works and how you can use it to produce a three-column page layout and an interactive menu bar that doesn't require the use of a graphics application.

As with the HTML examples used in the previous chapter, no special software is required to use CSS: Windows' Notepad editor is all you need.

Understanding CSS

If you want your website to have consistency and clarity, and you want to reduce the work involved in changing styles, CSS will prove invaluable

BENEFITS

Get an overview of the benefits of CSS

Learn how to keep the CSS code separate from the HTML

Cascading Style Sheets (CSS) can mean different things to different people. To some, CSS is the web-design equivalent of desktop publishing, providing far more precise control over the look and feel of a website than HTML alone. To others, it's the future of web design, providing the ability to add special effects that were previously impossible. To most people, though, it's the quickest, most widely compatible way of producing stunning online designs. CSS reduces the work involved in designing a website, enabling users to recycle their work and ensuring consistency across an entire site. It's easy to see why this language is becoming a standard.

THE PROBLEM WITH HTML
HTML is great for defining the underlying structure of a web page, and it offers a set of rudimentary styling tags. As we showed in Chapter 3, it includes tables for organising and aligning your content, and lets you tweak the appearance of photos and text, either case by case or across your entire page. However, it doesn't go as far as many would like.

Styling tags must often be applied to each element individually, so if you have a 15-paragraph page styled in Arial and you want to switch to Verdana, you'll have to make 15 changes to your code to get the job done. This is time-consuming and increases the risk of introducing errors and inconsistencies into your code.

As these tags are scattered throughout your code, it means that it's harder for less experienced users to make amendments, because the page's structural information and its actual content are muddled together.

STYLE CHALLENGE
CSS addresses these shortcomings. By separating these elements, a group of developers working as a team can assign styling tasks to a coding expert, while a writer works on the content. CSS offers a far greater range of options for styling your content and laying it out with pixel-perfect precision. It also simplifies many tasks, such as defining layouts. Rather than defining a clumsy table with columns, rows and cells, you need only specify where a box of content should begin and end, and how big it should be.

CSS code is infinitely flexible, allowing you to define how elements – such as links using the `<a>` tag, pictures using the `<img>` tag or headings using the `<h1>` tag – look across an entire website. Alternatively, you can give each element a unique name and assign it an individual style that doesn't appear anywhere else on your site.

Although you can write the CSS code directly into your page, the real benefit comes in separating it into a file of its own. With the style information separated from the content, you can focus your attention on producing excellent copy for your visitors to read when working with the pages themselves, and switch to a more visual mindset when it comes to defining the layout.

When you separate CSS in this way, you call it into each page with a single line of code in the `<head>` section. This means you can create a single stylesheet for your entire site, to which each page refers in turn. The benefit is obvious: by centralising your style and layout information in a single file that all your pages use as a resource, you can make radical site-wide changes simply by editing the stylesheet rather than having to change every individual page on your site. As a result, you will spend less time working on the code for each page, and reduce the chances of introducing errors in the process.

Professional web designers use CSS widely, and if you're serious about developing your website, you should make the effort to learn at least the basics. Fortunately, you don't need to do this wholesale from day one. As we explained in the previous chapter, browsers are a perfect example of how all software should handle backwards-compatibility, as they are happy to mix 10-year-old code with the latest CSS mark-up.

When you start using CSS to style your layouts, we recommend that you use layers rather than tables and, if you wish, stick with the HTML formatting tags we defined in the previous section before moving on from there. We also recommend that you work with elements that already exist within HTML, such as `<h1>`, `<h2>`, `<p>` and others, so that any visually impaired visitors who have defined their own stylesheet can apply that in preference to your own CSS mark-up if they find your choices difficult to read.

GETTING STARTED

CSS is most often applied to web pages, but you can use it to define the style of any XML-based document, including some graphics files. You can also use it to specify output devices, which means you can apply more than one stylesheet to your page and ask the browser to use the most appropriate one for the device on which it is running. With three stylesheets running in tandem, for example, you could produce specific pages for a regular PC screen, a portable device such as a PDA or Windows Mobile-based phone and even a printer, which would set

```
Untitled - Notepad
File  Edit  Format  View  Help
<head>
<title>Welcome to Redcot Barn</title>
<style type="text/css">
<!--
body {
                    behavior:url("csshover.htc");
        }
#container {
        width: 960px;
        margin-right: auto;
        margin-left: auto;
        text-align:left;
}
        #menu {
        float: left;
        width: 150px;
        margin-right: 10px;
}
#content {
        float: left;
        width: 590px;
}
#sidebar {
        float: right;
        width: 200px;
}
#footer {
        border-top: 1px solid #000000;
        clear: both;
        margin-left: 160px;
        padding-top: 10px;
}
-->
</style>
<!--
#widemenu ul li {
        float: left;
        list-style-type: none;
        padding-right: 30px;
        padding-left: 5px;
        padding-bottom: 5px;
        padding-top: 5px;
        font-family: Arial, Helvetica, sans-serif;
        font-weight: bold;
        font-size: 14px;
        display: block;
}
#widemenu {
        background-color: #dddddd;
        margin-bottom: 10px;
        height: 25px;
}
#widemenu ul li a {
        color: #000000;
        text-decoration: none;
        display: block;
}
#widemenu ul li:hover {
        background-color: #bbbbbb;
        display: block;
}
#widemenu ul {
        height: 8px;
        margin: 0px;
        padding: 0px;
        display: block;
}
-->
</head>
```

Left: Separating the style information from the content makes designing your website easier and more versatile

the page up for the optimum reproduction on paper rather than on a screen.

Unfortunately, not all browsers are the same, and the more you use CSS, the more you will see that Internet Explorer's interpretation of your code can vary widely from those of the other major (and minor) browsers, which render web pages similarly.

Over the next few pages, we'll show you how to get round some of these problems. Once you take things further, though, you may have to start applying special conditional classes that interrogate the browser and change the way an element is implemented on the page. There are so many different instances when you may need to do this that they merit a book of their own. We can't cover them in full here, but an online search for 'IE conditional CSS' will provide a wealth of results.

Applying the basics

CSS is complicated, but you can start using the basics straight away. Here we show you how to get started with this versatile language

BENEFITS

Learn how to make a simple stylesheet step by step

Create elements such as pullquotes

Customise the look of HTML tags throughout your site

It can help to think of CSS as a plain-English description of how elements on your page should look. The styles are split up according to the elements to which they apply. This can affect anything from a single item on your page to every tag of a certain style. Here we'll show you how to define a range of common styles using CSS, and how to apply those styles to your pages.

YOUR FIRST STYLE SHEET

Styles can be applied on a page-by-page basis and are defined within the head section of a page between a series of special characters that, in effect, turns styles into a comment. In this way the browser reads the instructions as the page loads, but they won't appear on the page itself.

If we were to use this method to embed CSS code that gives our page a grey background, we would insert this section between the <head> and </head> tags:

```
<style type="text/css">
<!--
body {
    background-color: #CCCCCC;
}
-->
</style>
```

The <!-- and --> lines define a section of your page that the browser should treat only as information. It could be a note you've written to yourself, a section of code that you want to remove temporarily from the page without actually deleting or, as in this case, the place where you define your CSS attributes.

However, this is only a partial solution to the problems we outlined in the opening part of this section on CSS. While we have separated the styling information

Right: Modern websites show how CSS can be used to good effect

from the actual content of the page, we are still including it in the page itself, at the very top.

A far more efficient method is to define the look of your page in a separate file – a dedicated stylesheet – which you then attach to your page by adding a line to its header section. This way, you can call the same stylesheet into every page on your site, ensuring greater consistency and saving you the task of changing the styles on every page in your site when you want to freshen it up. The code for calling a stylesheet into your page looks like this:

```
<head>
<title>This is the title of my page
 </title>
<link href="styles.css" rel="stylesheet"
```

```
type="text/css">
</head>
```

Here you're telling the page to use a stylesheet called styles.css. The browser knows this is stored in the same folder as the page on which you are working, as no directory information is included.

Like web pages, stylesheets can have any name you choose. You can also link several stylesheets to a single page by giving them different names, calling them in by repeating the `<link` line above as many times as you need and swapping out the `"styles.css"` part. This way, you can have a single master stylesheet that you use across your site, and several tailored sheets that apply to individual pages.

STYLES FOR LAYOUT

When switching to CSS, you also need to start coding your pages differently. You can mix and match old and new technology, but while you can still use tables to define your layout, you should really use them only for tabular data – such as timetables and small spreadsheets within your pages – and switch to using layers for the actual guts of the layout. These layers are defined using the `<div>` tag, and can be sized and positioned with just as much precision as a text or picture box in DTP.

Your page will have several layers, and each one needs a name so that you can target it precisely with the appropriate style. If we were working on a page called about.html, we might want to include a layer called menu, like this:

```
<div id="menu">Layer content goes
  here.</div>
```

We can now style it in our stylesheet:

```
#menu {
    background-color: #FFFF99;
    margin: 10px;
    padding: 5px;
    height: 300px;
    width: 450px;
    border: 4px dotted #333333;
}
```

This turns our layer into a text or picture frame 450x300 pixels in size, with a 10-pixel margin around the edge to stop other page elements butting up against it. It has a yellow background (FFFF99) and a four-pixel-wide border made up using dark grey (333333) dots. Looking at the code above, you can probably see how easily you could tweak this to meet your own needs.

As you can see, the style name in our stylesheet (#menu) is the same name we have given to the layer in

the file about.html, with the addition of the leading #. The hash tells the browser to apply this style only to layers of that name. This means we can use the name 'menu' again elsewhere for elements that are not layers.

You can also see that the styling information is contained between the { and } brackets and that each line ends with a semicolon. Make sure you follow both conventions when creating your own stylesheets, or your styling won't work.

TARGETTING STYLES

Just as we can isolate layers, we can also target specific elements in the general content of our pages. Imagine we have a long track of flowing text that we want to break up. We don't have any images at our disposal, so we'll use a pullquote to highlight an interesting point in the text. To do this, we would include the following code in our about.html page:

```
<p class="pullquote">My really important
  words go here</p>
```

As we want to use this text in the middle of a piece of flowing copy and we don't want to break it up with a new layer `<div>`, we have applied the new style only to a specific paragraph in the text by attaching a class that we will define in the stylesheet. We can use the class, called pullquote, with as many paragraphs as we like on any of the pages to which we have attached the stylesheet, ensuring a consistency of style throughout the website.

The formatting for the pullquote is defined in the stylesheet as follows:

```
.pullquote {
    font: 18px Arial, Helvetica,
```

Below: By applying CSS styling that floats our text to the right and applies borders above and below, we can easily turn a regular paragraph into a pullquote around which the rest of the content on our pages will neatly flow

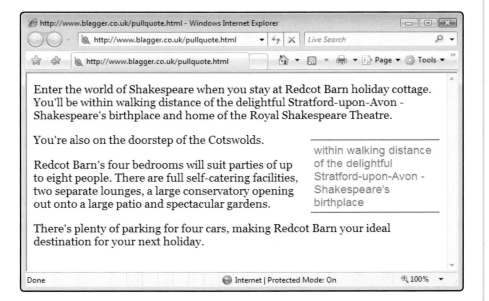

```
            sans-serif;
       color: #666666;
       width: 120px;
       margin: 10px 0px 10px 10px;
       padding: 5px;
       border-bottom: 2px solid #666666;
       border-top: 2px solid #666666;
       float: right;
    }
```

The dot that precedes the class name (pullquote) indicates to the browser that it should apply its contents only to a specific element with that class attached to it, and not to any layers we might also call 'pullquote'. You may think you would never do this, but consider that in the 'menu' example above, you may have a style for your menu layer, and want to define separately the font used to display different menus on different pages.

Our styling code for the pullquote defines the virtual box that contains the quoted sentence, and the actual styling of the quote itself. The box is 120 pixels wide, and as we haven't defined a height it will stretch to accommodate the words we put into it. This is important, because if we plan to use it on several pages throughout the site, we can never be sure that our quotes will always be the same length.

The box has a dark grey, two-pixel-wide solid border above and below, but as we haven't defined a background colour, the colour of the page will show through. It's

right-aligned (float: right;) so the rest of our text will flow around it and, because we want to give it some breathing space, we have applied a 10-pixel margin above, below and to the left. We do this in the line margin: 10px 0px 10px 10px, which is an abbreviation of the commands margin-top: 10px; margin-right: 0px and so on, in a single line to save space. The individual measurements in the line work in a clockwise direction, so the 10px 0px 10px 10px part tells the browser to apply those measurements to the top, right, bottom and left sides respectively. You can use this method to apply borders, margins and alignment to almost any element on your page, including images, by attaching appropriate classes.

We've also applied five pixels of padding. Padding is positioned within the dimensions of any layer; it is the area around an element. Here we're using it to keep the words away from the edges of the box.

The text is rendered in the same grey as the border and in 18-pixel Arial, Helvetica or sans serif, depending on which is installed on the visitor's computer.

CHANGING DEFAULT TAGS

You can use your stylesheet to make fundamental changes to the look of default HTML tags, such as paragraphs <p>, list items <li> or links <a>. You do this in the same way, but instead of giving each a name, you simply use its tag as the class name and drop the leading # or dot. For example:

```
a {
    font-weight: bold;
    font-variant: small-caps;
    color: #990000;
    text-decoration: none;
}
```

This will make our links prominent by rendering them in small, bold, dark red capitals. It also removes the underline from each one.

CONDITIONAL STYLES

Using CSS rather than plain HTML for styling allows you to introduce interactive elements that would otherwise require the use of Flash or advanced programming skills. The simple addition of the :hover tag makes named elements aware of the position of your mouse, and causes them to act differently when you move your pointer over them. Designers often use this to change the way links look when you point at them.

The following code, for example, changes the links in our page to adopt an underline and turn green as the cursor moves over them:

```
a:hover {
    text-decoration: underline;
```

Below: The full code for our web page with a pullquote is remarkably short, showing how simple CSS really is

```
pullquote[1] - Notepad
File  Edit  Format  View  Help
<style type="text/css">
<!--
.pullquote {
        font: 18px Arial, Helvetica, sans-serif;
        color: #666666;
        width: 200px;
        margin: 10px 0px 10px 10px;
        padding: 5px;
        border-bottom: 2px solid #666666;
        border-top: 2px solid #666666;
        float: right;
}
.style1 {
        font-family: Georgia, "Times New Roman", Times, serif;
        font-size: 18px;
}
.style2 {
        font: 18px Arial, Helvetica, sans-serif;
        color: #666666;
        width: 200px;
        margin: 10px 0px 10px 10px;
        padding: 5px;
        border-bottom: 2px solid #666666;
        border-top: 2px solid #666666;
        float: right;
        font-family: Georgia, "Times New Roman", Times, serif;
        font-size: 18px;
}
-->
</style>
<p class="style1">Enter the world of Shakespeare when you stay at Redcot Barn
holiday cottage. You'll be within walking distance of the delightful Stratford-
upon-Avon - Shakespeare's birthplace and home of the Royal Shakespeare Theatre.</p>
<p class="pullquote">within walking distance of the delightful Stratford-upon-Avon
- Shakespeare's birthplace</p>
<p class="style1">You're also on the doorstep of the Cotswolds.</p>
<p class="style1">Redcot Barn's four bedrooms will suit parties of up to eight
people. There are full self-catering facilities, two separate lounges, a large
conservatory opening out onto a large patio and spectacular gardens.</p>
<p class="style1">There's plenty of parking for four cars, making Redcot Barn your
ideal destination for your next holiday.</p>
```

```
color: #009900;
}
```

As you can see, we've defined only the parts that have changed, rather than writing out the entire style again from scratch. We've left the weight of the text (bold) and the case (small caps) unchanged from the original definition, as altering either of these would change the text's size on the page, and cause the text around it to shift position as your visitor moved their mouse around. If you've ever visited a website where this happens, you'll know how annoying it is.

So when a visitor's mouse pointer hovers over a link like this, the browser takes the style we have defined for `<a>` and uses it as the basis on which to make the changes detailed in `a:hover`.

Most browsers can apply a `:hover` state to any element on the page, allowing you to change not only links but also boxes, text areas, images and so on. However, Microsoft's Internet Explorer – which accounts for most of the browsing on almost all sites – restricts the use of `:hover` to links on a page. This means it's important not to rely on the `:hover` effect to such an extent that your content can be accessed only by users of browsers other than Internet Explorer, as we will show in the navigation bar example (page 62).

However, you can be even more specific in defining when certain styles apply to the various elements on your page. For example, you can style common features, such as lists, in different ways depending on where they appear within your page. This is another reason why you should make every effort to use layers rather than tables to lay out your pages.

GETTING TO THE POINT

As we will explain in greater detail later in this chapter, giving a full CSS description of the location of an element lets you restrict its effect to a single instance. For example, multi-level lists such as those you might use to outline points made in a meeting can have different bullet styles depending on whether the point made is a major point or just a sub-point of a bigger issue (or indeed a sub-point of that).

As we have already discovered, the HTML tag for defining a bulleted list is `<ul>`, and each entry within that list is defined using the tag `<li>`. To place a solid square next to the main points in the list, you would use the code:

```
ul li {
    list-style-type: square;
}
```

To define the bullets for subordinate points as small circles, which will be indented automatically, you would use the following:

```
ul li li {
    list-style-type: circle;
}
```

In effect, this tells the browser that for list items in an unordered list it should use square bullets, while for list items within list items within unordered lists it should use circles. You can go on adding further instances of `li` to the definition to target list items to an infinite degree within an ever-expanding list, although to be kind to your visitors we recommend breaking up your lists into more logical sections once they get deeper than two or three layers.

GOING FURTHER

Over the next eight pages, we are going to use CSS and a few other tools to create a classic three-column layout, which forms the basis of many websites. We'll then use this knowledge about interactivity to style up a list such as the one on page 45 as a menu for use throughout a site.

Above: Firebox is just one of millions of sites that use a classic three-column layout, which breaks the content up to make it easy to read

Putting CSS into practice

Creating the classic three-column layout favoured by modern web designers is quite straightforward with the help of CSS

Armed with the basics of CSS that we've covered so far, we can use layers and a stylesheet to build a floating three-column layout. This is a classic of modern web design, allowing you to have a header at the top of the page, a menu in a narrow column on the left, a wide area in the middle of the page for the main content and another narrow column on the right that acts as a sidebar for adverts or supplementary information needed.

This type of design is relatively easy to create using just a few lines of CSS, but because different browsers work in different ways, we need to tweak the code to ensure that all browsers interpret it properly.

CREATING YOUR BASE FILES
To form our three-column design we'll take a basic HTML page and style it using CSS. To do this we need just a plain-text editor, such as Notepad, to create two files: index.html and styles.css. The index.html

Below: After entering text in the layers of our layout, it's easy to see how they all run together without any styling. We need to divide them into three distinct columns

file will contain the content of the page, while the styles.css file will make it work.

It's worth typing in these examples, so you can get a real feel for how CSS works. The basic HTML page is the following short section of code:

```
<head>
<title>Welcome to Redcot Barn</title>
<link href="styles.css" rel="stylesheet"
 type="text/css">
</head>
<body>
<div id="container">
  <div id="header">Welcome to Redcot
   Barn</div>
  <div id="menu"></div>
  <div id="content"></div>
  <div id="sidebar"></div>
  <div id="footer"></div>
</div>
</body>
</html>
```

Believe it or not, that's the entire page. Everything we do from now on will be within the stylesheet. However, to make the different layers easier to differentiate onscreen, it's a good idea to enter some text into the menu, content and sidebar layers in the same way that we entered 'Welcome to Redcot Barn' in the header layer.

SETTING UP STYLES
As you can see from the code, the stylesheet for the page is defined within index.html. As it's stored in the same folder as the page itself, it's simply a case of specifying its name, rather than a full path to the folder in which it is saved.

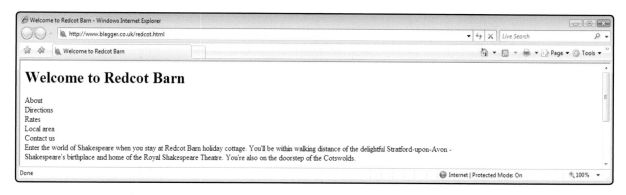

Left: Internet Explorer (top) renders centred layers differently to other browsers, as you can see when compared with Firefox (bottom)

As you don't know what screen resolution your visitors will be using, it's a good idea to design for nothing larger than 1,024 pixels in width. To allow room for scroll bars and application borders, you should confine your layout to a width of 960 pixels. Do this by defining a maximum size for the layer, called `container`, which contains every other layer on the page. You can then centre this onscreen by setting the margins on either side to `auto`, which tells the browser to split any unused width of the screen equally and position each half on either side of the layer. To do this, you have to add the following code to the file styles.css:

```
#container {
  width: 960px;
  margin-right: auto;
  margin-left: auto;
}
```

Again, the code is surrounded by { and } brackets, each line is terminated by a semicolon to show where the command ends, and a # is added to the front of the class name to apply it to a layer.

If you preview index.html in Firefox, you'll see that the container is indeed centred on the page. However, if you preview it in Internet Explorer it will stick stubbornly to the left-hand margin. This is because Explorer interprets the auto setting differently to other browsers when it's applied to the margins. Returning to styles.css, add the following, starting with a new line immediately below the } that closes the style:

```
body {
    text-align: center;
}
```

This centres everything on the page, including the container layer, which is what we want. Unfortunately, because it applies this formatting to the entire page and everything in any of the layers, it also centres the contents of the container. This is an unwanted side effect, as the text is now centred, which is not what we wanted. Returning to the styling for #container within styles.css, add the following line below margin-left: auto;:

```
text-align: left;
```

This will correct the text alignment in the container, and in any layers it holds. It does this because CSS allows styles to cascade from one section to any sections it contains, hence the name.

So, the browser loads the page and the stylesheet, extracts the styling for 'body', applies that to the entire page and then finds a layer called 'container'. It looks up the appropriate style for this (#container) and discovers that it overwrites the body commands within that section. It makes the necessary amendments to the text alignment until it gets to the end of the container layer and then switches back to the styling applied within 'body'. Anything you put on your page outside the container layer is centred unless you override that command again.

If you now preview index.html, you should see a properly formatted page in any browser, but it's still not a three-column layout. Assuming you have entered some text in your layers, you will see that they are stacked one above the other, and that each one stretches across the full width of the container.

We need to break up that width and apportion it to the various layers in our layout, giving the menu column 150 pixels, the sidebar 200 pixels and the main body copy 590 pixels. If you've been keeping count, you'll realise that this leaves us with 20 pixels spare, which we'll use to form two 10-pixel margins, one between the menu and the body, and the other between the body and the sidebar. The clever bit is that we'll define only one, and leave the browser to work out what to do with the other.

To begin, format the menu by adding this section of code on a new line immediately after the closing } in the body section of the stylesheet:

```
#menu {
    float: left;
```

Below: After styling the menu layer, we find that the text in the content layer flows around it like text in a newspaper flowing around a picture. It's easy to fix this by properly defining the content layer's dimensions

Bottom: The footer text is correctly positioned at the bottom of the page, but when we apply a border to the top edge, you can see that the footer layer actually starts immediately below the header

```
    width: 150px;
    margin-right: 10px;
}
```

This is fairly self-explanatory. It constrains the menu layer to a width of 150 pixels, applies a 10-pixel margin to the right-hand edge and floats it as close to the left of the container layer as it can. If you preview index.html in your browser now, you'll see that the content layer has jumped up to the top of the container layer and sits immediately below the header, alongside the menu. If you've entered enough text in this layer, it will flow down and around the menu like text running around a picture or a quote in a magazine.

We are going to fix this by styling the central content column in a similar way to the menu, adding the following immediately below the code for the #menu layer:

```
#content {
    float: left;
    width: 590px;
}
```

The styling information for the #content layer is even simpler than that for the #menu layer, even though it forms the main body of our page. Again, we have floated the layer to the left, but this time, because the #menu layer is also floated to the left and is in the way of the content column, the content can't get to the very left of the container. So its full 590-pixel width sits 160 pixels into the container, having been pushed there by the 150 pixels of the menu and the 10 pixels of the margin attached to the menu layer.

We'll now position the sidebar, and you'll see why we didn't include a margin to the right of the content layer. Add the following code to the styles.css file, immediately after the section defining #content:

```
#sidebar {
    float: right;
    width: 200px;
}
```

This fixes the width of the sidebar to 200 pixels and floats it to the right of the #container layer. A simple calculation shows where the margin between the sidebar and the content layer has come from: the menu was 150 pixels wide with a 10-pixel margin, and the content was 590 pixels wide. Adding them together, the total is 750 pixels. Subtract that from the width of the container – 960 pixels – and you're left with 210, which is 10 pixels wider than we need to contain the sidebar. Floating the sidebar to the right, therefore, creates a 10-pixel gap between its left-hand edge and the right-hand edge of the content layer.

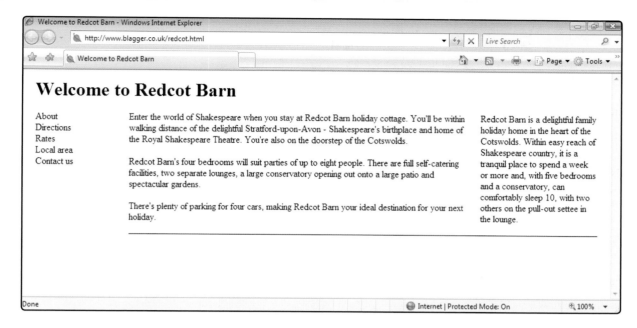

Left: After setting the footer's 'clear' attribute to avoid all elements above it, the footer layer is positioned under the rest of the content in the container layer

Now we just need to style the footer, which poses another interesting problem. We obviously want the footer to sit immediately beneath everything else in the container layer. However, if we add a top border to it using the following code, you'll see that while the text may have been pushed down by our other layers, the actual footer itself starts above them. Only its contents are pushed down:

```
#footer {
   border-top: 1px solid #000000;
}
```

This line adds a solid border (you could also use a dotted line, a dashed line or other options by substituting the word 'solid') one-pixel wide in black, which we specify here using the hexadecimal code #000000, as explained in more detail in chapter 3. If you now save the stylesheet and preview index.html, you'll see that while the line of text in the footer appears below the menu, content and sidebar layers, the upper border has become detached and appears above them.

To get round this problem, we need to tell the browser to keep the entire footer layer – including the border – clear of everything that comes before it by adding the following line above the closing } of the #footer definition shown above:

```
clear: both;
```

Save your stylesheet and preview index.html again and you should now see that the text and border have been united at the foot of the container layer, precisely where they should be. It's still not perfect, so shunt it in by 160 pixels from the left to line it up with the edge of the

content layer. Give the text some breathing space by adding some internal padding to the top of the layer by completing the #footer styling as follows:

```
#footer {
   border-top: 1px solid #000000;
   clear: both;
   margin-left: 160px;
   padding-top: 10px;
}
```

RECYCLING YOUR LAYOUTS

Your layout is complete, and you can concentrate on styling the text and image content of those layers using the CSS elements explained at the start of this chapter, or the HTML commands outlined in chapter 3.

Having established your stylesheet, you can easily re-use it elsewhere on your site by attaching it to other pages that are made using layers with the same names as those we have used for index.html. The immediate benefit is that you've halved the work of creating your new page, as the styles have already been defined.

This is small-fry, however, compared with what happens when you later decide to introduce an entirely new design across your website. As all the pages in your site use the same stylesheet, and each is structured using layers with matching names, you need to edit only a single file – styles.css – to apply your desired changes across the entire site. Suddenly what you may have imagined to be a several-day job that needed extensive planning and dedication can be completed in an hour or less, enabling you to concentrate on what really matters: creating compelling content that will have your visitors coming back time and again.

Developing your layout further

If you don't want your pages to have black text on a white background, you can add colours and effects with a little extra CSS

You now know how to create a well-structured, familiar layout. Your visitors will see your three-column layout and feel immediately at home, having seen other examples all over the web. The only trouble is that this one is dull.

Adding colours, images and textures to layers can make them more inviting. Compare Google news (http://news.google.co.uk) with the BBC News site (http://news.bbc.co.uk), for example, and you'll see how the BBC's use of colours makes its site look far more appealing than the rather strait-laced, text-based Google alternative.

We'll do something similar here to brighten up the design for Redcot Barn, still working solely with the stylesheet and never touching our HTML page.

ASSIGNING COLOURS TO LAYERS

Giving the page a coloured background is easy: you simply tweak the CSS that handles the body tag, which we used earlier to remedy Internet Explorer's problems in centring the container layer. We'll give the page a light green wash, bringing to mind the countryside that surrounds our holiday home. To do this, we'll rewrite the body section as follows:

```
body {
    text-align:center;
    background-color: #9EC7A0;
}
```

Now everything, including each of the layers, will have a green background (#9EC7A0). We don't want this to appear in the container layer, however, which should revert to white, so we need to change the styling of #container as follows:

```
#container {
    width: 960px;
    margin-right: auto;
    margin-left: auto;
    text-align:left;
    background-color: #FFFFFF;
    padding: 5px;
}
```

Right: Compare BBC's and Google's news services and you can see how adding some subtle background colours can make a page more appealing

This adds a pure white background and five pixels of padding around each side of the container layer. We added the padding because the menu, sidebar, header and footer were butting against the edges of the layer, and sitting uncomfortably against the green background. The five pixels of padding all round increases the overall width of the container layer by 10 pixels to a total of 970, but this will still easily fit on a 1,024-pixel-wide display.

ASSIGNING IMAGES TO LAYERS

Using images as backgrounds is just as easy. First, make sure they are properly sized and compressed. If you are using a photo as a background, you must also reduce its opacity so that the sharp contrasts don't interfere with the legibility of your overlying text.

However, image backgrounds don't have to be photos. Using subtle graphical elements such as fades and rounded corners can often be more effective, and give your layout depth. In the image on the right, MSN has used a light blue background that slowly fades out behind the main body of the page, and the sidebar to the right uses a graduated tint that fades smoothly from blue to white and back to blue.

We can easily do something similar to our design by using a light green background that fades to white behind our main #content section. This will help it stand out between the two white sidebars. The best way to do this is to create a narrow image which is then tiled across the full width of the layer. Because both the left and right sides of this image will be identical, we can make it very narrow. All we need is a thin strip just five pixels wide and 300 pixels tall that's solid green at the top and fades to white at the bottom. Save this as bgfade.gif in the same folder as the page.

Image backgrounds are designed to fill the entire background of a layer, regardless of its size, so they tile vertically as well as horizontally. This is a problem, as our graphic is designed to appear only at the top of the #content layer. As it starts out at 100 per cent strength and fades to nothing, it would look terrible if it then reappeared at full strength again immediately below the point at which it disappeared. We will therefore need to restrict its repetition to just the horizontal plane and not the vertical, which we can do with the line `background-repeat: repeat-x;`. If you wanted to repeat an image only on the vertical axis, you'd put a 'y' where the 'x' is. If you don't want any repetition at all, use `background-repeat: no-repeat;`.

With a background image in place, you need to consider how it will look behind some text. In our example, the text starts at the far left of the layer and runs across the very top. This was fine when there was no background, but now it would look uncomfortably tight. As such, we must add some padding – 15 pixels in this instance – to give breathing space. We do this in the same way that we added space to the #container layer.

Top: Subtle graphical backgrounds such as running faded images behind sidebars can look effective

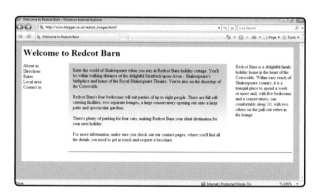

Bottom: Adding a faded graphical background to our #container layer focuses the reader's eye on the most important part of our page

As you may have worked out, this introduces problems of its own. When we define the width of a layer (590 pixels in this instance), we are, in effect, defining the usable area. Adding 15 pixels to each side increases its overall width to 620 pixels. This is a disaster, as the overall layout no longer fits within the #container and the result is a mess. We can fix this by reducing the size of the #content layer by 30 pixels, trimming it from 590 to 560 to pull it back into line.

If you've been following this section on CSS closely, you may be able to work out for yourself how the #content styling must be amended. If not, here is the code we used:

```
#content {
    float: left;
    width: 560px;
    background-image: url(bgfade.gif);
    padding: 15px;
    background-repeat: repeat-x;
}
```

The image, which we named bgfade.gif and saved in the same folder as the page and stylesheet, is called in using `background-image`. This is very similar to the `background-color` code we used when applying a light green wash to the page as a whole, and the white background we added to the #container layer.

Creating a navigation bar

You now have all the tools needed to create an interactive navigation bar. Using CSS, plus the list tags in HTML, it's well within your grasp

In chapter 3, we used the `<ol>` and `<ul>` tags to create lists of house rules for guests of Redcot Barn. However, confining these tags to mere list-making is a wasted opportunity, as they are the ideal starting point for creating CSS-styled menu bars. The tags already work in a hierarchical way, and each item in the list can be made to work as a little layer of its own, without the need to draw dozens of `<div>` tags.

List tags also provide an excellent example of the way browsers can skim over any commands they don't understand. This gives you a lot of freedom, as you can work on your designs safe in the knowledge that mistakes are unlikely to destroy your entire layout.

Once again, Internet Explorer diverges from the conventions used by almost every other browser in this area. As we saw when coding our three-column layout, only Internet Explorer is unable to centre our container layer when we split the redundant space on our page using the command `margins: auto;`. The same is true of the way older versions handle `:hover` states for

anything other than links; they don't handle them at all, at least not in IE7, which many people still use.

Over the next few pages, we'll create a menu that's compatible with all browsers, including IE. We can then expand this to introduce a level of interactivity for other browsers that would previously have been possible only using Flash or a graphics application. We'll also show you where you can find the resources to emulate the same effects in Internet Explorer using third-party open-source code saved elsewhere on your site.

In this example, we'll return to the index.html and styles.css files we used in the previous project to add an interactive menu to pages. If you want to follow this guide by typing in the code below and seeing how it works, make sure you download the files from the Advanced Projects section of our website.

ADDING THE MENU

First we need to add the menu entries to the index.html file. Open it in Notepad and add a new layer immediately below the header layer as follows:

```
<div id="widemenu"><ul><li>
<a href="">About us</a></li><li>
<a href="">Directions</a></li><li>
<a href="">Rates</a></li><li>
<a href="">Local area</a></li><li>
<a href="">Contact us</a></li></ul>
</div>
```

If you preview this in your browser, the menu appears as a bulleted list, because we've used the `<ul>` tag, denoting a list without ordinals (numbers). If we'd wanted to number each item on the list, we would have used an ordered list with the tag `<ol>`. For now we've also put empty links around every entry. We'll fill in their proper destinations later.

Below: The default styling for an unordered list gives each entry a bullet point and arranges them all in a vertical column

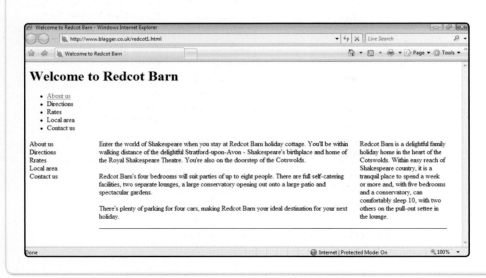

For now, the main problem with this menu is that it runs vertically and pushes all the remaining content of our page down. Save and close index.html and switch to styles.css, where we'll fix this as we start to style the menu to meet our needs.

Returning to a trick we used when creating a three-column layout, we'll arrange the menu entries side by side by floating them all to the left. As we discovered last time, if you float an item to the left and another item sits in its way, it will butt up against it. By floating every entry in the menu this way, we can easily get them to line up side by side in a single row. To achieve this, add the following section to styles.css, starting on a new line below the existing styles:

```
#widemenu ul li {
    float: left;
}
```

This compound class defines the target of our style very specifically. First, it tells the browser to confine the style data to elements found in the layer #widemenu. It then tells the browser to apply it only to list items (li) found in bulleted menus (ul). If we wanted to apply the style to items on any type of list in the #widemenu layer, we would leave out the ul section, and point lists with numbers would also adopt the style. If we wanted to apply it to all lists on our page, we'd leave out both the ul and #widemenu parts and open the tag with just li {.

Building up your targets in this way allows you to pinpoint precisely where you want your styles to apply, and to define multiple styles for identical elements used in different parts of the page. If you wanted to use a different style for list items in an unordered list in the main content area of the page, for example, you would start with #content ul li {. The browser will know to differentiate between this and the styling for the menu.

BITING THE BULLET

If you now review index.html, you'll see that while we've sorted out the alignment, we've introduced another problem. The bullets are no longer appropriate and, apart from the first one, each bullet overlaps the end of the previous item in the menu. We'll solve this problem in two ways: first, by removing the bullets, and second, by defining the amount of space each list item takes up. The code to do this is added to the #widemenu ul li style:

```
#widemenu ul li {
    float: left;
    list-style-type: none;
    padding: 5px 30px 5px 5px;
}
```

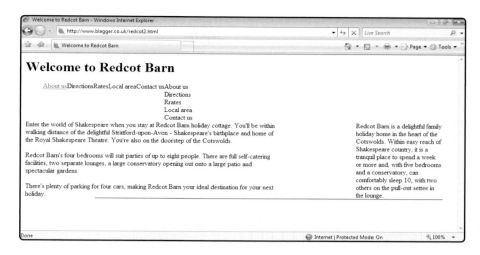

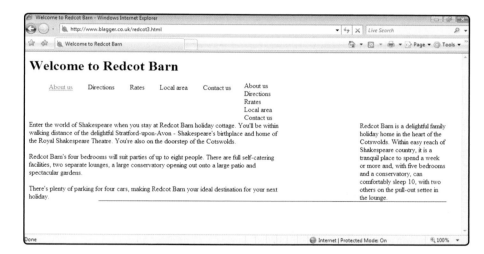

The list-style-type variable defines what should be used as the bullet for each entry in our list. Specifying none removes the bullet altogether. Alternatives include circle, square or a range of upper- and lower-case Roman numerals.

After removing the bullets, we also specified how the entries in the list should be padded, with five pixels of space above, below and to the left, and 30 pixels to the right of each. Alternatively, we could have specified a fixed width for the area each entry takes up – using width: 80px; for example. However, that would look uneven as longer entries such as 'Contact us' would fill their allotted area, while short ones such as 'Rates' would leave a lot of empty space.

Applying padding within each list item keeps them comfortably separate. When adding interactivity on those browsers that allow it, though, it also lets you simulate the effect of moving the mouse pointer over a large button that encompasses the entire area, not just the word itself.

We've almost finished working with the entries in our styled list, but there's one more task to complete. At the

Top: After removing the bullet and floating list items to the left, they line up side by side, but there's no space between them

Bottom: With some padding, the list items are nicely spaced out. Doing this rather than specifying a maximum area makes for a more comfortable effect. The left-most edge of each item may be a different distance from the left-hand edge of its predecessor, but the space between them, which is more obvious, is always equal

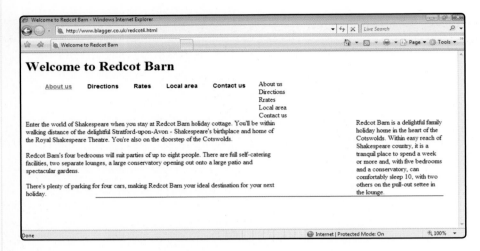

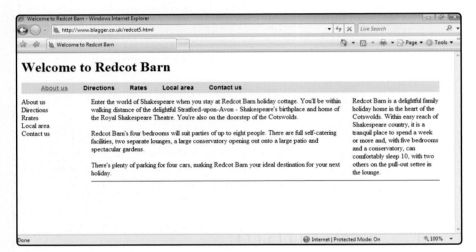

Top: Now that our list items have their own style, they stand out from the page

Bottom: The underlying #widemenu layer now stretches across the width of the page with a grey background that clearly differentiates it from the rest of the page

moment, the list uses the same font as the rest of the page, which means it blends in a little too well. A menu should be differentiated so that a visitor can find it quickly, making it easier to navigate the site. Add three lines between the `padding: 5px 30px 5px 5px;` and the closing } of the #widemenu ul li section:

```
font-family: Arial, Helvetica,
  sans-serif;
font-weight: bold;
font-size: 14px;
```

To remove the colours and underlines from the links so that they look more like part of the menu bar and less like plain links, we'll target the links (a) within list items (li) within bulleted lists (ul) in the #widemenu area:

```
#widemenu ul li a {
  color: #000000;
  text-decoration: none;
}
```

Then apply a dark red `:hover` state:

```
#widemenu ul li a:hover {
  color: #990000;
}
```

This looks better, but it's still not quite right. There's an obvious difference between the font used in the menu and the font used elsewhere on the page. Without clear limits around the menu, though, the two clash. Clearly the problem is no longer with the list itself, but rather the container in which it sits. As it's the same colour as the page, it's invisible.

We could apply top and bottom borders, but that might be overkill, so instead we'll apply a light grey background (hexadecimal code DDDDDD) to pull the menu slightly forward from the rest of the page, and add a 10-pixel margin to the bottom to separate it from the rest of the content:

```
#widemenu {
  background-color: #dddddd;
  margin-bottom: 10px;
  height: 25px;
}
```

The page is looking better already, but our horizontal list is still inset too far for our liking. It should begin near the left-hand edge of the #widemenu layer. As it's bound by the <ul> and </ul> tags that define its left- and right-hand edges, we should now turn our attention to these to reposition the list as a whole, rather than the individual <li> elements we've been tweaking so far.

The reason the list is inset at the moment is that all lists in HTML are indented by default to make them easy to spot in a tract of running text, and to differentiate them from any numbers you might use to organise paragraphs or flowing text. We'll get rid of this indentation by changing both the margin and the padding of the <ul> tag used within the #widemenu layer to 0, like this:

```
#widemenu ul {
  margin: 0px;
  padding: 0px;
}
```

The menu now springs back towards the left-hand edge of the layer, aligning itself with the rest of the page.

APPLYING INTERACTIVITY
Our menu is now complete, but without links to other pages, and should render properly in any browser. As we've already said, it's easy to introduce visual feedback in any browser through the judicious use of the `:hover` tag. You can do the same in Internet Explorer 9 using the

same commands, but version 7 only accepts `:hover` when added to the `<a>` link tag.

For the moment, we'll concentrate on those browsers that are compatible and apply the `:hover` class to `<li>` tags that define the entries in our menu list. We've already shown how to apply a `:hover` state to a link (page 54). CSS styles attached to an element remain active in any variation of that element unless you definitively overrule them, so we don't need to rewrite the code for the `li` style from scratch. Instead, we can allow the hovered-over element to retain its existing styling, and add a new style point that only ever comes into play when the mouse is over each element, using this code:

```
#widemenu ul li:hover {
   background-color: #BBBBBB;
}
```

Save styles.css and open index.html in any browser other than IE7 to see what effect this has on your page. Roll your mouse backwards and forwards along the menu line, and you'll see that every time you pass over an item in the menu its background gets darker. This background extends across the width we defined for the invisible box, which contains each entry in the menu.

To achieve such an effect before CSS, you'd have had to create two buttons for each entry in the menu: one that displays when the mouse is away from the menu, and one that appears as the mouse passes over it. This eats into your bandwidth and is needlessly complicated to code.

Potentially more serious, however, is the fact that if you were to change the structure of your site later and you needed to alter the menu to reflect this, you would have to re-create your buttons from scratch in your graphics application. Using the CSS approach outlined here, you can do the same thing with nothing more sophisticated than the copy of Notepad that's built into Windows.

You don't need to make any changes to achieve the same effect in Internet Explorer 7, but you do need to take advantage of its handling of 'behaviours' for onscreen elements. These are defined in separate files, which you include in your page as part of your stylesheet, and which in effect rewrite some of the browser's internal workings. One such behaviour rewrites every `:hover` state found on your page so that it acts as a JavaScript mouseover command. This is still a commonly used means of introducing more complex interactivity into your pages. You can download this behaviour from http://tinyurl.com/csshover, after which you copy and paste it into a new file and save it into the root of your site as csshover.htc.

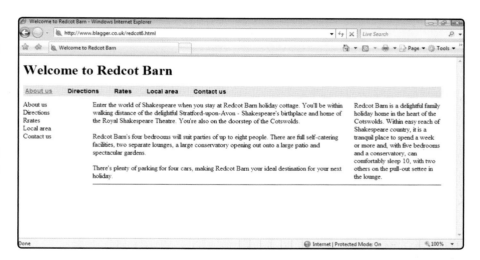

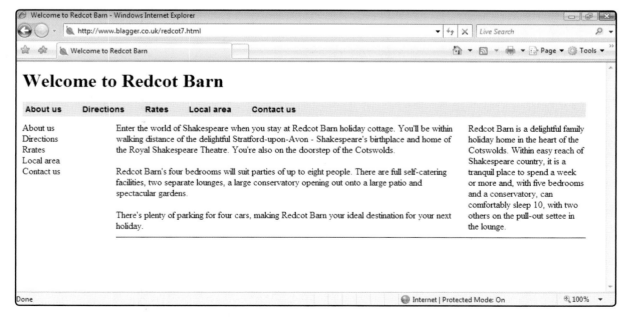

Above: After changing the padding and margin values to 0, the menu entries have the same left-hand margin as the text on the page

Left: Finally, we address the styling of the links in the menu by removing the text decoration and changing the colour to black, making the active elements look like proper entries on a menu bar

CHAPTER 5

IN THIS CHAPTER

Introducing HTML5 68

Building HTML5 pages.................70

Introducing CSS3 73

Create stylish text
with CSS3..76

Animation with CSS3....................79

Looking good

In the two decades since Tim Berners-Lee published the groundbreaking HTML tags, the technological world has changed, and our expectations of what the web should deliver have changed along with it.

The modern web user wants photos, podcasts and HD video. HTML5 delivers all this and more. In this chapter, you'll

MacBook Air

learn the differences between this new version and the older standard. Although it's perfectly acceptable to build your site with no HTML5 code, the latest version is even simpler to work with. If you've been put off coding a site by hand because you think it's too complicated, now's the time to take the plunge. You'll be surprised at how far things have moved on.

Introducing HTML5

The latest version of HTML brings many benefits, not just for web surfers, but also for anyone building a website

HTML5 may be the future of web design, but it's not yet a fully ratified language. It may therefore seem premature to embrace it, but HTML5 is already enjoying widespread adoption. The latest versions of the four most popular web browsers (Internet Explorer, Safari, Firefox and Chrome) already use HTML5, so it's safe to use HTML5 tags on your website.

HTML5 introduces a number of new tags and makes several others obsolete. That doesn't mean your site coded using HTML4.01 (the precise number of the HTML version we covered in chapter 3) won't display properly in the latest web browsers, as they all have excellent backwards compatibility. However, you should swap obsolete tags for their HTML5 alternatives.

From the last two chapters, you should be familiar with using <div> to define a block on the page, which you can then style up using CSS. This has been retained in HTML5, along with <span> (to pick out inline blocks for individual formatting) and joined by specific block types including <nav>, which is used to define a navigation element, such as a menu.

Many new tags help to define the content of a page rather than just position it within the flow. For example, <figure> ties an image to its caption, allowing you to style the pair as a single block and to sub-style the contents – image and caption – individually inside it.

Even if you don't intend to revisit existing sites and recode them using HTML5, you should stop using tags such as <frameset>, <frame> and <noframes> as they have been deprecated, along with <strike>, <u> and <font>. Most of HTML4.01's tag structure remains in place, however, with HTML5 building on it.

Beyond creating a clear distinction between content and presentation, HTML5 introduces elements that simplify the integration of non-textual material. The <canvas> tag, for example, provides a container for scripts that draw graphical elements such as shapes and graphs, while <audio> lets you embed audio directly on a page. The <video> tag does the same for visual content, with optional attributes for autoplaying, embedded controls, looping and a poster frame that displays before the video kicks in.

The code below will embed a file called barcelona. mp4 in your page, with accompanying controls. The video window is 640 by 480 pixels, and the movie file will load at the same time as the page. We've also specified a poster frame (barcelona.jpg) to display in the video box like a thumbnail on a DVD menu. No plug-ins are required. The text displayed between the opening and closing <video> tags handles errors, and is displayed if the visitor doesn't have a compatible browser:

Below: HTML5's semantic markup shows how the various parts of our page relate to one another

```
<video src="barcelona.mp4" controls
 width="640" height="480"
  poster="barcelona.jpg"
   preload="preload">Sorry - no video
    for you. Please upgrade your
     browser.  </video>
```

FIVE ALIVE

To demonstrate how easy HTML5 is to use, we'll build a simple page, using HTML5-native tags where possible. This should render properly in the latest versions of Internet Explorer, Firefox, Chrome and Safari. We'll then look at how CSS3 can style our on-page elements.

One benefit of HTML5 is evident in the new first line of every page: `<!DOCTYPE HTML>`. This is much simpler than its HTML4.01 equivalent. Following the head section, we'll add the new `<header>` and `<nav>` tags:

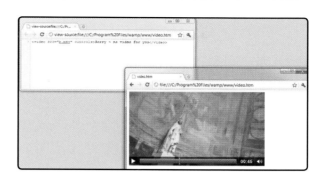

Left: New tags such as `<video>` enable you to use media content natively without any need for plug-ins

```
<!DOCTYPE HTML>
<html>
<head>
 <title>
 My first HTML5 page
 </title>
</head>
<body>
 <header>
 My first HTML5 web page
 </header>
 <nav class="topmenu">
 <ul>
 <li><a href="/">Home</a></li>
 <li><a href="about.php">About</a></li>
 <li><a href="email.php">Email</a></li>
 </ul>
 </nav>
```

The `<header>` tag lets you address this section in CSS while also defining the content. Aggregators and search engines will understand its contents, and can use it in place of the page title in a list of search results. Likewise, `<nav>` defines a container for navigational elements. It doesn't define the presentation of the navigation, so a properly linked menu should still be handled using CSS.

Because both these tags are semantic – defining content rather than formatting it – they can be used anywhere you like, several times on the page. You might want to use a `<header>` as a cross heading before each block of text, and another `<nav>` further down your page so visitors can jump to a subsection. You can therefore apply specific styles to each tag. We've done this with the `<nav>` tag, formatting it using a class within CSS called 'topmenu', to denote the menu that runs across the top of the page.

BODY LANGUAGE

With the menu and header out of the way, we can start to write the main body of the page:

```
<section>
 <h1>Welcome to HTML5</h1>
 <section>
 <h2>What is HTML5?</h2>
 <p>Body content appears here</p>
```

```
 <aside>
 <h3>Obsolete tags</h3>
 <p>Related content appears here</p>
 </aside>
 </section>
</section>
```

The `<section>` tags group together various elements on the page and define the start and end points of a discrete section. In our example, one overall section holds the body of our page, with smaller subsections to tie together the heading of each part (`<h2>`) and its body content (`<p>`). These are merely a semantic hint, letting readers see where one part begins and ends.

Our first subsection contains an `<aside>`. This semantic tag ties together a less important header and body content, and it might be styled to sit to the side of the main page flow. In HTML4.01, we could have achieved the same effect by drawing out a `<div>` and floating it to the left or right. However, it wouldn't have been clear that this was related content when examining the underlying code. We can now close off our page with `<footer>` and `<summary>` tags:

```
<footer>
 <section>
 <summary>Get in touch</summary>
 <p>Email us by clicking <a href=
 "mailto:editor@emailprovider.co.uk">
 here</a>.
 </section>
</footer>
</body>
</html>
```

In HTML4.01, footers were usually defined within a named `<div>`. As with `<header>`, having `<footer>` is a timesaver, helping to make the code readable and keeping elements addressable by CSS. The use of `<section>` ties together a summary and a paragraph. The summary defines the content that follows. You can have as many summaries as you want on the page and style them together or, by directly addressing 'footer section summary' in CSS, target one specific instance.

Building HTML5 pages

Here we take a closer look at the various ways in which you can organise and structure page content using HTML5

BENEFITS

Give pages a structure

Relate captions to images

Specify alternative sources

Now that we've built the skeleton of a web page using HTML5's new markup tags, we'll build on it with tags to define text types and formatting, and explain how to relate captions to images and other content, and how to specify live media sources.

THE GENUINE ARTICLE

Many changes in HTML5 relate to the way in which a page is put together. Most websites use `<div>` tags to mark out various content areas, as this makes them load more quickly than if content is laid out in a large table. The system is inefficient, though – without subsequently naming each `<div>` individually, it's impossible to tell one `<div>` tag from another. HTML5 overcomes this problem with `<header>`, `<nav>`, `<footer>` and `<article>`.

Instead of requiring descriptive names for each `<div>`, HTML5 code is more regimented, better organised and easier to navigate. If you want to differentiate between `<nav>` elements on a page, for example, you can apply id or class attributes to them, defined in your stylesheet.

Any content between the opening and closing `<article>` tags should be self-contained and still make sense to the reader if removed from the rest of the page in which it appears. It can contain its own headers, body copy and sub-articles, and probably include one or more `<section>` layers if its contents are particularly long.

TEXTUAL HEALING

Unless you're building a photography portfolio, the bulk of your content will be text, and in this respect HTML5 developers are well catered for. As well as `<aside>` and `<summary>`, HTML5 introduces the idea of highlighted text and specific time data. It also makes changes to the way the regular cite, bold and italic tags are used.

The new `<mark>` tag formalises the way in which text is highlighted, in much the same way that HTML5's layout tags standardise the naming of standard page sections. For example:

```
<p>The text between the mark <mark>and</mark> mark tags is highlighted.</p>
```

In itself, this doesn't make any difference to the text as displayed on the page – it just picks out the word 'and' for further processing. To change the way it's highlighted, you must define a style for `<mark>` in your stylesheet. The following would change the background colour of that word to emulate a highlighting pen:

```
mark {
background-color: #FFFF00;
}
```

The `<b>` and `<i>` still apply bold and italic formatting to text, and can be defined specifically using a referenced stylesheet. For your site to be fully HTML5-compliant, however, these tags should no longer be assumed to mark

Left and Below: Additional time and date data is embedded, but isn't rendered when the text is displayed in the browser

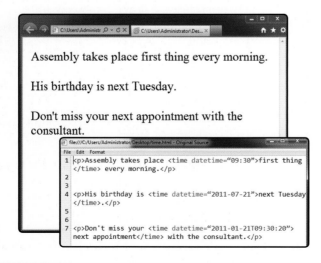

out the text as being of any greater importance that the text that appears around it. Likewise, where `cite` used to pick out the name of a person who originated a quoted work, it is now used solely to name the work itself, such as a book, film or radio programme. Like `<mark>`, its styling would need to be defined within your stylesheet.

The `<time>` tag marks out sections within your content as times or dates, with two variables – `datetime` and `pubtime` – more clearly defining an element as a specific moment that relates to the content wrapped inside the tag. At its most basic, you would use the `<time>` tag without any variables to mark up a particular part of your content as being a time or date, so:

```
<p>The bus leaves at <time>22:15</time>.
</p>
<p>Your rent is due on <time>2011-06-28
</time>.</p>
```

By adding the `datetime` variable to the tag, you can add extra information to the tagged text. This information isn't displayed, but as it's encoded within your document it's made available to any application that scrapes your code for content, such as a calendaring application.

The following are all valid uses of the `<time>` tag, combined with its datetime attribute to provide detailed information that supplements the text:

```
<p>Assembly takes place <time datetime=
  "09:30">first thing</time> every
  morning.</p>
<p>His birthday is <time datetime="2012-
  02-21">next Tuesday</ time>.</p>
<p>Don't miss your <time datetime="2012-
  04-16T09:30:20">next appointment</time>
  with the consultant.</p>
```

In the third example, we've specified both a date and a time, with the control character 'T' used as a separator between them. Each variable within the `<time>` tag is denoted in order, from the largest to the finest division – from years down to seconds, in other words – in line with the proposal set out in RFC3339 (http://tools.ietf. org/html/rfc3339). This avoids any problems thrown up in translating from European to US date formats.

Pairing the `<time>` tag with its `pubdate` variable allows you to specify the date and time on which a particular part of your page was created. This would allow you to indicate the currency of certain data such as share prices or, as in this example, the viewing times for films at a cinema in the coming week:

```
<time pubdate="2011-08-12">
 <article>
  <header>This week's showing times
   </header>
```

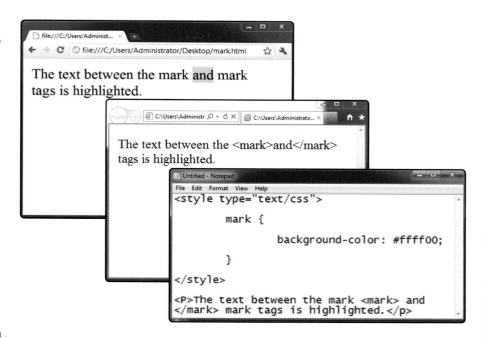

```
   <b>Amelie</b> <time>19:30</time> /
    <time>21:00</time><br/>
   <b>Bourne Ultimatum</b> <time>21:30
    </time><br/>
   <b>Carry On Camping</b> <time>12:30
    </time> / <time>15:00</time>
 </article>
</time>
```

Here we are combining both the pubdate variable, as a means of telling visitors (or at least their browsers) when the data within the article was published, and the plain `<time>` tag to mark out the showing times of each film. This element could easily be automated when outputting data from an underlying database, or used as the publication date marker on a blog post or news story.

Above: The <mark> tag lets you define how text should be highlighted. It works in Chrome but not in IE9

Above: The <article>, <section> and <time> tags make short work of formatting this table of film times

GOOD RELATIONS

In HTML4.01, there's no way to tell anyone who looked at the underlying code – or any search engine spider – how an image relates to the text around it. Captions on the rendered page don't exist outside the finished content and aren't fundamentally linked to the images themselves. HTML5 introduces the concept of figures and captions to establish a proper link between the two. The `<figure>` tag works as a container for a loose collection of related elements, in much the same way that `<aside>` can bundle together a header, content and footer to sit outside the main flow of the page.

There are other similarities between `<figure>` and `<aside>`. The W3C draft describes `<figure>` as representing "a unit of content, optionally with a caption, that is self-contained, that is typically referenced as a single unit from the main flow of the document, and that can be moved from the main flow of the document without affecting the document's meaning".

The key difference is the level of importance to the reader's appreciation of the main body of the page. If the content is directly related to the page but could be positioned anywhere, use `<figure>`. If it's only tangentially related to the main body, use `<aside>`. The `<aside>` used on page 69 presented a box of obsolete tags that replicated content within the main body, but could easily be removed as the information was available elsewhere. The `<figure>` in the example below might illustrate a Contact page on a site with a photo of a building. It would be an important element, helping those who visit the office to locate the relevant building, but could be positioned anywhere on the page – it needn't be anchored within a specific block of text.

You add a captioned image to your page using:

```
<figure>
   <img src="office.jpg" alt="ACME
     premises">
```

Below: By specifying several video sources, the HTML5 Demos site caters for a wide variety of platforms and web browsers

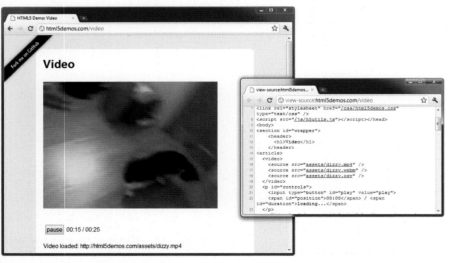

```
<figcaption>ACME's central London
  offices</figcaption>
</figure>
```

The term `<figure>` shouldn't be taken literally, as the tag can be used to bundle together a general illustrative item, such as a block of code, a table or a `<div>` layer that merits its own caption.

MEDIA STUDIES

We've already touched briefly on embedding media using HTML5. There are four primary media tags: source, audio, video and embed. The `<embed>` tag is a catch-all, allowing you to use a plug-in to handle media that can't be played back natively within the browser. The only required attribute is the media file (you don't need to point to the plug-in used to render it), but you can add height, width and a media type. The media type helps visitors' browsers to pick the appropriate plug-in to play the file, and the height and width enable browsers to leave a gap of the required size to hold the media while it loads the rest of the content. This means browsers on slower connections will be able to render most of the page properly, and therefore reduce the chances of your visitors clicking away.

```
<embed src="bikeride.flv" height="50"
 width="150" type="application/
  x-shockwave-flash">
```

There's no need to close off the embed tag with a matching `</embed>` in this instance.

By contrast, the `<audio>` and `<video>` tags can take a closing tag, allowing you to specify multiple source files; your visitor's browser will pick the first one in the list that it can play, much as it would choose the first available font from a specified family.

The following would be used to embed an AAC audio file for which there are no alternatives, complete with transport controls:

```
<audio src="podcast.m4a" controls=
  "controls">
```

If you've provided Ogg Vorbis and Wav versions of the file for those whose browsers can't handle AAC files, you can take the attributes out of the tag itself and list all the possible source files, with those you'd rather be used first higher in the list. You end the list with the closing `</audio>` tag as follows:

```
<audio controls="controls">
   <source src="podcast.m4a" />
   <source src="podcast.wav" />
   <source src="podcast.ogg" />
</audio>
```

Introducing CSS3

CSS3 builds on the functionality and flexibility of its predecessor. Here's how to use it to style your pages and add effects

---

By now you should be familiar with the idea that all styling elements must be removed the main flow of code in HTML5. From now on, pure CSS is used to define the layout and look of your pages.

CSS3 is being developed alongside HTML5. Here we'll explore two of the most radical effects applied with CSS – shadows and rounded corners – and how CSS3 addresses these commonly requested features of modern web design in a clean and simple manner.

BORN THREE

Just as HTML5 improves on HTML4.01, CSS3 takes the best of what was already in place in CSS2 (the version we looked at in chapter 4) and adds new elements such as drop shadows, rounded corners and animations that allow designers to build more flexible pages in native code, rather than resorting to third-party image editors and plug-ins. CSS3 lets you lay out textual content in columns, as in a magazine, specify where breaks fall and how wide the gaps should be between columns. You can use images as borders, stretching them as appropriate, and target elements specifically on the page.

The `:hover` modifier already possible for an action to be carried out only when a visitor's mouse is in a particular position in relation to the content on your page. New modifiers such as `:checked`, `:enabled` and `:not` let you apply styles to selected radio buttons, enabled page elements and even objects that are not of a specified kind.

The first elements of CSS3 were published in 1999, but it's only now that browser support has advanced sufficiently to allow us to use it with confidence on a live website. However, the degree to which different browsers render the various elements varies greatly. Luckily, you can target specific browsers with fixes by isolating each rendering engine. Let's take rounded corners as an example, which we could apply to a container called `boxout` as follows:

```
.boxout {border-radius: 20px; }
```

This element isn't universally supported, and won't render properly on older browsers. You'll have to make allowances for this by targeting the earlier Webkit (Safari 3 and earlier) and Mozilla (Firefox) engines using the following code:

```
.boxout {
    border-radius: 20px;
    -moz-border-radius: 20px;
    -webkit-border-radius: 20px;
}
```

Left: Firefox and Chrome render the button well, but IE9 can't handle the rounded corners without extra code

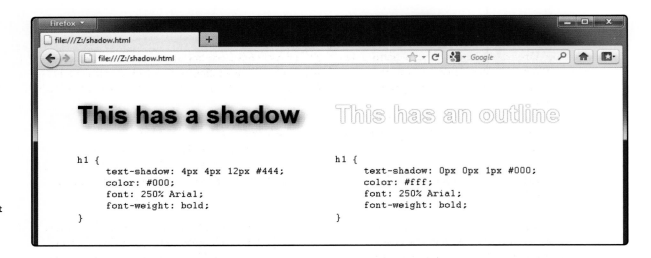

Right: By changing the offset of your shadow, you can quickly and easily create outlined text using CSS3

Web browsers that don't need the specific `-moz` and `-webkit` targets will simply ignore them. This workaround is easy to implement, compliant and won't throw up an error.

BUTTON IT

We'll put this into practice by creating a simple CSS3 button using code instead of graphics. You may wonder why we'd do this when we could just make a button in Photoshop, compress it and embed it within the page. There are two very good reasons. First, it makes lighter demands on your server. The code below that defines the two button states is 285 bytes in length. Doing the same with images would require two graphics – one for the up state and one for the down – and that would total several kilobytes each. Savings of this type soon pay dividends when implemented across every page of a busy site.

Second, the content of the button itself – the words 'Download Linux' – is already search engine-optimised. If you were using a graphic, you would need to use `<alt>` tags to describe the content to search engine crawlers, and possibly also apply a 'title' attribute to the `<a>` tag to further improve its indexing. Screen readers will see our button as nothing more than a standard link to which we've applied some styling, which will greatly ease navigation for visually impaired users.

```
<!DOCTYPE HTML>
<head>
<title>A 3D button</title>
<style type="text/css">
#button a {
    background-color: #39F;
    border: 5px outset #6CF;
    border-radius: 10px;
    font: 24pt Arial;
    font-weight: 900;
    color: #fff;
    padding: 10px;
```

```
    text-decoration: none;
}
#button a:hover {
    border: 5px inset #6cf;
    padding: 9px 11px 11px 9px;
}
</style>
</head>
<body>
<br />
<div id="button"><a href="download.
html">Download Linux</a></div>
</body>
</html>
```

The button has no fixed dimensions, so will always be 10 pixels larger than its contents in each direction, allowing us to re-use the code wherever we want to create a button by simply placing a link inside a `<div>` tag called 'button'. By combining the 10-pixel padding with CSS3's new border-radius attribute, we've given our button rounded corners and then we've given it a sense of depth by extruding the whole thing by five pixels, using the border outset and inset attributes on the up state and down state buttons respectively.

One further change made to the downstate button – which is displayed when the visitor hovers their mouse over the link – is to shift the text one pixel up and to the left. We have done this by reducing the top and left padding to 9px in each case, and increasing the right and bottom padding to 11px to maintain the overall size of the button. The text now follows the motion of the button in stepping back into the page.

When specifying the padding on each of the sides of our button, we are able to use just '10px' once on the up state button as each is the same, but on the down state button we have to specify the padding on each size individually ('9px 11px 11px 9px'), starting with the top and working around in a clockwise direction. Previewing the results in Chrome, Firefox and Internet Explorer, we can immediately spot a problem here. Chrome (which uses Webkit) and Firefox (which uses Gecko) perform as we would expect, but IE9, which uses the Trident rendering engine, doesn't, despite supporting the border-radius class.

To overcome this problem, we have to notify IE9 of the document coding by adding the following line to the document's <head> area:

```
<meta http-equiv="X-UA-Compatible"
 content="IE=9" />
```

Reloading the page, we can now see that it correctly renders with rounded corners in all three browsers. Although IE9's support for CSS3 is better than that of its predecessors, it's by no means perfect, and it lacks support for many elements that remain draft proposals. Microsoft maintains a list of the current supported CSS classes in each version of its browser from IE6 to IE9, which you can find at http://bit.ly/lBbsvV.

CASTING SHADOWS
Our button is complete, but rounded corners are just one of the new features open to us by switching to CSS3. Firefox, Safari and Chrome support drop shadows on both text and graphics, allowing you to apply these effects to your content, again without needing a graphics tool to render them as a JPEG image. The formula for applying shadows is as follows:

```
text-shadow: x-position y-position
 blur-amount colour;
```

To apply a mid-grey shadow to the bottom right of a heading (as though cast by a light positioned above and to the left of the text), you'd use the following code:

```
h1 {
    text-shadow: 2px 2px 4px #bbb;
}
```

To cast your shadow upwards, as though lit from below, you would change the second pixel measurement (the y-position) to a negative figure, such as -2. However, by removing both offsets and darkening the shadow colour, you can modify this effect to produce a keyline around the text. Changing the font colour to white (#fff) would then result in outlined characters; for example:

```
h1 {
    text-shadow: 0px 0px 4px #000;
}
```

IE9 doesn't currently support text shadows rendered in CSS3, so it ignores these commands when parsing the stylesheet. The result will be solid text without a drop shadow or an outline.

You can apply a shadow to any onscreen element within a virtual bounding box, such as an image or a div layer. Here we'll define a class called 'imageshadow' to do just that:

```
.imageshadow {
    box-shadow: 8px 8px 12px #ccc;
    -webkit-box-shadow: 8px 8px 12px #ccc;
    -moz-box-shadow: 8px 8px 12px #ccc;
}
```

Internet Explorer 9, Opera 10.5 and Firefox 4 natively support the box-shadow attribute, but Safari, Chrome and earlier editions of Firefox (up to 3.5) don't, and so they need the -webkit and -moz variants detailed above. To apply this effect to an image, simply call the class from the image tag:

```
<img class="imageshadow" src="picture.
 jpg" />
```

As a live effect, we can combine our shadow with other effects, such as the border radius that we used earlier, and it will follow the contour of the element to which it's attached.

SAVING GRACES
CSS3's enhancements will considerably reduce the amount of work that's involved in building a website. What would once have involved the use of graphics and animation tools can now be achieved natively using nothing but code, thereby tightening the development cycle, reducing server load and ensuring that pages load faster for your visitors.

Below: Shadows follow the contours of the box object to which they are applied

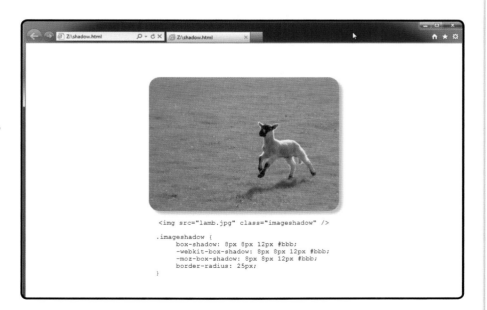

Create stylish text with CSS3

You can make onscreen text more attractive with the help of shadows, banners and rotations

BENEFITS

Make text stand out

Add flashes to your page

Build tables of contents

CSS3 allows you to build more engaging page layouts and reduces the amount of coding involved in putting a page together. It can also be used to achieve some fantastic typographic effects, rotate text, add flashes and tables of contents.

We've already shown that shadows can be very useful on web pages, particularly for creating pressed and embossed text. You could combine the pressing with coloured text, but here we're going to emulate paper that has been pressed without any ink applied, as it gives a more realistic result.

When you're working with shadows, your first consideration should be where your virtual light source will be positioned; in most cases, this will be above your visitor's monitor. We're going to set ours above and slightly to the left, in which case the light would catch on the inner bevel on the right and bottom of each letter. No light will fall on the other two edges, as they will be facing away from the light source. The formula for casting shadows on text is:

```
text-shadow: x-axis offset, y-axis
 offset, amount of blur, colour;
```

The amount of blur is optional. To cast a sharp shadow to the lower right of a line of text, you'd use:

Right: By darkening the letters, the pressed text looks a lot more realistic

```
.shadow {
    text-shadow: 0.2em 0.2em #ccc;
}
```

To soften that shadow for a more realistic result, you'd add a small amount of blur:

```
.shadow {
    text-shadow: 0.2em 0.2em 0.2em #ccc;
}
```

With that in mind, we'll define a new <div> to hold our text, and apply a light shadow to the specified edges to emulate lightfall. The code for the HTML is:

```
<div id="layer">
<p class="shadow">Computer Shopper</p>
</div>
```

And for the CSS, the code is as follows:

```
#layer {
    background: #900;
}
p {
    padding: 2em;
    color: #600;
    font: 3em Arial;
    font-weight: 900;
}
.shadow {
    text-shadow: 0.03em 0.03em 0.03em #D00;
}
```

The result is subtle, but recognisable, and is helped by the fact that we've darkened the letters slightly by picking a darker tone of the red we used for the

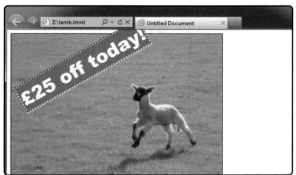

Left Incorporating a shadow can make your text appear to be embossed

Right: As the image remains untouched, it's easy to enable or disable overlays such as this

background of our `<div>`. Selecting a different colour would have spoiled the effect. Use a colour picker, such as the table maintained at http://en.wikipedia.org/wiki/Web_colors#Color_table.

To create the illusion of embossed text, we need only swap our text and background colours, and the sides on which our light falls. There's no need to change the HTML. Our amended CSS looks like this:

```
#layer {
   background: #600;
}
p {
   padding: 2em;
   color: #800;
   font: 3em Arial;
   font-weight: 900;
}
.shadow {
   text-shadow: -0.03em -0.03em 0.03em
   #D00;
}
```

THE REAL DEAL

This is a decent start, but if you were to increase the size of your text – to 8em, say – and look closely at the corners of each character, you would see a disconnect between the shadow and the characters that cast it, so the effect works only on smaller text sizes. To create a more believable feeling of depth on larger characters, we must take advantage of CSS3's ability to layer several shadow styles, each one on top of its predecessor, by putting a comma between them.

We don't need to touch our HTML to achieve this, but we will increase the text size in our CSS from 3em to 8em and rewrite the `.shadow` class as follows:

```
.shadow {
   text-shadow: -0.01em -0.01em #D00,
   -0.02em -0.02em #D00, -0.03em -0.03em
   #D00, -0.04em -0.04em #D00, -0.05em
   -0.05em #D00, -0.06em -0.06em #D00,
   -0.07em   -0.07em #D00, -0.08em
```

```
   -0.08em #D00;
}
```

Here, we've laid eight shadows on top of each other; each one is offset 0.01em from its predecessor, which gives us a total depth of shadow of 0.08em at the deepest point. Even with large font sizes, this creates a believable sense of depth as the characters recede into virtual 3D space. For clarity, we changed the colours in the CSS, so that the results in our image appear as grey on white.

PAGE TURNER

Our text stands out more clearly now, but shadows aren't the only tool we can use to draw our reader's attention to our text. CSS3 makes provision for rotating elements on the page, and here Internet Explorer's support is up there with the best of them. Rotation, which can be applied to images and text, needs to be done individually for each browser architecture; the transform command must be preceded with `-moz` for Firefox, `-webkit` for Safari and Chrome, `-o` for Opera and `-ms` for Internet Explorer 9.

To rotate the text in all the paragraphs 30° counter-clockwise, we add this code to the previous CSS listing:

```
p {
   -ms-transform: rotate(-30deg);
   -moz-transform: rotate(-30deg);
   -o-transform: rotate(-30deg);
   -webkit-transform: rotate(-30deg);
   color: #800;
   font: 3em Arial;
   position: absolute;
   top:75;
   font-weight: 900;
}
```

Because the text rotates around its central point, we have introduced two new lines to our CSS – for position, and for top – to stop it swivelling beyond the edges of the browser window.

As you'll remember, our paragraph is contained within a `<div>` called 'layer'. We want it to take its measurements with reference to that layer, so we specify

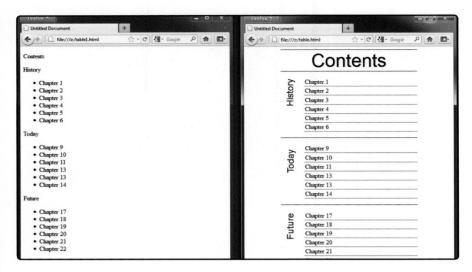

Above: Building a good-looking table of contents requires a minimum of CSS code

'position: absolute'. If we were to use 'fixed' instead, the element would rotate around a point relative to a position within the browser window rather than the layer that holds it. The rotation point is 75 pixels down from the top of whichever object it is using as its reference point, as denoted by the line 'top: 75;'.

CLASS DISTINCTION

You may think that being able to rotate your text is just a fun novelty, but it does have some very practical real-world examples. Take the following code, for example:

```
<style>
#layer {
  width: 450px;
  height: 320px;
  border: 1px solid black;
}
.sheep {
  background-image: url('lamb.jpg');
  top: 1;
  left: 1;
}
.sticker {
  -ms-transform: rotate(-30deg);
  -moz-transform: rotate(-30deg);
  -o-transform: rotate(-30deg);
  -webkit-transform: rotate(-30deg);
  color: #fff;
  font: 2.5em Arial;
  position: absolute;
  top: 55;
  font-weight: 900;
  background-color: red;
  padding: 0 10;
  border: 3px dotted white;
}
</style>
```

```
<div id="layer" class="sheep">
<p class="sticker">&pound;25 off
today!</p>
</div>
```

This code could be used as the basis of an online catalogue, with a general #layer attribute used to define the proportions of a <div> (450 by 320 pixels with a one-pixel solid border) that can be recycled for each product by applying a class. Our example catalogue deals with livestock and happens to be selling sheep. We've applied the class 'sheep', which, in our stylesheet, positions it one pixel from the top and left of the browser margins and adds an image of a lamb as the background.

Remember that named <div> elements ('layer' in this case) are defined in the stylesheet with a leading #, while classes applied to layers, text, images and so on should be preceded by a dot; this is why we can apply multiple styles to this <div> while only drawing on a single class.

BANNER TIME

We can draw visitors' attention to one of the items by applying text within a banner, overlaid on top of the image. Here, there's a £25 discount on lambs if bought the same day. We'll apply the class sticker to the text, which is then rendered by the stylesheet in white on a red background, rotated by 30°.

We've also applied padding (padding: 0 10;) to each end of the sticker, so the characters don't bump into the edge, and a dotted white border. Consider the following:

```
padding: 0px 10px 0px 10px;
```

We could have used this to define the padding applied to the top, right, bottom and left sides, but by cutting it to just '0 10' we've styled the top and bottom (0 pixels) and the two sides (10px), reducing the length of our code.

As well as making our text more dynamic, there's no need to use an image editor. Because the image of the lamb remains untouched, we can remove the text when the offer expires, without having to swap out the picture.

UNDER THE TABLE

Finally, we can use the idea of rotated text to build a contents table for an online reference book. It will have three sections – past, present and future events – and each will contain a number of individual chapters. We can achieve this by corralling our sections within DIV layers and our chapters in an unordered list.

The results may lack professionalism and do little to mimic a printed table of contents. However, by offsetting the contents so that they sit beside – rather than below – the section headings, and rotating those headings, we can improve the finished layout enormously, without requiring graphics, and with text that remains selectable and editable at all times.

Animation with CSS3

Animation can help to bring a website to life. You can use the tools built into HTML5 to achieve something flashy without the need for Flash

When used judiciously, animation is a useful tool. Its implementation can be purely decorative – as is the case with most animated web ads – or functional, controlling the behaviour of specific page elements.

To demonstrate how animation works, we'll show you an example that you can implement on any site: a floating panel that slides in from the edge of the browser. Such panels are common on sites that encourage feedback from visitors, but we're going to use our panel to provide supplementary information. If you want a feedback form, simply swap the panel content for the necessary form and apply a regular submit button tied to your form-handling routine. If this isn't provided as part of your hosting package, try CoffeeCup's Web Form Builder, which you can download from www. coffeecup.com/form-builder.

Our panel is a simple flat graphic – a GIF created in a photo editor and saved with a transparent background. The transparency is important, as we want the body of our page to remain visible behind the empty areas of the panel when it slides into position, giving the pull-down tab a greater sense of realism. The only parts of the panels that should be opaque are the background on which we'll place the content and the tab that will poke down from the top of the browser window.

Our graphic is 300 by 242 pixels, but yours should be large enough to fit whatever content you need it to accommodate.

BUILDING YOUR PAGE

Our page is deceptively simple. We're coding it using HTML5 so that we can take advantage of the simpler header structure but, beyond that, the remainder of the page is the same as it would be in HTML4.01.

We have just two elements: the primary content, which is organised in a layer called 'mainbody', and the panel itself, which is split into two parts – one that defines the physical dimensions encompassing the panel and the protruding tab, called 'menutab', and one for the contents that sit on top of the panel, called 'menutabcontents'.

For the time being, we have filled the body of our page with dummy text, and positioned an image, some text and a button on the tab, as follows:

Left: CoffeeCup's new Web Form Builder lets you quickly and easily create HTML5-compliant forms for your website

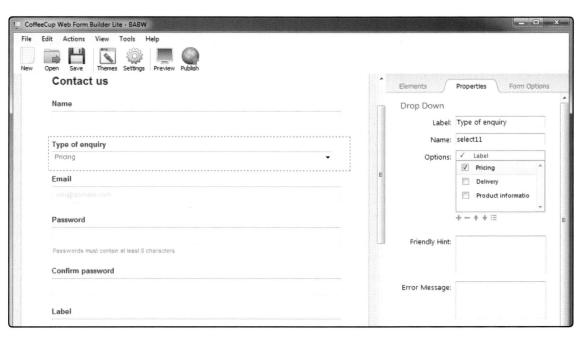

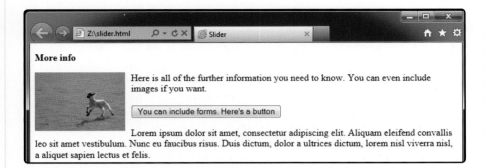

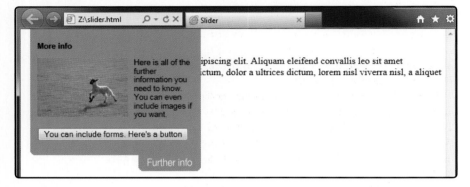

Top: The contents of our panel and our page are the same thing. We just need to split them on to separate layers

Second down: Hover the mouse over the tab and it drops down the full panel; this becomes an active area so the visitor can move their mouse around within it

```html
<!DOCTYPE html>
<head>
  <meta http-equiv="X-UA-Compatible"
    content="IE=9" />
  <title>Slider</title>
  <link href="slider.css"
    rel="stylesheet" type="text/css">
</head>
<body>
  <div id="menutab">
  <div id="menutabcontents">
    <p><b>More info</b></p><img src=
    "lamb.jpg" align="left" width="150"
    height="100" style="margin-right:
    10px;"/>Here is all of the
    further information you need to
    know. You can even include images
    if you want.<br /><br /><form>
    <input type="button" value="You can
    include forms. Here's a button">
    </form>
  </div>
  </div>
  <div id="mainbody">
    <p>Lorem ipsum dolor sit amet,
    consectetur adipiscing elit. Aliquam
    eleifend convallis leo sit amet
    vestibulum. Nunc eu faucibus risus.
    Duis dictum, dolor a ultrices dictum,
    lorem nisl viverra nisl, a aliquet
    sapien lectus et felis.</p>
  </div>
```

If you preview the page in your browser, you'll see that while the image sits to the left of the panel contents, everything else on the page flows on from what precedes it. We want the panel and its contents to slide into view, but there's no 'intelligence' on this page yet, and nothing to tell the browser how to handle the panel animation.

You could conceivably add animation to your page using JavaScript, but it's far more efficient – in terms of the amount of bandwidth consumed when displaying the effect, and in the amount of code required to implement it – to look to CSS instead and define its behaviour at the same time as the page layout.

DOING THE MATHS

We've designed our panel with a tab on the bottom as it will drop down from the top of the browser window. This tab will remain visible at all times, but when the mouse isn't hovering over it, the remainder of the panel will be kept hidden. In order to achieve this, we need to position the main portion of the panel beyond the browser boundaries. We'll do this by setting a negative upper margin in our CSS code. The top of the tab, where it joins the main body of the panel, is 215 pixels from the top of the image canvas, so the upper margin will be set at -215px.

To write the CSS for this page, we need to think in three dimensions. We need to specify the horizontal and vertical positions of the elements on our page (we can usually leave these alone, unless we specifically need to anchor objects within the layout). In addition, we need to consider their relative heights, as though they were coming out of the screen towards us.

We want our panel to slide down over the main page body, so we need to tell the browser to position it there using the z-index attribute. Z-index describes the third axis on a page (x-axis, y-axis, z-axis), which in this case comes vertically out from the page. Each object that you want to stack is given a value, with higher-valued objects appearing further up the stack. To position our panel higher than the body of our page, we can either give the menutab layer a z-index of 2 while giving the mainbody layer a z-index of 1 or, as we'll do here, give the mainbody layer a value of -1 while leaving the menutab on layer 1.

Z-index works in conjunction with the position element. If you don't tell the browser whether your positioning is relative, static, absolute, fixed or inherited, your stack won't be rendered properly. Therefore, we need to decide what the browser should use as the point of reference when positioning each element.

In the case of the mainbody layer, it's the document body. We're going to set this to start at the very top of the browser window with a top margin of 0px; by setting the mainbody layer to 'absolute' and its top to 30px, we can be absolutely certain that the mainbody will leave a gap of exactly 30 pixels at the top of the browser window.

This is sufficient room to display the tab of our panel, which is always visible, even when the panel is hidden – without the tab fouling the page contents.

We want to position the panel in relation to the browser window, not in relation to the page. If we positioned it in relation to the page, it would disappear as soon as the page was scrolled to read any excess body content that didn't fit within the browser window. By anchoring the panel to the browser window, it will ignore any scrolling.

The 'position' attribute for the menutab is therefore set to 'fixed', and we have also called in the graphic that we created earlier to be displayed as its background. Our initial CSS, which is saved in an attached file called 'slider.css', as referenced in the header of the HTML page, looks like this:

```
body {
  margin-top: 0px;
  overflow: scroll;
}
#menutab {
  width: 300px;
  height: 242px;
  background: url(tab.gif) no-repeat;
  margin-top: -215px;
  z-index: 1;
  font: 0.8em Arial;
  position: fixed;
}
#menutabcontents {
  padding: 10px 20px 10px 20px;
}
#mainbody {
  z-index: -1;
  position: absolute;
  top: 30px;
  left: 20px;
}
```

As you can see, the menutabcontents layer has been padded to keep the contents away from the very edge of the panel and improve its appearance.

CHANGING YOUR POSITION

The page is starting to take shape. We can now see the panel tab hanging down below the top edge of the browser, and its contents are hidden because they have been moved up by the negative top margin value to a position above the browser's viewable area.

To get the tab to roll down, we need to use the :hover class variable. Unlike our previous uses of :hover, we don't want to change the styling of an element; we just want to change its position. So we'll add a new :hover-specific class that's attached to the menutab layer that normalises its position:

```
#menutab:hover {
  margin-top: 0px;
}
```

Reload the page and move your mouse over the protruding tab, and you'll see that the whole panel now pops out, overlaying the main body of the page without disturbing the main body's position, and that you can also move your pointer around within the popped-out panel without the panel disappearing, which it does when we move our mouse away.

We're halfway there, but the result could still be improved. We can slow down the transition using the transition-duration element and its -moz, -ms and -webkit variants to target Firefox (-moz), IE (-ms) and both Chrome and Safari (-webkit).

We're doing a bit of forward-planning here as far as Internet Explorer is concerned, because version 9 doesn't support transition durations fully, although work is under way to integrate it into future releases. Still, any work done at this stage will put you in good stead as the browser is upgraded.

We don't need to slow the animation down much to achieve the result we're after. In this case, we're going to set a duration of half a second on all browsers by adding the following lines to the styling of the menutab layer:

```
-webkit-transition-duration: 0.5s;
-moz-transition-duration: 0.5s;
-ms-transition-duration: 0.5s;
transition-duration: 0.5s;
```

Save your changes and reload the page. When you move your pointer over the tab and away again, you'll see that the panel animation now slides smoothly into view.

APPLYING EFFECTS ELSEWHERE

The key to achieving a realistic result in all animation tasks is to control the speed at which the motion completes. When using this technique elsewhere, the one consideration that should remain uppermost in your mind, beyond the start and end position of your assets, is the speed at which the assets should transform from one state to the other. Master this, and you will afford your site a degree of polish that puts it several steps ahead of the competition.

Below: Hover the mouse over the tab and it drops down the full panel; this becomes an active area so the visitor can move their mouse around within it

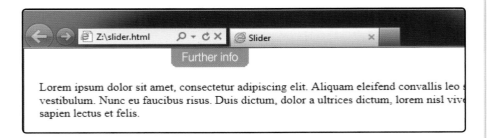

CHAPTER 6

IN THIS CHAPTER

Using WordPress to build
  your site..84

Content management

A content management system, or CMS, is a convenient way of managing lots of web pages. You determine the content, such as a diary entry, and the 'system' manages the way that the posts are shown and provides you with a way of creating new posts.

If your site has a lot of pages, you won't want to create every single one by hand. In this chapter, we'll show you how to create

MacBook Air

a website using WordPress. Although WordPress is primarily aimed at helping people to write a blog – an example of a simple CMS – it can also be used to assist in building a large website. To use WordPress, you just need a database for storing the content, which your web host should provide. Best of all, WordPress is free, so it won't cost you anything to use.

Using WordPress to build your site

WordPress's straightforward content-management system is ideal for helping you to put together an effective and eye-catching website

ESSENTIALS

SKILL LEVEL
Beginner
Intermediate
Expert

HOW LONG
3-5 hours

Below left: The WordPress Dashboard is where you manage your website

Below right: You can switch between themes (templates) whenever you like

WordPress was originally designed to help with building blogs whose content is arranged chronologically. However, it's also a powerful content-management system (CMS) and is ideal for creating traditional websites. Best of all, it's free and easy to use – you just need a web-hosting account that supports PHP and MySQL. It comes with a huge number of templates and you can download thousands more, customise them or even create your own. In this chapter, we'll walk you through the process of installing WordPress and creating a stunning, feature-packed site.

Building a website from scratch using HTML and CSS code allows you precise control over how everything looks and works. However, this approach isn't for everyone; it takes a little while to learn these coding languages, and once the site is complete it's relatively time-consuming to update it. What's more, it's virtually impossible for a non-technical person to update it by tweaking the text and images on existing pages, let alone create new pages.

WordPress is extremely easy even for web novices to use, yet still provides precise control over how your website looks and works. As it's free and massively popular, there are lots of professional-looking templates you can download to get your site up and running in next to no time, while plug-ins let you add features such as photo slideshows or videos.

Another of WordPress's strengths is that it runs entirely in your web browser. This saves you the cost of buying website-creation software or a decent HTML editor, such as CoffeeCup.

WordPress has its rivals, including Joomla and Drupal. While these are arguably more powerful content-management systems, neither is as easy to use.

INSTALLING WORDPRESS
Many web-hosting providers support one-click installation of WordPress using tools such as Fantastico, while others require you to install it manually. If you're choosing a hosting provider, it's worth opting for one with good WordPress support such as www.dreamhost.com or, if you prefer a UK-based host, www.webhosting uk.com or www.tsohost.co.uk. If your host doesn't have a one-click installer, visit http://wordpress.org and

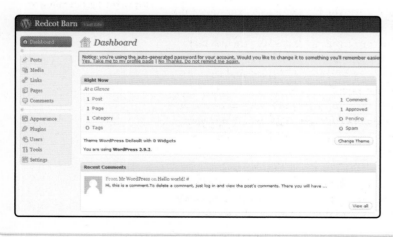

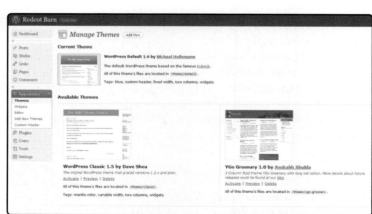

download the latest version of the software, which is currently 3.2.1. You'll need to download the .zip file if your host is Windows-based, or the .tar.gz for Linux hosts. Check with your provider if you're unsure.

Log in to your website's FTP server using the details supplied by your hosting provider and copy across the contents of the WordPress folder (not the folder itself) to the root of your web space. Your web host needs to support PHP and at least one MySQL database.

Set up a MySQL database using your website's control panel. You'll need to enter a database name, username and password. Again, check with your web host if you can't work out how to do this. Edit the wp-config-sample.php file on your web space to reflect the details of your database, and rename it as wp-config.php. One of the fields you may need to change is DB_HOST. Some hosting providers, such as FastHosts, require you to enter the IP address of your MySQL database here; for most others, you can leave the field at its default 'localhost' value. There are support forums on WordPress's website, where you should find experienced users to assist you quickly.

In your browser, visit your website but add /wp-admin to the address. You'll then be presented with a welcome screen, where you'll need to choose a title and enter your email address. Click the Install WordPress button and, assuming your wp-config.php file has been filled out correctly, you should see a Success! screen with a username and a randomly generated password that you must use to log in to the Dashboard. Note these down – they will be emailed to the address you entered on the welcome screen – and click the Log In button. You'll find yourself at the Dashboard, which you use to create new web pages and change the way your site looks and works.

CONFIGURING WORDPRESS

The first thing you'll notice is a red box at the top of the screen, warning you that you're using an auto-generated password. Click the link to take you to your profile page to change this password to something memorable, then click the Dashboard link in the top-left corner to return.

In order to configure WordPress as a traditional website rather than a blog, you'll need to create a new page which will be your homepage. To do this, click Pages in the menu on the left-hand side. Click 'Add new' and type 'index' into the blank white box below Edit Page. Then click the Publish button on the right-hand side. Click Settings in the left-hand menu, then Reading. Select the 'A static page' radio button rather than the default 'Your latest posts'. Under the 'Front page' drop-down menu, choose 'index' and then click Save Changes.

EXPLORING THEMES

We don't want to use the default WordPress theme for our site and you're probably none too impressed by it,

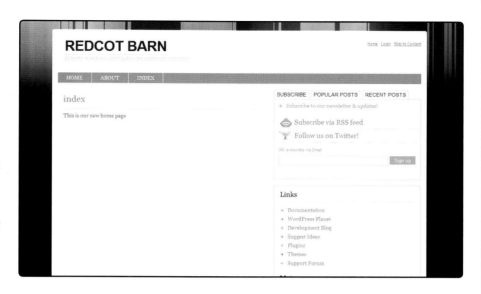

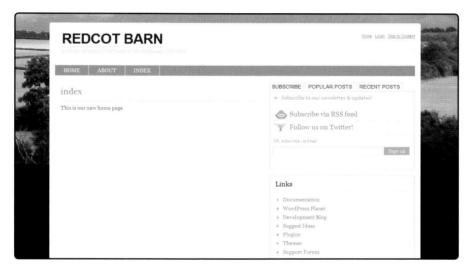

either. While we could create one with some PHP and CSS, it's actually far easier to download a free theme that someone has already created and tested in various browsers.

Click Appearance in the menu, then Add New Themes – you can use the filter tool to narrow down the search results. Then click Install or Preview on a theme you like. Bear in mind that most are blog themes that aren't suitable for traditional websites. We searched Google for non-blog WordPress Themes and we downloaded one called Urbane from www.blogohblog. com/wordpress-theme-urbane. You'll need to unzip the theme, and copy the folder and its contents using your FTP application to the wp-content/themes folder on your web space.

When you click on Themes in WordPress's Dashboard, you'll see Urbane in the list. Simply click Activate to switch to it. To view your site, click the Visit Site button at the top of the Dashboard. If you see a

Top: The basic homepage using the Urbane Theme. Now we add text and images

Bottom: Changing the background image gives the page a totally different look

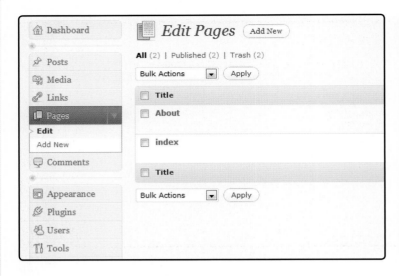

landing page for your web host, you may need to delete a default homepage that your provider places in the root folder of your web space, such as index.htm. You may see the homepage of an existing website if you've previously uploaded a website on to your web space; you'll need to remove or rename the files in order to see your WordPress homepage.

CUSTOMISING THE HOMEPAGE

We need to improve the appeal of the homepage by adding body copy, images and so on. First of all, we'll change the background image, as it doesn't fit in with the subject matter of our site, which is a holiday cottage.

If you look in the urbane folder you unzipped, you'll see a folder called images – in this, you'll see a file called bg.jpg with a resolution of 1,280x418 pixels. This repeats

Above left: Adding new pages is simple using the Add New command in the Dashboard

Above right: Create links easily using WordPress's page editor

Below: When adding images, you can determine alignment, size and alternate text

horizontally, so you can't simply replace it with a photo, as it will look awful for those with screen resolutions over 1,280 pixels wide. Instead, you can create another image that will tile well, or resize a photo to the maximum width you think your visitors' monitors will have; 1,920 is a sensible choice. We'll make one that fades to black like the existing image on page 91, but you don't have to do this. Save your new image as bg.jpg; overwrite the file in urbane/images, or save it in another folder. Then use your FTP application (we used FileZilla) to upload it to the wp-content/themes/urbane/images folder in your web space.

We'll now fill out the front page with content. Return to the WordPress Dashboard. If you haven't done so, create a bookmark for it in your browser. Click Pages, then Edit. Click on the 'index' page, and you can type or paste in your copy. The two tabs on the right-hand side of the main text box are called Visual and HTML. Make sure the Visual tab is selected, unless you plan to include HTML tags. To create a link, highlight the text that will form the link and click the chain icon in the toolbar. Enter the link address, and whether it will open in a new window or the current one.

On the right-hand side of the page is an Attributes pane. This allows you to set whether the current page has a parent or not. If it doesn't, a new link will be created on the main horizontal menu bar. If you select another page as the parent, a new drop-down menu item is added to the parent link on the menu.

INSERTING MEDIA

To insert images, videos or audio to your pages, click the appropriate icon to the right of Upload/Insert – these look as though they're greyed out, but they are in fact active. When you do this, a window opens with four tabs: From Computer, From URL, Gallery and Media Library. If you haven't used any images, the Gallery option will be missing. If you haven't uploaded any

media, you must choose between the first two options. The Flash-based uploader works well, as you can select multiple images from your computer, and it will automatically create thumbnails of images based on the size as defined in Settings, Media.

To insert an image, click the Show link to the right of an image's thumbnail. You'll see more options, such as alternate text (which you should fill in for accessibility), size and alignment. When you've done this, click Insert into Post and the image will be inserted wherever your cursor happens to be. If the image position isn't quite right, hover your cursor over the image and click on the Edit Image icon – in our example, the text was too close to the image, making things cramped. Click Advanced Settings and enter 10 in the Horizontal space box. This adds 10 pixels of padding either side and gives some breathing space. Changes are applied in the preview window. Click the Update button to save your changes.

You should now be familiar with the WordPress Dashboard, and be able to create new pages and change the theme of your site. We'll now turn our attention to modifying the template and installing plug-ins to make our pages more interesting for visitors.

UNDERSTANDING TEMPLATES

We've added text (with links) and a photo, but the template we've chosen has some features that we don't want. Fortunately, these are easy to remove by modifying the code in the template.

If you've logged out, navigate to your site and click the login link in the top-right corner. You should find yourself back at the Dashboard, where you need to click Editor under the Appearance heading in the left-hand menu. On the right, you'll see a list of Theme Files. Their names are self-explanatory and make it easy to locate the area you want to change. If you click on a file, its contents will be displayed in the middle of the screen where you can edit them. Unless

you're familiar with HTML and PHP, the code won't mean much, but you should still be able to get an idea of what's happening as most of it is in plain English.

Below the list of templates are two style sheets: style.css and ie.css. The former contains all the CSS that defines the look of the site, while the latter contains just two lines that apply if the browser is Internet Explorer. The other files control individual elements on a page.

We want to remove the tabbed box in the upper-right corner. Click on the tabs-content.php file and comment out the entire file: add <!-- before the first line, and --> after the last one; this will tell the browser to ignore all the code in between. Finally, click the Update File button, and the tabbed box will disappear from the site.

Above: The homepage looks more polished as we've sorted out the background image, but there's still work to be done

Far left: You can install plug-ins from within WordPress; ratings enable you to find the best

Left: Plug-ins such as this contact form have numerous options so you can configure them to your liking

details about the plug-in – just click the red Install Now button at the top to install it. If you see a timeout error, try again in a few minutes; you should see an Installing Plugin message in WordPress.

If this still doesn't work, you can manually download the file from http://downloads.wordpress.org/plugin/ si-contact-form.zip. Unzip the file and copy its contents to the /wp-content/plugins/ folder on your web space.

Next, you need to activate the plug-in. Click Installed in the Plugins menu in WordPress's Dashboard. You should see the contact form plug-in in the list; just click the Activate link beneath it. This will turn into a Settings link – click this to configure the form.

CONFIGURING THE FORM

There are many options when configuring the form, so read through them to set up the form in the way that best suits your needs. As we've entered some text in the Contact Us page, we'll remove the text in the Welcome introduction box, as it's duplicating our message.

We particularly like this plug-in because it uses the popular CAPTCHA security mechanism, which prevents spam. Visitors must enter the code from an onscreen graphic (or from a noisy audio clip, if you enable the Flash Audio option). A link at the bottom of the CAPTCHA section tests whether your PHP installation will support it. This link also provides troubleshooting advice if the CAPTCHA image doesn't appear beneath your form. There could be a variety of reasons for this, but the most common reason is that the file permissions on your web server have been set too tightly.

You can enter default text into the subject line, as well as pre-loading a list of alternative subject lines. This can help you to filter incoming emails into different folders, depending on their content, as you'll know in advance what the subject lines will be. By default, the redirect option is enabled; this takes visitors to the homepage three seconds after they submit their form.

You can enter the email address to which you want the forms sent; by default, this is set to the email address that you entered when configuring WordPress. Test that everything works by entering an email address in the 'Send a Test E-mail' field near the bottom of the page.

To make the form appear on the Contact Us page, you need to copy the shortcode at the top of the settings page; this is [si-contact-form form='1']. Paste this into the body section of your Contact Us page. Untick the Allow Comments option and click the Publish button.

When you go to your website, you should see a new menu item at the top for the Contact Us page. Click on this to see your new form. To make changes, go back to the settings page of the plug-in to add or remove fields.

SETTING UP A SLIDESHOW

Our website is coming together nicely, but it would be nice for visitors to get a better idea of our guest house by

Check this by opening a new tab and browsing to your website. To remove other elements from the template, select the relevant file and comment out its contents, update the file and look at your site to see the changes. If you don't like what's happened, return to the file and remove the commenting to reinstate that page element.

INSTALLING PLUG-INS

Now we've updated the template, we're going to create a new page and install a plug-in that allows potential holiday makers to contact us. Click Add New under the Pages menu heading. Enter Contact Us in the title bar and enter some text in the body of the page that explains how visitors can use the form to get in touch with you.

Click Save Draft and then click Plugins in the left-hand menu. This will display the Manage Plugins screen. Click Add New and use the search bar to search for 'secure contact form'. Then find Fast and Secure Contact Form in the results list and click the Install link to the right of it. A pop-up window will show more

Above: This is how the contact form appears on our site

Below: You can change the links that appear in the right-hand box by clicking on the Links section in the Dashboard menu

watching a photo slideshow. To add one, we'll install another plug-in. In the Plugins section of the Dashboard, click Add New and search for 'showtime slideshow'. Click the Install link, then Install Now and – once it's successfully installed – the Activate Plugin link.

We need a new page for our slideshow, so create one called Gallery. Click the Settings link for the ShowTime Slideshow plug-in in the Plugins section, and you should see a wealth of options. You may not need to change any settings apart from the default size, which is 640x320. On our site, this is too wide as it overlaps the Links section on the right of each page, so we've changed it to 480x320. Don't forget to click the Save Settings button at the bottom of the page to apply your changes.

When visitors hover their cursor over the slideshow, they can control it by moving the cursor to the left or right and clicking to skip a photo, or clicking the photo to pause it. Clicking at the top or bottom puts the slideshow in full-screen mode. These controls aren't immediately obvious, so you may need to add some text to the page for the benefit of visitors.

UPDATING THE LINKS PANEL

To change the default links in the right-hand panel of each web page, just click on the Links heading in the menu in the Dashboard. This brings up an Edit Links page where you can add, edit and delete links. To remove all existing links, put a tick in the box next to each one, choose Delete from the Bulk Actions drop-down menu and click Apply.

When adding a new link, you'll need to enter a name for it as well as the web address. It's useful to provide a description that can be shown below the title, or when visitors hover their cursor over the link. You can choose whether the new page opens in a new tab or the same one by selecting an option in the Target section.

WORKING WITH WIDGETS

Many WordPress themes come with widgets, which are little tools such as search bars, calendars, site maps and so on. Our Urbane theme has three panels at the bottom of each page where you can add widgets. As this is part of the template, these will appear on every page of your site and help to give a unified look and feel, as well as helping visitors quickly navigate to the page they're looking for.

At the moment, the three panels are visible, although they simply have the words 'Widgetized Section' in them. To choose widgets for these, click on the Widgets subheading under the Appearance heading in the Dashboard – a list of available widgets will appear. Each one has a brief description beneath it explaining what it does. On the right is a list of the locations where you can place widgets; of these, we'll be using Bottom Section Left, Bottom Section Middle and Bottom Section Right. Expand these by clicking the arrow to the right of each name and you'll see that each one is empty.

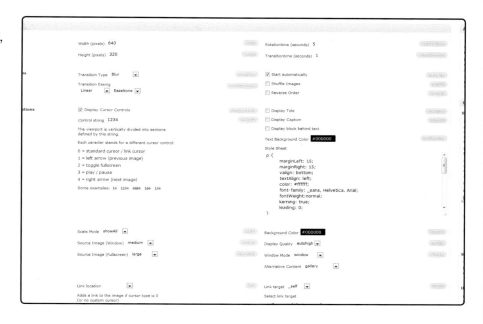

To add a widget to a section, click on its title, drag it to the blank grey area beneath a section heading and a dotted outline will appear. Release your mouse button and the widget will be added. You can add multiple widgets to each section, and you can even add the same widget to multiple sections if you want to. Reordering widgets is as simple as dragging them around within each section.

When you've dropped a widget on to one of the sections, it becomes active and will appear on your website. It will also display any options; you can show or hide these by clicking the arrow to the right of the widget's name. For the Search widget, for example, you

Top: There are lots of options for the slideshow plug-in, but you probably won't need to change them

Bottom: Here we see the slideshow in action; it can also show images fullscreen

can only enter a title, but for the Pages widget, you can also select how to sort the list of pages as well as exclude certain pages from the list. If you make any changes to a widget's settings, don't forget to click Save or your changes won't be applied.

If you want to remove a widget, simply drag it from the section on the right back to the list of available widgets. You can also drag it to the Inactive Widgets pane and this will save any settings you've made so you can enable the widget again at a later date.

A useful widget is Text. It's easy to overlook this as it doesn't sound very exciting. However, as you are able to enter any text or HTML into it, it can be very useful. You could use it as a pull quote to draw people's attention

to a fact that you don't want them to miss, or to highlight some positive customer feedback. As this isn't an editor, you'll need to enter HTML code to style your text. We wrapped our customer quote with <h1> tags (the large heading style) to make the text jump out of the page.

ADDING GOOGLE MAPS

There are many reasons to put a map on your website, but a static image isn't the best choice. For a start, you need to source the map and copyright issues usually mean you can't simply take a screenshot of an online map and use it on your website. You could draw your own map, but this takes time and skill.

A better solution is to embed an interactive Google Map, which is both legal and simple. What's more, since it's interactive, visitors can zoom in and out to get a better idea of the exact location and also get directions and an estimate of how long their journey will take.

There are a number of plug-ins for WordPress that can add a map, but we recommend Aaron Campbell's Google Maps for WordPress. To install it, head to the Plugins section and click Add New. In the Search box type 'Google Maps' and you should see Google Maps for WordPress fairly near the top of the list of results.

Click the Install button to the right, and then Install Now on the window that appears. When it's installed, click the Activate Plugin link. The next step is to sign up for a Google Maps API key, as you can't use Google Maps on your website without one. Go to http://code. google.com/apis/maps/signup.html and type in your website's URL in the box towards the bottom of the page. Tick the box to agree to the terms and conditions, click the Generate API Key button and your key will be displayed in a box at the top of the next page. Copy this and return to your WordPress Dashboard.

Above: A widget is a tool or content that appears in sidebars or footers on your site

Right: Three widgets have been enabled on our site in the footer area: a search tool, a calendar and a sitemap

Far right: The text widget can be used to display any text or HTML you like; we've used it for customer feedback

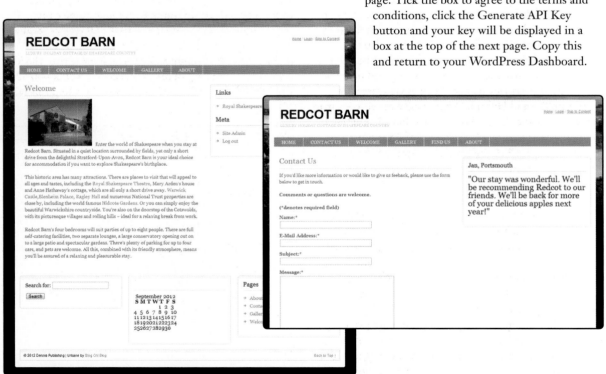

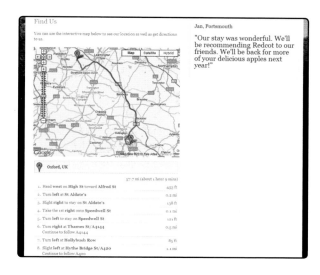

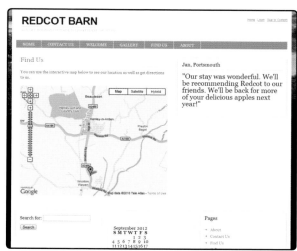

There should be a warning at the top of your Plugins list saying Google Maps won't work until you have an API key. Click this link and paste the key you just copied into the box. Click the Update Options button and you'll see a message saying that your key appears to be valid.

Now create a new page or edit the page on which you want your map to appear. You'll see a new section at the bottom of the page for Google Maps; this is where you specify the map options. You can enter a location name, which becomes the title for the marker on the map, plus the address, which appears in the callout box over the map. You can also enter a description, if relevant, and specify the width and height of the map in pixels or percent. However, these can be left blank.

One of the best aspects of this plug-in is the ability to display a box where visitors can type in an address from which to get directions. The map is redrawn to show the route and the directions are displayed in a list below it. You can choose whether to allow zooming and panning and whether users can change the map view between Map, Satellite and Hybrid. When you've set all your map options, click the Send Map to Editor button and the necessary code is entered into the text editor box at the top of the page. Click the Preview button on the right and check if the map is displaying properly on your page.

STRAIGHT TO VIDEO

The final element we want to add to our site is a video, which will give visitors a much better idea of what it's like to stay at our guest house. To do this, we need to install one final plug-in called WordPress Video Plugin. If you search for this using the search facility in the Plugins section, you'll be able to locate and install it just as easily as the other plug-ins we've installed.

The plug-in supports every common online video service, including YouTube, Google Video, Facebook, Vimeo and Dailymotion. Click on the link in the plug-in description to go to the instruction page; this describes

how to embed each type of video into your page using WordPress short code. So to embed a YouTube video, enter the following at the point where you want the video to appear: [youtube id], where id is the unique code for the video. In the URL www.youtube.com/watch?v=8DHOZW_8OPk the id is 8DHOZW_8OPk. You can also specify the size of the video in pixels by including the horizontal and vertical figures after the id code. For example, [youtube 8DHOZW_8OPk 480 320] would produce a video 480 pixels wide by 320 pixels tall.

Top left: Directions are shown without visitors having to leave the page

Top right: Our custom Google map shows a marker to pinpoint a location

Above: You need an API key in order to use Google Maps on your WordPress site, but this can be downloaded for free from http://code.google.com

Left: Embedding a YouTube video into a page is easy when you've got the WordPress Video plug-in installed

CHAPTER 7

IN THIS CHAPTER

YouTube video.................................94

Driving directions..........................95

Weather forecasts.........................96

Photo slideshows...........................97

Make the most of RSS feeds.......98

Internet forums 100

Adding sparkle

By now, you should be more confident about creating a good-looking website that your visitors can navigate easily. You're now in a position to go a step further and make your website really special by adding a few flourishes here and there.

In this chapter, we'll show you how to add video, panoramic images, slideshows, weather forecasts and even driving

A GOURMET EUROPEAN MARKET & DELICATESSEN

Gene's SAUSAGE SHOP & DELICATESSEN

CLICK TO Shop Gene's

SAUSAGE VARIETIES
Gene's carries over 40 varieties of homemade natural wood-smoked tasty delicacies. Check out descriptions of our favorites!
Learn About Our Sausage →

GIFT BASKETS
Piled high with imported European goodies, our beautifully handcrafted baskets are the perfect holiday gift for the food lover!
Learn About Our Gift Baskets →

Gene's $25

OUR SPECIALTIES
With a full delicatessen, fresh produce,

GIFT CARDS
A tasty gift for any occasion! Stop in our

Anniversary Specials	
Smoked Ham	$3.99/LB
Pastrami	$3.99/LB
Roast Beef	$3.99/LB
Corned Beef	$3.99/LB
American Cheese	$3.99/LB
Swiss Cheese	$3.99/LB
Veal & Pork Wieners	$1.99/LB
Tony Chacher's Creole Injectable Butter (17 oz.)	$2.99 ea.
Tony Chacher's Creole Seasoning (8 oz.)	$2.19 ea.

MacBook Air

directions to your pages. If you know you're going to be updating your website frequently, you'll also benefit from creating an RSS feed to let people know when there's something new to read. Finally, if you're setting up a website for a club, we'll show you how to add a forum so members can chat, give advice, arrange meetings and stay in touch.

YouTube video

A video can give your website added appeal and bring a page to life in minutes. Here we show you how to turn those thoughts into action

Hosting a video on a website used to be a complex process. Thankfully, this has changed. Adding a video clip to your site can be done in a few minutes, and all for free. Here we show you how to add a YouTube video to your site.

1 Prepare your video for uploading. YouTube accepts videos in a range of formats, including AVI, MPG and MOV. For the best results, use an MPEG4 format such as AVCHD. A free video encoder such as Any Video Converter (www.any-video-converter.com) will change your video to one of these formats. Choose a resolution that matches your source video, since YouTube supports up to 1080p. Depending on your account, clips may be limited to 15 minutes long.

2 To upload your clip, you need a YouTube account. If you don't have one already, sign up for free at www.youtube.com. Once you're registered, click on the yellow Upload button on the right-hand side. You must add a title, description and tags, but go to town with these only if you want YouTube users to find your video easily. Click the 'Upload a video…' button and select the file. Uploading takes a while, since your broadband connection's upload speed is likely to be much slower than the download speed. For this reason, we recommend keeping your video's file size below 50MB.

3 Once your video is uploaded, YouTube processes it. We now have to embed it into our website. Even before the processing is done, you'll see a message saying that the upload is complete. Below it, you'll see a box containing some code. Copy and paste this code into one of your web pages, where you want the video to appear.

4 Visitors to your website can now see the video when they look at your website, and can click the large play button overlaid on the video to play it.

Driving directions

If visitors to your website need to know how to get somewhere, you can easily provide the tools necessary to show them the way

O ur Redcot Barn website is the perfect example of a website where driving directions are relevant. Rather than including a map of the local area as a JPEG image, you can easily add a driving directions gadget, thereby saving your visitors time and hassle.

1 Visit http://tinyurl.com/directionsgadget and click the 'Add to your webpage' button to load the configuration page.

2 First, change the default Location to the country in which you will be requiring directions. You should also change the Language in the drop-down box to your preferred language. In our example, the gadget will be used only to direct people to Redcot Barn, so the most important detail for us to include is the address, and this goes in the End Address box. A nice touch is to add a helpful message to the Start Address box so, for example, you could type 'Enter your postcode, eg DA4 2HW'.

3 The last step to customising the gadget is to change the colour and size of the box. If you're placing the gadget in a sidebar, you can tailor it to fit perfectly by editing its width and height. If the gadget is the focus of a page, you can leave the width at its default value, but it's worth increasing the height from 91 to 100 pixels to avoid the clutter of a vertical scrollbar.

Next choose a border for the box. You can add a title for the gadget, or leave the box empty if you don't need one. At any point, you can click the Preview Changes button to see how your options will look.

4 Once you've customised everything, click the Get the Code button to reveal the code in the text box below. Cut and paste this code into the page where you want the gadget to appear, and save the file. The resulting directions appear in a new browser window, since this gadget redirects visitors to Google Maps (see page 150 to find out how to add Google Maps to your website).

ESSENTIALS

SKILL LEVEL
Beginner
Intermediate
Expert

HOW LONG
30 minutes

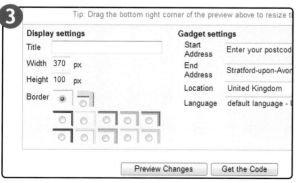

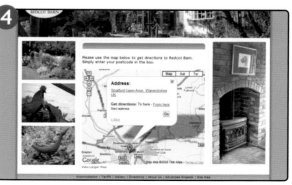

Weather forecasts

Including a weather forecast on your website is easy to do, won't cost a penny and is another helpful way to keep your visitors up to date

ESSENTIALS

SKILL LEVEL
Beginner
Intermediate
Expert

HOW LONG
30 minutes

Adding a weather forecast would be ideal for our Redcot Barn website, as potential customers can see at a glance what the local weather is like.

It's easy to add a forecast to your website using the myWeather gadget, which takes data from www.weather.com and displays it in an easy-to-read format. This is far better than updating your site every day by hand. Other weather widgets enable the user to change the location of the forecast, but the myWeather gadget allows you to fix the forecast area; this is useful if you want to prevent people searching for other forecasts.

1 Go to the myWeather gadget's homepage at http://tinyurl.com/myweather and click on the 'Add to your webpage' button to see the Preferences page.

2 To configure the gadget, you need to look up the location code of the area for which you want a weather forecast. Go to the myWeather website (www.notkewl.com/myWeather) and enter a UK town or city. The nearest town to Redcot Barn is Stratford-upon-Avon, which returns a code of UKXX1549. Copy and paste this code into the Zip/Location Code box on the gadget's configuration page. Click on the Preview Changes button to check the gadget is displaying the forecast for the next three days in Stratford-upon-Avon.

3 Delete the title, as you won't want this on your web page. Increase the height to 270 pixels to remove the vertical scroll bar. Most importantly for a UK-based forecast, select Metric Units in the drop-down box so temperatures are displayed in Celsius, not Fahrenheit.

4 Once you've customised everything and the gadget is showing the forecast for the correct area, click on the Get the Code button to display the code. Cut and paste this into your web page, where you want the forecast to appear.

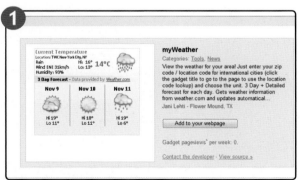

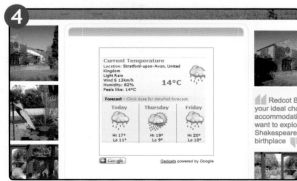

Photo slideshows

A slideshow is a charming way to showcase a selection of photos, and it doesn't take long to create a simple one using Picasa

Sometimes you'll want to show visitors to your site more than just a couple of photos, and that's when a slideshow works wonders. On page 138, we'll explain how to create a customised show using JavaScript, but here's how to create a simple slideshow using Picasa.

Picasa is a Google application for organising photos online. You can upload images, give them descriptions and arrange them into albums. You can also use Picasa to create slideshows for use on your website.

1 To create an online gallery, you'll need a Google account. Visit http://picasaweb.google.com/home and create a new account, or log in if you already have one. Accept the Terms and Conditions and click the Free Download button, if you haven't already installed Picasa.

2 In Picasa, create a new album by clicking on the Upload button. Add a title and any other details you want, and choose the Public or Unlisted option.

On the next page, you'll be prompted to install the Picasa Uploader. Once this is installed, choose photos to upload. Next, click on to the album's page and make a note of the RSS feed address by right-clicking on the RSS link at the bottom of the page and choosing Copy Shortcut.

3 Go to http://tinyurl.com/picasagadget and click the 'Add to your webpage' button to see the Preferences page. Paste the feed you copied in Step 2 into the Picasa Web RSS Feed box on the Preferences page. Remove the text from the title box, and increase the size of the gadget so the image can be seen without cropping. View the effect of any changes made by clicking Preview Changes.

4 Once you're happy, click the Get the Code button and copy and paste the code into your web page, where you want the slideshow to appear. If you update the images in the Picasa Web Album, the new images will appear on your website automatically.

ESSENTIALS
SKILL LEVEL
Beginner
Intermediate
Expert
HOW LONG
1 hour

Make the most of RSS feeds

An RSS feed keeps people up to date with new content on your site, so that they know about fresh updates as soon as they happen

ESSENTIALS

SKILL LEVEL
Beginner
Intermediate
Expert

HOW LONG
3 hours

RSS stands for Really Simple Syndication, or Rich Site Summary, depending on who you ask. Beyond the acronyms, an RSS feed is a way to view or publish frequently updated content such as news stories, blogs or podcasts.

Adding an RSS feed to your website lets your visitors keep up to date with news and events without having to check back continually to see if anything has been updated. Therefore, there's little point in including an RSS feed on a static website, where little of the content changes from day to day. RSS is better suited to news sites and blogs, where feeds can be used to alert readers each time a new story or blog post is uploaded. Similarly, RSS can be used to tell media player software such as iTunes when a new podcast is available.

The idea behind RSS is a complex one to get to grips with, but once you understand it, it soon becomes indispensable. An RSS feed is simply an XML file

(XML being similar to HTML) that is stored on your web server. The file contains a list of the most recent articles, blog posts or podcast files on your site. When your visitors use an RSS feed application such as Google Reader on their PC, they can see at a glance if any of their favourite websites have been updated. It makes the task of keeping up with multiple websites a lot easier, and ensures that visitors never miss a new article.

CREATING A FEED

Adding an RSS feed to your website can be difficult, because it needs to be programmed to update automatically whenever you add a new post. Thankfully, you don't need to do this yourself. If you're using a blogging tool such as WordPress (see chapter 6) or a content-management system for a news-based website, you'll almost certainly have an RSS feed already. If you don't, the easiest way to get one is to use a service that provides one (see the Tip opposite).

All you need to worry about, therefore, is changing the settings to suit your website. The most important aspect to consider is whether to include the full text of your posts in the feed. If you do, visitors won't need to go to your site to read the full details. Including just an excerpt will force them to go to your site to get the full story; this is a crucial manoeuvre if you intend to make money from advertising, or from the services or products that you provide. Having said that, adding the complete text to the feed makes it more convenient for readers.

There's only so much you can tweak from within your CMS, and the basic RSS feed has its limitations. If people aren't visiting your site to read the content, it can be hard to track the number of readers you have. There are free tools you can use to get more from your feed, though. In the walkthrough opposite, we'll take you through setting up and using the excellent FeedBurner. You'll need an RSS feed configured before you can do this.

Below: Google Reader is a good RSS feed application, and it's free to use

How to... Use FeedBurner to get more from your feed

1 Go to http://feedburner.google.com and sign in using your Google account details (or sign up if you don't have one). Enter the URL of your RSS feed. This can be found by right-clicking on the RSS link on your site and selecting Copy Link Location. Alternatively, enter the URL of your site, such as blog.computershopper.co.uk. Click Next and verify which feed you want, if your site has more than one.

2 On the next screen, give your feed a title and a feedburner.com address, which will be used instead of the standard feed on your site. This lets you use the advanced FeedBurner features, but will be transparent to your readers. Click Next and you'll be told your new feed is live. You get the option to monitor clickthroughs (how often people click items back to your site), downloads (such as podcasts) and other statistics. Click Next and you'll be taken to the main control panel. Click the Analyze tab and you'll see the Feed Stats Dashboard, although it will take a day or so before you can see the figures.

3 Instead of using a plain-text link to this new RSS feed, FeedBurner can automatically create HTML that you can insert into your web pages to give you a more noticeable and attractive icon. Click on the Publicize tab and the 'friendly graphic' link to reach the oddly named Chicklet Chooser. From here, you can select the style of icon you want to use, and cut and paste the code into the web page, where you want to include the RSS feed. Usually, this will be your homepage. Alternatively, you could choose to make it part of the header on your site, so it's visible on every page.

4 There are other ways that FeedBurner can publicise your new RSS feed and give your readers an easy way to stay up to date with your news and blog posts. Click on the Publicize tab again and select Email Subscriptions on the left. This will provide you with the code to place a small box on your site where users can sign up to receive email updates about your posts. This is perfect for visitors who are unsure what RSS feeds are, or who don't want to install an RSS reader.

Checking back on FeedBurner periodically will allow you to track how many readers your RSS feed is attracting; this is something that a standard RSS feed alone doesn't provide. Be warned, though: checking statistics can become addictive.

TIP
To get an RSS feed for your site, you'll need additional services such as Blogger, WordPress or TypePad. To learn how to use their RSS features, visit http://tinyurl.com/aboutrss.

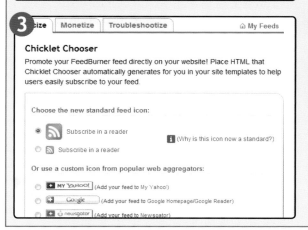

TIP
If you like the statistics FeedBurner provides, you'll probably like Google Analytics. See page 107 to find out how to use this useful tool.

Internet forums

Providing a place for a community to chat on your website is easy, and it won't cost a penny if you install some open-source software

ESSENTIALS

SKILL LEVEL
Beginner
Intermediate
Expert

HOW LONG
45 minutes

Having a regular group of visitors to your site is great, but giving them a way to converse makes them stay on your site for longer, potentially earning you more advertising revenue, and it adds value for users who share a common interest. For example, if your website is for a local mums and toddlers' club, a forum offers a way for members to chat to each other, arrange meetings, swap tips and offer advice.

It's sensible practice to make people sign up with an email address and password, to prevent spam posts. To prevent libellous or nasty posts, you must also moderate the forum, or delegate the job to someone you trust.

In this walkthrough, we'll show you how to get a forum up and running using phpBB, a popular open-source forum program. You'll also need a web-hosting account with a MySQL database and PHP support.

1 See if your web host has an automatic installation service. Sometimes phpBB can be installed at the click of a button using a tool called Fantastico; look for it in your hosting provider's control panel. If you find it, use this install method and go to Step 7. If not, download the latest version of phpBB from www.phpbb.com/downloads and extract the files to a folder on your desktop.

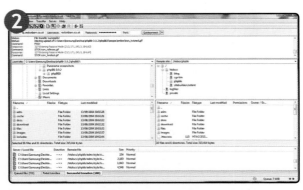

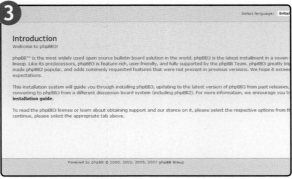

2 Next, upload the files to a new folder on your web server using your FTP software. If you don't have FTP access, upload the single zipped file using your host's file manager and then unzip the file from the online control panel.

3 Once the files are uploaded, you need to configure the installation. Open your browser and enter the address of your forum. This will be your domain name, followed by the name of the folder containing the phpBB files; in this instance, www.redcotbarn.co.uk/forum. This will take you to the main installation page for phpBB.

4 Click on the Install tab, then click on the 'Proceed to next step' button. This will take you to the requirements page for the installation, where phpBB will run several tests to see that you have all the appropriate features and permissions to run the software. Once these tests have been completed successfully, click the 'Start install' button at the bottom of the page.

5 On the Database settings page, you'll need to go back to your hosting account and create a database, which phpBB will use to store your users' details and their posts. If you're not sure how to create a database, contact your hosting provider. Name the database 'forum', without the quotes. Create a new user, assigning them read and write permissions on the database. Once you've done this, go back to the phpBB installation page and enter the database details. Proceed to the next page and enter the user details you just created.

6 The rest of the settings in the installation pages can be left at their default values. When all the steps are complete, you must delete the installation directory. If you don't do this, the forum won't be visible.

7 You'll then be taken to the Administration page. Here the forum can be customised and controlled when it's up and running. Only one thread is available by default. To add more, click on the Forums tab at the top of the page and then click the 'Create new forum' button before entering a name and description for the section.

The first time you create a forum, you need to assign permissions. These define who can do what on this part of the message board. It's best to assign the standard permissions to only registered users when you're starting out. You'll get a better idea of how to tailor this once your community starts to grow. With every thread you create from then on, you can select the permissions from an existing thread on the 'Create new forum' page by using the drop-down box.

8 You can now view your forum. Click on the 'Board index' link in the top right of the page. This will take you to the same page your visitors will see. You can place a link to this – either in the text of another web page or as a link in the main navigation bar – so visitors can access the forum without having to type its URL into the address bar in their browser. The forum will look plain at first but you can customise it, placing your own header on the page or using one of many phpBB themes that can be found online for free (see the Tip, below).

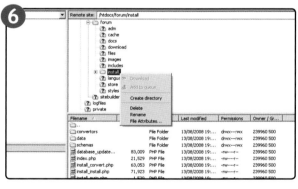

TIP
To spice up the look of your forum, browse the styles and themes at www.phpbb-styles.com, www.phpbb.com/styles and www.phpbb3styles.net.

CHAPTER 8

IN THIS CHAPTER

Legal considerations.................. 104

Bringing visitors back................ 106

Understanding Google
    Analytics...................................... 107

Making money from
    your site...................................... 108

Finishing touches

Now the bulk of your website is in order, there are just a few things left to consider to make it work for you. First, you must ensure there are no legal issues with the content you publish. Images, text, logos, audio and video can all be copyrighted, so you'll need to know the content is your own, or that you have permission to use it. We'll explain the pertinent details, so you stay on the right side of the law.

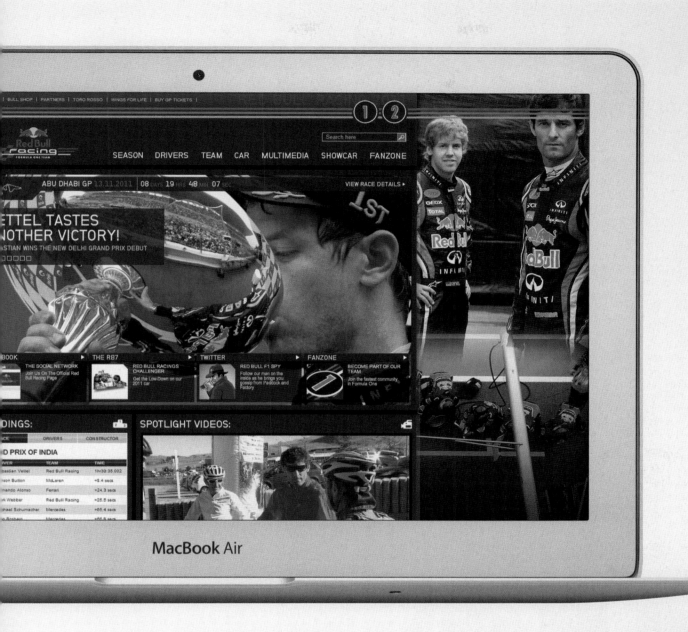

MacBook Air

We'll also help you to improve the chances of visitors returning to your website. This is enormously beneficial, especially if you intend to sell products or services. We'll show you how to use your site to make money, even if it's just to cover hosting costs. Finally, we'll explain how you can check your site to ensure that it continues to look and work at its best.

Legal considerations

Before you publish anything online, be absolutely sure it won't land you in hot water with the law. We explain the main issues to bear in mind

Below: Flickr has plenty of Creative Commons material on its site, but bear in mind that not all of it is free to use

E ven if your website is designed for the pleasure of your friends and family, you should never forget that the World Wide Web is exactly that. Unless you password-protect it, your site can be seen by anyone. For this reason, you need to be clued up on the law and fastidious about every single detail you publish online.

PROPERTY RIGHTS

First, you need to be familiar with the concept of copyright. Just because some text or an image is publicly accessible online, it doesn't mean anyone and everyone can copy and use it. Makers of commercial websites pay a lot of money for the words and photos that appear on them, and they won't take kindly to people ripping them off, even people who aren't out for commercial gain.

When you're looking for images to use on your site, it's best to assume that the pictures you find online are copyrighted unless you can prove otherwise: this is the best way to avoid expensive legal wrangling. However, there are ways to find legal-to-use images. Flickr (www.flickr.com) is a great place to find Creative Commons-licensed pictures (see the box below). Just remember that a copyright owner can waive their rights at their discretion. If you see an image that you simply must have, email the owner and politely ask permission. However, most professional photographers will charge you for using their images; it's their prerogative.

If you decide to go down the route of paying for the images on your site, you could try a microstock site. These are large image libraries that charge either per image or on a monthly or yearly basis for a set number of image downloads. Examples of image libraries are Shutterstock (www.shutterstock.com) and iStockPhoto (www.istockphoto.com). These sites allow you to buy photos for as little as 50p each. In return, you have the right to use the image on your site, although you can't then sell the image on to someone else.

The best way to avoid copyright issues altogether is to take your own pictures to use on your website. There are a few things to bear in mind, though. First, if you intend to make money from your images, make sure the people in them are happy about this. If a picture is primarily of one person, ask them first. If things are really taking off, it may be worth investigating a model release. This is a contract, signed by your subject, that allows you to sell the image. Remember that it's legal for you to take – and sell – pictures in public places, even if the resulting shots contain identifiable people.

ON YOUR MARKS

Trademarks are logos, symbols, images, words or phrases that are owned by a company. Even sounds can be trademarked; just think of the Intel Inside sound that accompanies the company's TV adverts.

You should be careful of accidentally creating a website element that will remind people of a trademark. It will make you look unoriginal, and you certainly don't want to attract the attention of high-powered lawyers. You can even infringe a trademark with the URL that you choose for your site.

Some people register domain names that are almost identical to those of popular websites. For instance, www.georgewbush.org is the URL of a satirical website. This site gets plenty of hits simply because people haven't realised that they should have gone to www. georgewbush.com, which is the former president's real address. However, if you try this tactic, it will be obvious that you're trying to pass yourself off as someone associated with the real site and the company may take legal action.

FREEDOM OF SPEECH

If you're running a news website, or anything that references current affairs, remember that quoting people is acceptable, as long as you cite your sources. Never make it appear as if an interviewee were talking directly to you if you're actually quoting words from another site.

Put simply, creating and running a website makes you a publisher, and so you should be mindful of the kinds of legal issues that can affect newspapers and magazines. The main one here is libel, which is where something written about someone is untrue and hurtful to that person's reputation. A good rule is to determine whether the story you're about to publish online is true. Have your checked your facts? Or are you publishing opinion without any facts behind it? Unless you have thousands of pounds to spare, you can't afford to get involved with any lawsuits.

Even repeating libellous claims is enough to get you into trouble. In 2007, Conservative MP Esther McVey

published claims about rival MP Stephen Hesford's plan to go on a taxpayer-funded sporting tour of Australia. He didn't intend to go. Although McVey was only repeating claims made in *The Mail on Sunday* months before, Hesford sued her.

AND FINALLY...

Remember that although running a website can give rise to legal confusion, most of it can be cleared up with a simple email. If in doubt, contact the person whose content you'd like to use; you may be surprised at how far this can get you. Beyond this, you can always consult a lawyer, although it will probably cost you. Of course, if you can't afford to consult a lawyer, you certainly can't afford to publish questionable material, so don't risk it.

Above: Wikipedia is a wealth of information that is free to all. You can do what you like with the content, as long as you credit your source, and make sure your final work has the same licensing restrictions as the original

Artistic licence Understanding Creative Commons

One way of avoiding the pitfalls of identifying content to use on your site is to find work licensed through Creative Commons. Creative Commons is an organisation that has developed a set of licence agreements that offer more flexibility.

Previously, work was either totally off-limits (copyrighted) or free-for-all (public domain), neither of which is particularly useful. Copyrighting work makes it too hard for people to use, and it reduces the chance of it finding a large audience. Conversely, however, public domain work is too easy to use, and reduces the chances of the author getting credited for the work they've done.

For more information, as well as a free set of icons to use if you decide to license your work with Creative Commons, you should visit www.creativecommons.org. Here are the main Creative Commons symbols to watch out for, and what they mean:

Content can be used, even for commercial gain. Derivative works can be made. Copyright must be attributed to author.

As above, but any work released must have the same Creative Commons licence as the original.

Content can be freely used, even for commercial gain. No derivative works. Original author must be cited.

As for attribution licence (top), with the added restriction that use must be non-commercial.

The most restrictive licence. No commercial use, no derivative versions and, of course, attribution.

Bringing people back to your website

A truly successful website relies on a steady, growing base of repeat visitors. Here's how to convince people to keep coming back

BENEFITS

Learn what makes visitors keep coming back to a website

Find out what to avoid when trying to build a repeat readership

You've published your website and the visitors are pouring in, but to make sure your website is a hit you must secure repeat readers. While the number of unique hits (different visitors) is the figure advertisers look for in a website, you'll want people to keep coming back, whether you're selling goods or services, hoping to make your name as a blogger or creating an informative site that offers up-to-the-minute news and information.

If you run a small business, a professional-looking website can help mask the fact that your products are produced in your shed. That doesn't mean you should set out to mislead people, rather that you can gain their trust by providing valuable, accurate information. The way you conduct relationships with readers is important; it's better for your site to have a friendly atmosphere rather than a hard sell. After all, it's easier to sell to loyal customers than to acquire new ones.

KEEP IT TOPICAL

If you're a blogger, never forget that people search for newsworthy topics. During an election, for example, they'll search for the names of the candidates involved.

During big sporting events such as the Olympics or the World Cup, people search for the names of prominent performers, while the stars of new cinema releases are always a top search term on sites such as Google. If your readers get to know that they can count on you for the analysis of breaking stories, then they are more likely to make you their first stop whenever they come online.

The corollary of this is to keep your site updated. There's little more off-putting than realising the blog you're reading was last updated three months previously: the whole point of the format is that you keep people informed. If people find you don't update frequently, they simply won't bother coming back.

This brings us on to consistency of quality. People often start their websites with the greatest of care and the best intentions, only to find a year in that it has lost its allure. Lacklustre content is off-putting – people won't return to your site if they're uninspired by what they see.

JOIN THE CLUB

People will be more likely to return to your site if they have an incentive. A good way to create one, particularly if you have nothing to sell, is to create a community on your site. This is easy if you're making a site for a local club or church where people already know each other.

If you have a forum (see page 100) or host a blog, you should get people to register before they post comments. This small action allows them to continue to voice their opinions on your site. Also, if you gather their email addresses, you'll be able to send out an email notifying them when your site's been updated. Just make sure you have a strong privacy policy, so people know how many emails they'll be receiving, and also that you won't give their addresses to anyone else. And remember, badgering people with spam certainly won't entice them to come back.

Right: Telegraph.co.uk readers know that whenever they visit, the site will be up to date with the latest news and analysis

Understanding Google Analytics

Find out how many visitors your website is attracting and analyse their movements around your web pages with Google's invaluable tracker

Wouldn't it be great if you knew how many people were visiting your site every day? It would be even better to know which pages visitors were viewing, how long they spent reading each page and when they left your site. Using Google Analytics, you can find all this out free of charge. All you need is a Google account, which is also free. Analytics logs a small amount of information about the people that visit your site. It runs invisibly and, in most cases, has no effect on how fast your site loads or runs.

Go to www.google.com/analytics and sign in. If you don't already have an account through a service such as Google Docs or Gmail, you need to sign up first. Once you're logged in, Google will give you a small piece of JavaScript code to include on your site. Simply paste the code somewhere on your home page; the sidebar will do if you're using WordPress. Analytics takes a day to start reporting.

ANALYSE THIS

When you log in to Analytics, you'll see the Dashboard displayed prominently. The top graph shows the number of visitors per day. This is a useful number for telling, at a glance, whether traffic to your website is rising or falling, but there's a wealth of information besides this headline figure.

At the bottom right of the screen is the Content Overview, a useful panel that shows you which of the pages on your website are the most visited. This information can help you to figure out where you need to place advertising on your website for maximum effect. You can also give close attention to less frequently visited pages to try to determine what is wrong with them.

The navigation bar on the left is the best way to get around Google Analytics. For instance, click on Content, then Top Exit Pages. This view tells you which pages people looked at immediately before leaving your

website. If you spot a pattern, you can check the page or pages in question to see if there's anything obvious that might be causing people to leave. Perhaps you could add more links as a way to keep visitors interested for longer.

Traffic Sources is another helpful tool that can tell you which websites and search engines are directing traffic to your site. The search engine data is useful, as it tells you which keywords lead to your site, and how often they do so. This should help you optimise your website for search engines (see page 132 for more on this).

Finally, the Content tab has a small link called Site Overlay. This is one of Analytics' best tricks. It launches your website, with Analytics data pasted over the top, giving you a visual impression of where people are clicking when they're viewing your pages.

BENEFITS

Determine the visiting patterns of the people coming to your website

Find ways to improve your site so that people keep coming back

Below: Google Analytics is easy to use, phenomenally powerful and, best of all, it's free

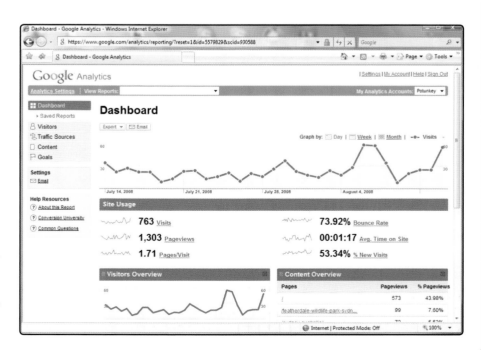

Making money from your website

If you don't mind allowing some advertising on your site, you can turn your interest into a commercial venture and earn some cash

I f you're creating a website to promote a small business, money will be your ultimate goal. If you're making a website for a local club or about a particular hobby then profit probaby isn't high on your list of priorities, but that doesn't mean your website can't earn you a little pocket money. Hopefully, this will be enough to cover your hosting costs, plus something extra to reward you for the time and effort you've spent creating and maintaining it.

If you find that your website is receiving a large amount of traffic, you could turn this to your advantage, and approach companies whose products or services tie in with your site. However, it's unlikely that you'll be able to pull off any advertising deals like this unless your website receives many thousands of hits per month. Having said that, even if you have fewer visitors, you can still earn some revenue with the help of Google AdSense or an affiliate program such as Amazon Associates.

AdSense will pay a small amount every time a user clicks on targeted advertising on your site. You should bear in mind that small sites might earn only £50 per year – the minimum needed to withdraw cash from the scheme. The Amazon Associates scheme works in a similar way, by displaying adverts on your page, but it shares with you a portion (up to 10 per cent) of any sales made as a result of people clicking on a particular advert.

Allowing adverts on your site is often a compromise. It's no secret that surfers don't like to be bombarded with advertising. Furthermore, adverts can clutter your pages and make them look untidy. But if you are careful and the adverts are subtle, they shouldn't put people off.

HOW TO... USE GOOGLE ADSENSE

1 Go to the homepage at www.google.com/adsense and create an account; a normal Google account won't do. You'll need to provide details such as your name and address. You can then set up a banner ad for your site. Click on the AdSense Setup tab at the top of the main page. Here you'll see various ways to earn revenue from AdSense. We'll be using the AdSense for Content option, which produces banner advertising for products and services related to the content of your site.

2 On the AdSense for Content page, you're given two options: Ad units and Link units. Ad units are used to give actual adverts, either text-only or image-based, while Link units are used to give text links to broader topics that take the user to a page of search

How to... Use Amazon Associates scheme

The Associates scheme lets you earn up to 10 per cent of any sales made when a visitor clicks on an Amazon advert on your site and subsequently makes a purchase. You can choose which products to promote from the millions in Amazon's catalogue.

1 First you need to register an account with the Amazon Associates scheme by visiting the homepage at http://tinyurl.com/amazonassociates.

2 Once you have created an account, go to the Associates Central page and click the Links & Banners link menu at the top of the site to see the different types of adverts that you can create. Some options are as simple as text links to products on the Amazon website, and these are particularly useful for targeted items. So for our holiday cottage website, we might choose to display a link to a popular tourist guidebook of the local area to help visitors.

Other options are more complex, such as the Self-Optimising Links option that we're using here. This works in the same way as the customisation options in AdSense, by tailoring the banner to suit the content of the site on which it appears.

3 Click on the Widgets link, scroll down to Self-Optimizing Links and click the 'Add to your Web page' button. You will see the configuration page. On this page, you can adjust the dimensions and colour of the banner. You'll see a warning if you change it too much, as Amazon requires the advert to be recognisable. You can also choose whether to show the Amazon logo, product images or a border.

4 Once the banner is ready, copy and paste the code from the box below the configuration tool into your site. The optimisation means that the adverts will become more relevant over time.

results. On the Redcot Barn site, an Ad unit will provide links to specific guest houses and a Link unit will redirect to search pages for guest houses. We're selecting Ad units.

3 The next page offers several customisation options. These allow you to change the appearance of the ad box to fit in with the colour scheme and layout of your site. We're making the border of our banner green to blend in with the Redcot Barn website. An advert that looks out of context is unlikely to get many clicks. Once you're ready, click the Submit and Get Code button.

4 Cut and paste the code into your site, where you want the ad box to appear. Google will analyse the content of that page and put relevant adverts in the box. Log in to the AdSense page periodically to see how much your advert is earning, and make any changes. AdSense lets you tweak banners without having to re-insert code.

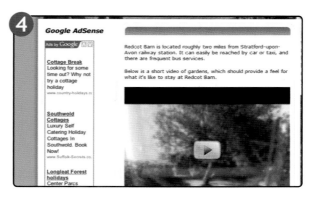

CHAPTER 9

IN THIS CHAPTER

Identifying your needs 112

Getting your business
    online 113

Creating an online shop 116

Google Webmaster Tools 120

Making your website local 126

Business websites

These days, most businesses benefit from having a website. Whether you're George the painter and decorator or Michael Dell, you'll find potentially millions of internet users who want your products or services. And as a website doesn't have to cost anything, you can get an online presence for your company even if your budget is tiny.

You don't have to be an HTML expert, either. There are plenty of packages available to help you create a professional-looking website in very little time and with the minimum of hassle.

In this chapter, we'll discuss the best options for getting your small business online. We'll also lay out your options if you want to set up a web shop.

Identifying your needs

Before building a business site, you need to consider your brand and the services you wish to provide. Here we look at the main options

Below: The choice of shopping-cart software is plentiful, with lots of UK-based options such as Volusion and Mr Site Storefront

A recent survey of 530 small UK firms found that almost half still don't have a website to promote their business, while 80 per cent of the companies that have a website say it generates extra sales as a result.

Clearly, it makes sense to have a website for your business. The site doesn't have to be updated constantly – a small, static site can provide all the information your customers need. An online presence means that anyone searching for the services you offer will know you exist, and this could make a massive difference to your revenue. Furthermore, you don't have to hire an expensive web designer to create a professional-looking site. Services such as 1&1's MyBusiness Site (see our guide opposite) can help you design a website in minutes.

The best way to make a website is to spend a little time learning HTML and CSS, as we explained in Chapters 3 and 4. However, if you're running your business full time, you may not be able to create a site this way. Plus, you may want to sell products as opposed to services. This is where online services such as UK2's E-commerce (see page 117) and Mr Site Takeaway Website Pro (www.mrsite.com) come in.

The biggest challenge when building a business website with a shop is handling money. The payment method you choose will depend on volume of sales, and whether you have a merchant account with your bank – if you don't, you won't be able to accept payments via credit or debit card. There are companies that can handle this for you – the big four bureaux are PayPal (www.paypal.com), WorldPay (www.worldpay.com), Google Checkout (http://checkout.google.co.uk) and Nochex (www.nochex.com). However, they charge up to five per cent per transaction, so they're suitable only for high volumes.

Google Checkout doesn't require an e-commerce front end; you can just paste the required HTML code near a description of the product for customers to buy it immediately. Alternatively, you can use some e-commerce software, which is integrated with the bureaux listed above, enabling customers to buy multiple items more easily.

If you don't already have a website, you should choose a web-hosting provider that offers a web shop, as you'll then have the complete package: a domain name, space to store your site (including the shop), integration with a payment bureau to handle money, email addresses and a single control panel where you can do your web admin.

BIG BUSINESS

For larger businesses with higher volumes and merchant bank accounts, you may need to ask your bank to add internet merchant services to your account. You'll also need a payment service provider to handle transactions – collect a customer's name, address and payment details, and transfer them securely to your bank. Having an online payment method makes your company look more professional than sites where customers get redirected to a payment bureau's site to make a payment. However, the combination of setup costs, monthly charges and commission fees could work out more expensive than these bureaux if your sales volume isn't high enough.

Getting your business online

The right online presence will increase sales and attract new business. Here we show you how to create a professional website in minutes

Although it wasn't the case several years ago, a website is now affordable to all small businesses. For example, 1&1's MyBusiness Site costs £10 per month excluding VAT, and this includes everything from technical support to a .com or .co.uk domain name. There are templates for over 100 business sectors, and it's easy to tailor the content, layout and design. Here we show you how to create a professional-looking site for a car repair garage.

1 Access any browser and go to http://mybusiness. 1and1.co.uk. Note that older versions of Google Chrome aren't fully supported.

2 Choose your business sector by clicking the link below the Your Business Sector heading, which displays all 125 sectors. If yours isn't listed, just choose the best match, as you can always adjust the wording on the site later. Below this, choose your colour scheme. Now enter your company name, address and contact details. The information you enter will be used to fill in the blanks in the default text on your new site. Make sure you use capitalisation correctly and enter a postcode for your address, as this will help to generate a Google Map of your location.

3 You'll now see a screen asking you to choose a domain name. The list will show some suggestions based on your name, industry and location. If you don't like these, click the 'Check another domain name' link and type in your desired web address. It pays to choose a name that's memorable and short. Picking a '.co.uk' domain lets people know your location and sounds more professional than '.info' or '.net'.

If you already own a domain name, you can move this to your MyBusiness Site account. It's possible to choose a web address later if you're undecided at this point. When you do choose a domain name, it will take up to 24 hours to become live.

4 Next, enter your payment details. Click Continue and enter a password for the account. You can have

TIP
You can test 1&1 MyBusiness Site free for 30 days. You will need to supply payment details but no charge is made in this time and unsubscribing is quick and easy.

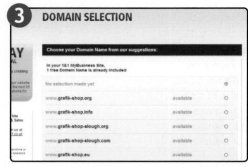

up to 200 email addresses, with the domain name you chose appearing after the @ symbol. Finally, click the 'Order' button.

5 1&1's servers will now create your website. Once the process is complete, you can click the button to view your site. Hopefully, you'll see a complete, working site with multiple pages, an interactive Google map of your location, an image gallery and a contact form. However, there's plenty of room for improvement. The company name's legibility on the banner image is poor, and while the text is good you'll want to personalise it.

6 Click the small red Login link at the bottom-right corner of the page. Type in the password that you entered as part of the signup process and a small control panel will appear in the top-right corner of the page. You're now in edit mode. Hovering your mouse over the different page elements will bring up a set of controls. Just click on the element you want to edit. Before you do this, it's worth looking through the list of layouts by clicking on the Layout button at the top of the control panel. You can preview layouts before choosing one.

7 Once you've chosen a layout, start customising the home page by editing the About us element. Hover over the paragraph and click to open the editor, which will appear below the paragraph. You can now edit the text just as you would in a word processor; there are controls for text alignment, bullets and numbering, font colour and bold and italic buttons. If you want more precise control, you can edit the raw HTML by clicking the HTML button on the far right.

Highlight the text you want to delete, but don't delete the More link, as this will stop people navigating to the page to which it links. Type or paste in the new text, and click Save. The page will reflect the changes you've made.

8 As we didn't enter any opening times when we signed up, we'll do that now. Hover the mouse over the white space below the Opening times heading, and the editor controls highlight the blank area – don't select the heading or the divider line below it. Click on the editor and it will open to allow you to enter the text you want. You can't use the Tab key to align text in the editor.

9 We'll now address the main banner. Click on it to open the editor. Choose an image from the Photo Gallery, or click the Own photo button to upload a photograph to which you own the copyright – usually a photograph that you've taken. On the right-hand side, you'll find a size guide to help you crop and resize your image rather than uploading needlessly large files straight from your digital camera.

To adjust the position and size of the header image, click the Settings button on the right. You can alter the height of the image as well as zooming in on it. You may also be able to move it horizontally and vertically.

Next click on Title and alter the colour, font and position. Alternatively, you can delete the default text and leave it blank in order to use your own company logo. You can upload an image for your logo by clicking the Logo button. When you've picked and uploaded an image, you'll see the size and position controls to move it around. It's also possible to click and drag the logo and title around instead of using the sliders.

10 You can easily alter the navigation bar at the top of the screen. Hover over the bar, and click the Edit navigation button that appears. You can change the position of menu items in the list that pops up by clicking the up and down arrows, and change the names, too. If you change a name, don't forget to edit the text on the page to which it links. To delete a menu item, click on the dustbin icon to its right – this also deletes the page to which it links. To hide a link, and make it visible later on, use the eye icon. If you click one of the icons that looks like a page with a + sign, a new page is created below – type a title in the blank box. Add a page to a submenu by clicking the + icon of a page in the submenu.

11 We've created a new menu item called Window tinting. This page is blank except for the right-hand column, which stays the same on every page. When you navigate to the page, you'll see options allowing you to choose a page element – everything from a simple text box to a photo gallery or a YouTube video. It's best to keep the same format you used on other pages, so start with Heading. When you've typed one in, click the + symbol to add another element, perhaps Image with Text. It's easy to reorder elements; use the up and down arrows that appear when you hover over an element.

12 When you've finished editing your site, you should optimise it so that it appears high in search engine results. You can do this using page titles, descriptions and meta tags. Each of these can be added by clicking on the Settings button in the control panel.

Look under the Search Engines section and you'll see Page title, Site Description, Meta Tags and Alt Tags. Click on Page title and you can change the text that appears at the top of the visitor's browser window. By default, this is what you entered as your company name. The rest of the title is made up from the name of the current page, for example Services – Martin Automotive.

The second box lets you change the title of the home page, so you could add a description of your business or a company slogan. This text will be stored when someone bookmarks your site, as well as by search engines, so it pays to make this as descriptive as possible.

Entering short descriptions of each page in the Site Description section is useful, as these will appear as the snippets of text that accompany search results. Search engines use these to match your pages to search terms, so include as many relevant keywords as possible. You don't have to write a description for each page, but if you don't, you may as well copy the general description from the home page and paste it into each of the others.

You can enter meta tags by clicking on the link of the same name. These are keywords, separated by commas, and should be kept specific to the page to which they refer.

SHOP TO THE SYSTEM

By now, you'll have a website that gives your business a professional-looking shopfront on the internet. Customers should be able to find your website when they search for services or products your business provides, and while browsing they'll be able to find your location, get in contact and learn more about what you offer.

Creating an online shop

It's easier than you might think to sell products through your site. We explain how to set up shop so your customers keep coming back

Left: Part of Amazon's success lies in its range of products and its easy ordering system

Right: Shop4giftsonline is an example of a shop made with Mr Site Takeaway Website Pro

Whether you're a sole trader or a larger business selling products, the internet is an obvious way to attract more customers. A site such as the one we created over the previous few pages is great for businesses that offer services – such as a car repair garage or a hairdressers – but if you sell products you need an online shop where people can browse your catalogue and order items for delivery.

One of the great things about an online shop is that it never closes. Having a shop front on your local high street is all very well for customers who want to buy an item during opening hours, but you could lose out on sales when your shop is shut. Customers buying online may have to wait for them to be delivered, but they can order whenever it suits them, whether that's 3pm or 3am. They don't have to travel to your shop (only to discover you're out of stock) and they don't need to be local – you can have a worldwide customer base.

Many companies exist only online and depend on the internet for all their sales. There are plenty of advantages to this approach, not least the amount saved by not renting a shop front. Selling solely online also means you don't need to man your shop for eight hours per day, and you can sell products when you're away on holiday.

PAY AND DISPLAY
Before you make any decisions about your online shop, it's important to understand that there are two main components of e-commerce. The front end is the shop itself – the web pages that allow customers to view items and decide what to buy, put items in a shopping cart and click a Checkout button. The back end is the mechanism for accepting money; it takes the customer's details, calculates the total price (including the shipping method the customer has chosen) and then securely transfers the payment details, usually from a credit or debit card.

There are many such packages to choose from; the best one for you will depend on the number of products you expect to sell. Most systems take care of the technical aspects behind the scenes, so don't be put off.

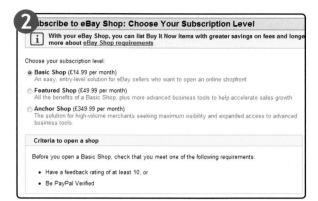

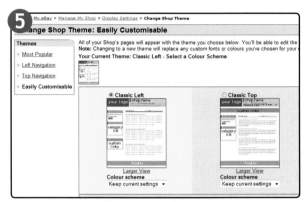

For most people, the easiest option is to buy an off-the-shelf web shop, which is completely self-contained and will allow even novices to list products for sale and accept payment through companies such as PayPal, WorldPay or Google. This is only a problem if you already have an established company with databases of existing products, stock levels and prices. Adding a web shop to this system isn't easy, and would require professional help to integrate the two.

SET UP AN EBAY SHOP

If you're just starting a business, eBay is a quick and effective way to begin selling physical products. You don't even need to market your shop: eBay does it for you. A Basic eBay shop costs £15 per month and can be set up in minutes. But spending time configuring it and getting your listings right can have a huge impact on your success. You pay a listing fee whether your product sells or not, so you need all your listings to result in sales.

To open a Basic shop, you must have an existing eBay membership with a minimum feedback score of 10. In other words, you must have received ten feedback ratings from purchases you've previously made on the site. Alternatively, you must be PayPal Verified. In any case, you need to be PayPal Verified to be able to run any sort of business online. This is just a matter of connecting your PayPal identity to a bank account.

Don't start building your shop until you have your product ready. Online buyers expect next-day despatch at the latest, so if you haven't got an initial stock you're risking embarrassment and, worse, negative feedback. Feedback – the ratings you're given by those who buy products from you – is an incredibly important element of eBay trading.

Make sure you're very clear about the cost of making your product. Keep this in mind as you add your product listings, because eBay presents you with all sorts of opportunities to enhance your listings. These may help sales, but they cost money and reduce your profit margin. On the plus side, listing fees are per listing, not per product: if you're selling ten products in the same listing then – assuming you sell all ten – the actual cost per product is a tenth of the total fee. Selling fees, however, accrue on top of this and are paid on each individual sale.

1 Go to www.ebay.co.uk and sign in, then head to http://pages.ebay.co.uk/storefronts/start.html and click the Open a Shop button.

2 You'll almost certainly want to begin with a Basic shop. Featured shops are more expensive but have lower fees to compensate, so you need to sell a lot of products to make it worthwhile. Featured shops tend to appear higher than Basic shops in the product listings for any given search.

You need to decide on your shop name. In most cases you should be using a name that includes your search keywords, and the shop name should be very similar to the domain name you've chosen for your website. Once you're done, click Continue.

3 You'll then be asked if you want to perform a Quick Shop Tune-up of your nascent emporium. Decide for yourself which of the options makes sense to you. To manually specify your shop settings, go to My eBay and select Selling. Under Shortcuts, click Manage my Shop. This should bring up the summary screen.

4 Click Display Settings to edit the appearance of your shop. If you have a logo, make sure you include it in your design. The aim is for your eBay shop and future website to share a similar design, even if that only really amounts to the colour scheme.

5 Click the 'Change to another theme' link to browse through the available shop structures. Although there's a reasonable range of themes, they all tend to be similar. This is a weakness of selling on eBay, but everyone's in the same boat. We prefer the Classic themes, which are cleaner, more appealing designs that you can more easily customise to your liking. Click Save when you're done.

Click on 'Edit current theme' to modify the colour scheme. Choose colours from your palette and pick plain fonts (Verdana is a good choice from the limited options available). Click Save Settings and then go through the other links under Shop Design to customise your shop. The most important one to sort out at this point is Product Categories. When you've finished tweaking, click the Shop Summary link to go back to the Manage my Shop screen.

6 Finally, click the View My Shop link to see your shop in all its glory.

WORDPRESS

If you'd prefer to avoid eBay and have a relatively limited product range – up to 100 products, for example – then a WordPress plug-in should do the job (your website will need to be built in WordPress, which we've already covered in chapter 6). WP e-Commerce (also known as WP Shopping Cart) is a free plug-in with additional modules that can be purchased later.

You then need a way of collecting your customers' details and receiving money from them. The simplest choices are Google Checkout (http://checkout.google. com) and PayPal (www.PayPal-business.com). To use these services you'll need either a Google Checkout Merchant account or a PayPal Business account; both of which are easy to set up. In each case, a small sum of money is automatically deposited in your nominated bank account. This is used to verify that you own the account; to complete the setup, you're asked to type in the amount of the deposit that was made. You should allow two working weeks to complete the process.

Both Google Checkout and PayPal allow non-members to pay by credit card. However, PayPal traditionally doesn't allow a credit card that has been registered against a PayPal account to be used independently. So if you are a member, you can only pay via PayPal, not directly by card. This can cause confusion and irritation to customers, particularly if they've forgotten their PayPal details, so you should add another provider besides Google Checkout and/or PayPal. One option is the PayPal Payments Professional scheme, which allows your customers to use any credit card, whether or not it's been registered against a Paypal account.

Another option is WorldPay (www.worldpay.com), which allows your customers to pay by credit or debit card with the minimum of fuss. WorldPay can be expensive, though; another option is Nochex, which offers similar facilities and could reduce your costs.

One final note on payment: think very carefully about accepting payment by cheque. It's likely you'll attract extra orders that way, but accepting cheques is usually more trouble than it's worth. A high percentage of orders are never paid for, and they take longer to process and require more administration work.

SETTING UP SHOP

Install the WP e-Commerce plugin in the same way as we describe on page 88. You should then hide all the pages created by the plugin. Under the Pages heading on the left, choose Edit and you'll find a series of new entries: Products Page, Checkout, Transaction Results and Your Account. For each, click Quick Edit and tick Private Page to ensure that only you, not visitors, can see these pages during development. You'll see a new section in the Dashboard called Products. Go to Settings and, under General Settings, enter your regional information.

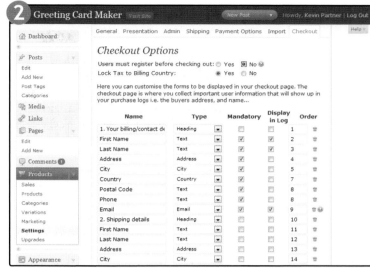

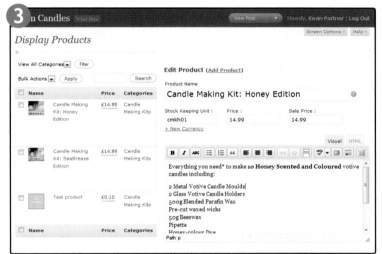

1 Click Payment Options. We've found that the easiest payment provider to get started with is PayPal. Anyone with a PayPal Business account can offer PayPal Payments Standard, and to get that working all you need is your PayPal address. Enter this here.

2 Under Checkout, ensure you include all the relevant fields. If you need an extra field (for example, to let customers add special requirements) you can add it at the bottom. The other important tab is Shipping Options. Under Shipping Modules, select one of the Internal Shipping Calculators options, hover your mouse over an option until Edit appears and click it. Usually you'll want to choose Weight, and you can then add Layers, which specify cost bands.

3 Now click Categories under Products on the left. You must set up at least one category, and in most case you'll need lots. Categories make it easier for customers to browse your shop since not everyone likes to use search. You want to have multiple products per category, but not too many. It's also a sign of credibility if you have various categories.

It's now time to add your first product. Click Products > Products and complete the form. In the Stock Keeping Unit field, type in the stock code you want to use for the product. Write a complete description using the Rich Text Editor, making sure you include everything your potential buyer needs to know. Select the category it belongs to and add any search tags that make sense.

The remaining fields are obvious. Finally, upload your product images; the more the better. Customers need the online equivalent of picking up and trying the product and that, generally speaking, means plenty of photos.

4 You should add a test product, at a low price, that you can use to make sure it all works. Then see how your shop is shaping up by editing the Products page and clicking Preview. Make sure you thoroughly test the entire process before it goes live.

Google Webmaster Tools

Google provides a number of tools to help you optimise your website so that others can get more from it. Here's how to hammer your site into shape

Google uses many different methods for ranking websites, so it can be difficult to work out why your site isn't appearing as a top result, or even at all, in searches. A number of strategies have been developed to exploit loopholes or flaws in search engines to boost your site's position in search results. Generally, this involves trying to deceive Google's indexing service by providing different content to search engines than to users. Another popular strategy is a link-sharing scheme, which takes advantage of the fact that Google ranks well-linked sites more highly than others. You should avoid tricks of this type, though: if Google thinks you're trying to play the system, it can reduce the ranking of your site or even remove it from its index entirely.

This is why the Webmaster Tools service is invaluable, as it gives you an insight into how Google is viewing

Below: The Dashboard includes the top searches that your website featured as a result

your website, allowing you to fix problems and optimise your search ranking without resorting to underhand tricks. Webmaster Tools will also help your website's ranking in other search engines such as Yahoo! because many of the rules for Google apply equally well to them.

To start using Google Webmaster Tools, go to www.google.com/webmasters/tools and sign in with your Google account; you can sign up for one first if you don't have one. After logging in, you need to add your website so that you can start using the tools. To do this, you have to click the 'Add a site' button and type in the full URL of your website. For security reasons you need to prove to Google that you really are the owner of the website. This is most easily done by uploading a verification file to your website's root folder using an FTP client, as we explained on page 46. You can then access the Dashboard and start using the tools to optimise your website.

MAKING A DASH FOR IT

After logging in to Webmaster Tools and selecting your site, you're taken to the Dashboard. This shows a brief overview of how well your website is currently being indexed by Google as well as any urgent errors. If this is the first time you've used the tools after adding your site to Google, the Dashboard will be empty as data won't have been collected yet. It may take a few days for useful data to start appearing.

It's worth spending a little time looking at the Dashboard when you log in as it can help to keep your site optimised. The screen is divided into several reports, each of which has a more detailed tool that can be accessed from links on the left of the page. In particular, you should review the Search queries and Keywords reports. These give an indication of the searches that found your website and the keywords that Google has identified from analysing the content of your pages.

The Crawl errors report details any problems that were encountered when indexing pages from your site.

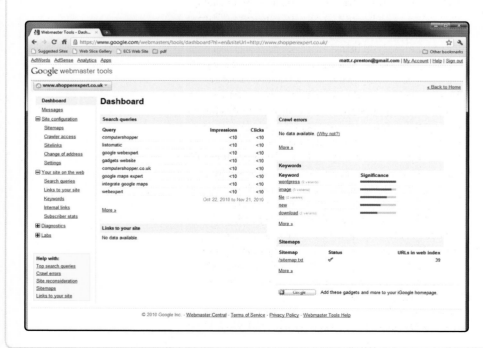

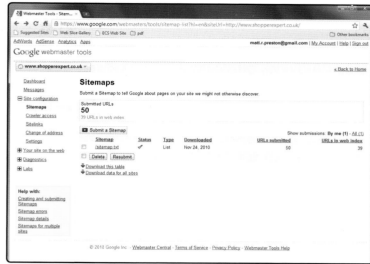

This includes problems with dynamic content such as failing PHP scripts, but more commonly it will show you any broken hyperlinks in your pages. It's important to fix these things as quickly as possible: visitors don't like broken links on sites, and Google can't index pages it can't reach.

After reading the overview, you can start using the Site configuration tools to optimise the way Google accesses and indexes the content in your website.

MAP READING

One of the biggest problems you'll encounter when adding a site to Google is that certain pages might not show up in the search results at all. This can happen as the Google indexing service locates pages to index by following links from within the content of your pages. If some pages aren't reachable, have links that are created dynamically by a script or are part of a Flash movie, then Google won't be able to locate them. Sitemaps can solve this by providing a list of all the pages in your website.

In its most basic form, a Sitemap is a text file with a list or URLs to pages in your website, one per line. This is enough to inform Google about the pages available on your website. When making the Sitemap, you need to make sure that you specify all URLs consistently. So if, for example, you registered your site as www.pandafacts.co.uk, you should ensure that all URLs in the Sitemap begin with www.pandafacts.co.uk/. When you've created the sitemap, make sure it's named with a .txt file extension and upload it to your website. Then, in Webmaster Tools, under Site configuration, click Sitemaps and then the Submit a Sitemap button, and type the correct path to the file.

If you have a very large website, you need to make sure that your Sitemap doesn't exceed 50,000 entries. If it does, split it into several smaller files and submit them separately. You can reduce the size of your Sitemap

files by creating Zip files of them, but the limit of the number of URLs per file still stands.

There is a more descriptive format for Sitemap files that lets you specify more about the pages and assets in your website, using an XML format. This style of Sitemap allows you to annotate resources such as images and videos with subjects and running times. Adding this metadata for images is particularly useful for good integration into Google image searches. There are plenty of websites that will attempt to generate XML Sitemaps automatically, including www.xml-sitemaps.com and www.hotwebtools.com/gmap.

CALL OFF THE SEARCH

The opposite problem is when you have content in your website that you don't want to appear in search results, such as confidential or out-of-date information. This is where crawler access tools come in useful. The method for preventing URLs being added to the search index is to create a file named robots.txt in the root directory of your website. This file contains instructions to search engines about which files and directories it's allowed to process. The syntax of this file can be a bit confusing, but Webmaster Tools has a 'Generate robots.txt' utility in the Crawler access section to help you out.

In most cases, it's best to start by selecting 'Allow all' for the default crawler access. Disabling this would prevent your website appearing in any search results. You can then use a series of block actions to exclude specific URLs from being indexed and appearing in search results. Select 'All robots' to block all search engines. When you have finished adding block rules, click the Download button to download the finished robots.txt file. You then need to upload the file to the root directory of your website.

Webmaster Tools also includes a utility to test your robots.txt file, to make sure that it's working as you

Above left: You can exclude certain pages of your website appearing in search results using robots.txt

Above right: The Sitemap page shows how many URLs were found in your Sitemaps

expect. To try this, select the 'Test robots.txt' tab and paste the contents of your robots.txt file into the box. Click the Test button to see the results. You can also experiment with changes to your robots.txt here. When you're happy with the changes, make sure you update the contents of robots.txt on your website with the new settings.

THE MISSING LINKS

Sitelinks – also under Site configuration – are the links shown below some websites in Google search results. They make it easier for users to navigate your site from search results – for example, by jumping straight to the 'Contact us' or 'Support' pages. These links are created by Google by analysing the structure of your website.

Although there isn't currently any way of creating these links in Webmaster tools, there's a simple guideline for helping Google to discover the structure of your website. Make sure that important pages in your website are always available within one or two clicks from the homepage. Also, if users arrive at a page in your site from a search engine, make sure they can navigate to the homepage and the main sections easily. With this structure in place, Google should be able work out relevant sitelinks for your website.

On the off-chance that Google has made a mistake and created a sitelink for a section of your website that you don't want to appear in search results, you can remove it by using the Demote button. Simply copy the URL of the sitelink you want to remove, paste it into the Demote this sitelink URL box and click the button. Google doesn't guarantee that a demoted page won't appear as a sitelink, but it will take your request into account when generating sitelinks.

CHANGE OF ADDRESS

If, for some reason, you need to change the domain name of your website, Webmaster Tools provides a tool for telling Google about the new URL. There is a series of steps to follow that can help Google to update its indexes faster and make the transition smoother for your visitors.

After setting up your new site at the new domain, you must make sure that you add it to your Webmaster tools account and verify that you are the owner. Next, you need to redirect all traffic from the old site to the new one. If your site is using the Apache web server, you can do this using by setting up an HTTP redirect in an .htaccess file. Finally, using the 'Change of address' tool, tell Google that your site has moved from one address to another.

Right: Sitelinks help users navigate your website directly from search results

DRIVING IN TRAFFIC

The success of a website relies on the quality of its ranking in searches such as Google – it doesn't matter how excellent the content is, people won't use it if they can't find it. If you're running a business from your website, adding it to Google is an essential step. Fortunately, adding your website to the Google index is easy. Just go to www.google.com/addurl and enter the full URL to your site. Within a few days, your website should start appearing in search results. However, getting the most from Google requires more than this. You need to make sure that Google is able to access all the content from your website to ensure good coverage in searches.

Some of the most useful Webmaster Tools include the ability to check which search terms are driving people to your site, who's linking to it, and the most commonly used keywords people type in to view it.

SEARCH PARTY

The Search queries tool provides details on the top Google search queries that returns results containing pages from your website. By default, only the top queries from the past 30 days are shown, although the date range used is configurable.

Three key pieces of information are shown: Queries, Impressions and Clicks. The Queries number shows how many search terms (as entered into Google search) were relevant to pages from your website. Impressions is the number of pages that were actually viewed, while Clicks, as you might expect, are how many times a link on your page was clicked on. Impressions and Clicks also show a percentage increase or decrease since the previous time period, so you can see how your website is developing. In all cases, higher numbers and increasing averages are better, as it means that your website is frequently appearing in searches and is well ranked.

You can also see information about each of the top queries by clicking on them to see how many impressions and visits to your site each one has generated. Each query shows the average position where your page appeared in the search result for that query. The higher the position, the greater the chance that it is being viewed and clicked, which, in turn, will lead to people visiting your website. By default, this view shows queries found from all Google searches, but by using the Filters button you can narrow the results to a specific search type, such as mobile, image or web. The Top Pages tab shows similar statistics but allows you to narrow the data for individual pages within your website.

Analysing the top queries can help you to improve the content of your site. In conjunction with this, you can use the Keywords tool to see the top keywords that Google has identified from your website. Clicking on any of the keywords will show more details, such as the number of occurrences and the variations. Google can identify spelling variations, including plurals – such as

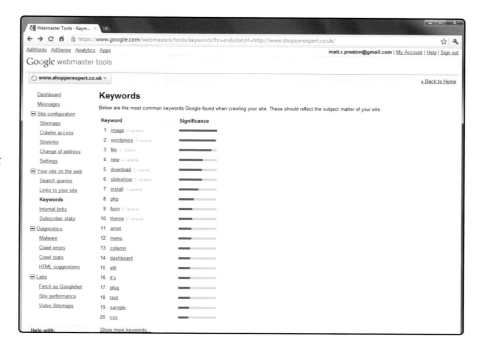

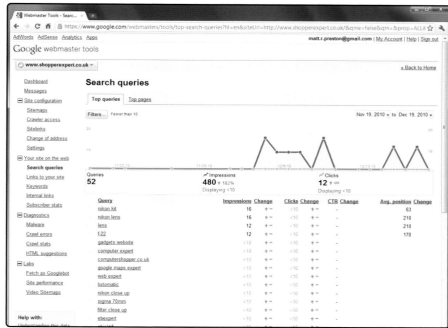

'image' and 'images' – and group them together. If a keyword isn't ranked as highly as you expected, this suggests that your content needs more work to make it more relevant. Highly unexpected keywords such as 'Viagra' can indicate that your website has been hacked and needs immediate attention.

THE LINKS EFFECT

In order to work out the relevancy of search results, Google measures how well a website is linked to from others. The 'Links to your site' section shows an

Top: Review the most relevant keywords identified by Google from your website

Above: See the top queries that matched pages in your website

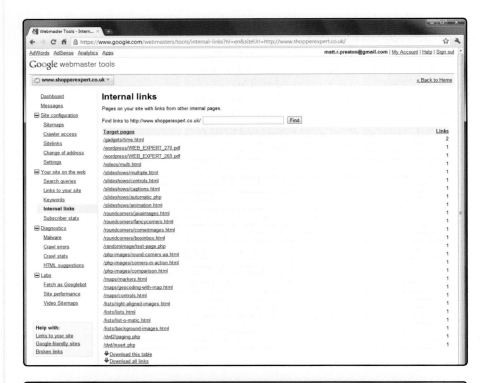

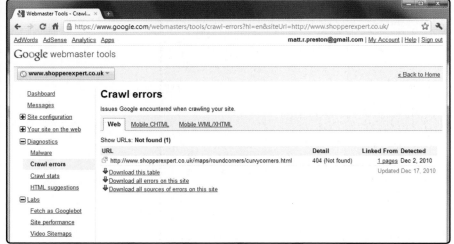

Top: Review the internal links in your website

Above: Check and fix broken links in your website

overview of your website's links, where those links are coming from and which are your most linked pages. This is useful data to track as it directly influences your search ranking and the availability of links to your website.

The Internal links section shows a slightly different aspect: the links between pages in your own website. Each page that has internal links to it can be clicked on to show details of where the links are from. Google uses this information in its relevancy calculations. If important pages do not appear in this list, or have significantly fewer links than other less-important pages, you may need to reorganise your link structure. Use this tool before renaming pages to prevent creating broken links in your website.

MAL PRACTICE

Google is also able to detect malware, which is any malicious software designed to access computer information secretly without the user's consent. If found, Google will provide detailed information in the Malware section of Google Webmaster Tools. If your website has been hacked, it can be used to host viruses, worms and spyware. To protect users, Google will mark search results that point to infected sites, warning users about the potential dangers of visiting them.

If your website has been infected with malware, you'll need to take immediate steps. First, you should take your website offline to prevent the malware from spreading. You should then update all your passwords and set about removing the malware. If your website is small, this could be as simple as looking for new pages or suspicious content that has been added. The larger the website, the more difficult this process is. If you have a recent backup, it's probably best to replace your live site with that. If your website is based on a CMS such as WordPress, Joomla! or Drupal, consider checking online for the latest updates and security fixes.

After you've removed the malicious code, you can request that Google reviews your site by clicking on the 'Request a review' link. Google will check your website and, if doesn't find any malware, the malware warnings will be removed from search results to your website.

FORWARD CRAWL

The 'Crawl errors' and 'Crawl stats' sections provide feedback from Googlebot, which is the tool Google uses for downloading content from your website to build its search index. Crawl errors are created whenever Googlebot is unable to download pages, usually because of broken links. The Crawl errors tool lists all the broken links found so that you can correct them; broken links annoy users and prevent Google indexing your content.

Crawl stats are useful to check as they can show you how frequently Google is visiting your site to check for updated content. As you improve your website, add new pages and gain in popularity, Google will increase the frequency of visits to index your content.

Fetch as Googlebot is a utility that allows you to check the content Google is seeing from your website when it's being indexed. Type in the URL for a page in your website to see the content Google is going to download when indexing. This can be useful when you're making changes to your site, and for checking that your site is clean after removing malware. It can also be useful as a method for checking that URLs forbidden in your robots.txt are being blocked correctly.

LANGUAGE BARRIERS

The HTML suggestions tool shows information about any HTML problems Google finds while indexing your website. These problems won't prevent your website being indexed, but they can affect the descriptions of any web pages that appear in search results. Problems detected tend to fall into three categories: Title, Meta data description and non-indexable content.

Snippets of web pages that appear in search results are generated automatically, but where possible they include the title and description from the `<title>` and `<meta name="description">` tags in the HTML. Google will make suggestions about these tags if they're missing, too short or too long, or duplicated between pages. Pages that include non-indexable content, such as some rich media, are reported here for your information.

LAB WORK

The Labs section is a testing ground for new tools with which Google is experimenting. From time to time, these tools may get promoted to one of the other main sections of the Dashboard, or removed. Instant Previews are the page snapshots that are displayed in Google search results. These preview images are generated when you site is crawled. You can use this tool to compare an Instant Preview with your live page.

The 'Site performance' section displays the average load times for pages in your website over the past few months. The page load time is calculated as the total time between when the user clicks on the link in their browser to when the page is fully loaded. This information is automatically collected from users who have installed the Google Toolbar and enabled the PageRank feature. Improving your page load times is useful, as many people avoid slow sites.

Besides paying to increase the bandwidth for your site, there are many other ways in which you can improve performance and make your pages load more quickly. For example, adding GZIP compression can reduce the size of web pages significantly, reducing the transfer time and making them load faster.

Several browser plug-ins can analyse the performance of your site and offer suggestions. Google Page Speed (http://code.google.com/speed/page-speed) and Yahoo! YSlow (http://developer.yahoo.com/yslow) are free open-source Firefox browser extensions. Both provide a set of best practices that can drastically improve the performance of your website.

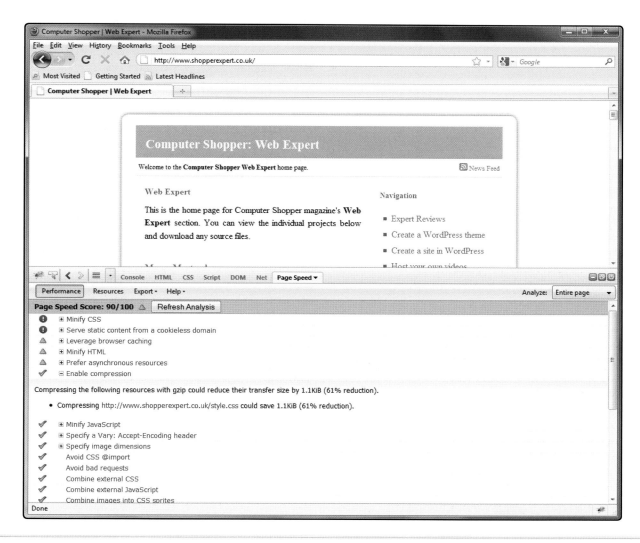

Left: Use Google Page Speed to fix performance problems

Making your website local

Use Google's local search engine to make sure visitors find the services relevant to their location

Below left: Google Places lets you add lots of information about your business, making it easy for people to find it

Below right: You can access the Google Webmaster Tools if you've got a Google Account

One of the best things about Google is that it provides local search engines, such as www.google.co.uk, so people in one country can find businesses and pages relevant to their location. This is crucial, particularly if you're running an online business. If you can get your website to appear on the right local searches, you'll find an increased amount of relevant traffic flowing to it. Fortunately, it's not hard to ensure that this happens. Using the tools, tips and tricks we've highlighted here, you can make your website visible and appealing to the local population.

When Google works out where a website is based, it uses a wide range of features. Getting a match on as many as possible will ensure that you get the most relevant visitors. One of the primary sources Google uses is your website's domain name. For sites in the United Kingdom, a '.uk' domain name, such as those ending in '.co.uk', should be considered an essential. It immediately tells Google your website is aimed at people in Britain. This should help your site appear in

the www.google.co.uk rankings, particularly when people select the 'Pages from the UK' link.

However, there are other factors. Where your web host has its servers is also crucial, as Google can identify their location by the server's IP address. That's not to say that all web hosts with foreign data centres are bad, though – 1&1 Internet has servers hosted in Germany, but customers that order a site through the UK website are automatically given a UK IP address. As far as Google is concerned, your 1&1 website is located in Britain, even if it's physically stored in Germany.

If you've bought your domain name and hosting package through a foreign website, your site could appear in the wrong local search engine results. If this is the case, you should seriously consider moving your website to a UK hosting company. It may cost a bit more per year, but the gains you'll get from more customers will be worth it in the long run.

You should also tell Google exactly where your website is located: the more information you give, the

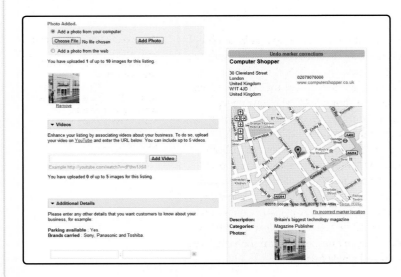

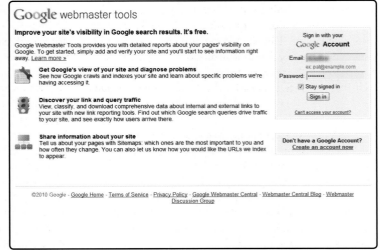

better the result. The submission service at www.google.co.uk/addurl lets you tell Google that your website exists and should be added to the index, so that people can search for it. Include the 'http://', and add a comment explaining what your site's about, type in the CAPTCHA phrase and click Add URL. The next page will tell you that your site has been added.

Google makes no promises about when your website will appear in search results, or if it ever will. That said, provided your site has relevant information stored on it, Google should accept it into its search engine.

PINPOINT ACCURACY

One of the best ways to tell Google where you're located is to use the Webmaster Tools to set a geographic target for your website. We've already covered this in depth on pages 120-125, but here we'll use it to tell Google in which country your site is based. Be aware that you can apply this information only to non-specific domains such as '.com', as '.co.uk' addresses are assumed to be country-specific. To set a Geo Location, go to www.google.com/webmasters/tools. You'll need to log in with your existing Google Account, but you can click the 'Create an account now' link if you don't have one.

Once you've logged into your account, you'll need to add your website before you can use any of the tools. To do this, click the 'Add a site' button and type in the URL of your site. Click Continue when you're done. On the next page, you'll be asked to verify that you're the owner of the website. Until you've taken this step, you'll be unable to use the tools properly.

There are a few options you can use to verify your site with Google, each of which comes with its own instructions. The easiest method is to select 'Upload an HTML file to your server'. This requires you to download a verification HTML file and upload it to your website's root folder. Once you've chosen your method and followed the instructions, click the Verify button to have your site verified.

Now you can set your website's country. Click on your website from the Webmaster Tools main page, expand the Site configuration section on the left-hand side, then click on Settings. Tick the 'Target users in' option and select your country from the drop-down list and click Save to apply the settings. It may take a while, but your website should start appearing on the local search results.

RETURN OF THE MAP

While the above steps should help ensure that your website appears on the correct local search results, there's another way for people to find local businesses through Google: Google Maps. The integrated search in Google Maps means people can find an area and search it for local businesses. It's important, then, that your business appears correctly on the map if local business is important to you.

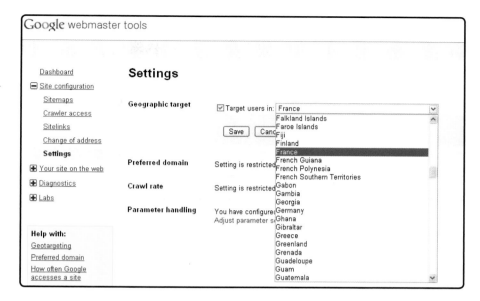

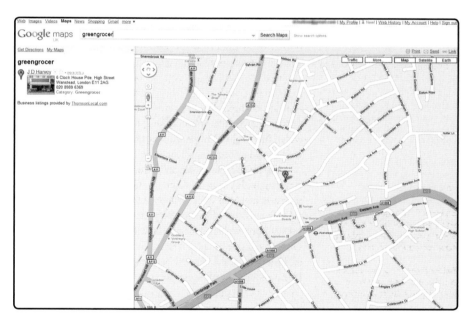

Getting listed on this search is easy thanks to Google Places, which is free to use. Start your web browser and go to www.google.co.uk/places. You'll need to be logged into a Google account to use the service. Click the 'Add new business' button. On the next page, United Kingdom should be selected as the country, but select it from the drop-down menu if it isn't. Type your company's phone number into the Phone number box and click 'Find business information'.

If Google currently holds any information on your company it will be listed, and you can edit an existing entry or add a new listing; if your company doesn't have a current listing, you'll be taken straight to the 'Add a new listing' page. For the purposes of this column, we'll show you how to add a new listing.

Top: Setting your Geographic target can help your site appear in the correct local search results

Above: If you want to get a lot of local business, it's worth making sure that your company is listed on Google Maps

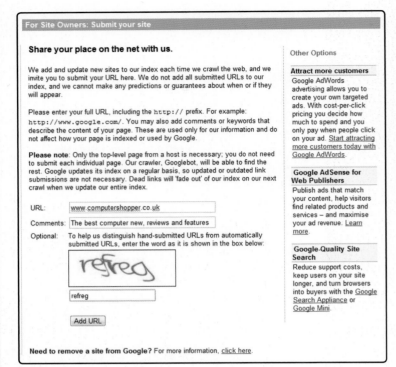

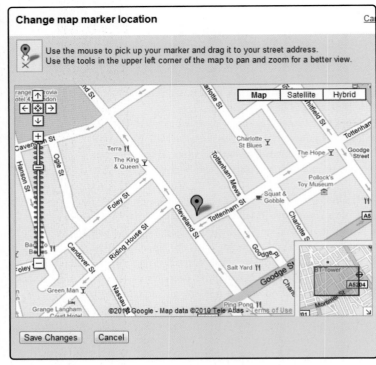

Above left: You can request that your website is added to the Google index so people can search for your content

Above right: Update your company's location manually by dragging the marker around the map

Below: You can view any information that Google has about your company in Google Places

You'll be asked to provide some basic information about your business, including its name and location. As you start typing in the address, the small Google Maps window will zoom into the same location. However, sometimes postcodes can point to the wrong address. If it does, click the 'Fix incorrect marker location' link and drag the red 'pin' to where your business is located, and click Save Changes. Make sure you get this address correct, or people will be unable to find your company.

You can tell Google if your company only operates from one location, or if it will serve customers elsewhere. You can tell Google how far from your location you're willing to travel. You can then set your hours of business and the payment types you accept, and add a photo of the premises. Finally, you can upload a video about your company to YouTube and add additional information, such as whether you have parking or not.

When you're done, click Submit. You'll be taken to a screen to choose a method to verify your listing: by phone, SMS (if you provided a mobile number) or postcard. Select the correct method and click Finish. You'll be sent a PIN by the requested method, which you need to type into the Google Places site. Once this is done, your company will appear on Google Maps.

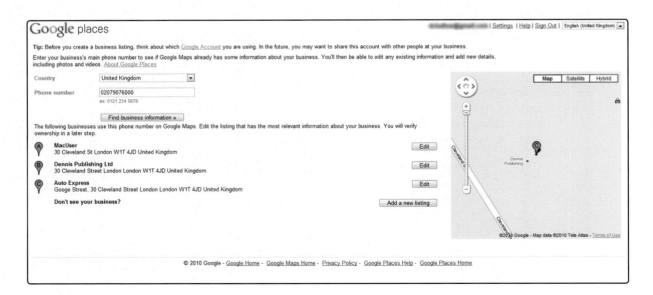

3 ISSUES FOR £1
on any of these great magazines

MacUser
If you use an Apple Mac, then MacUser is essential reading for you. Packed with buying advice, world exclusive reviews, breaking news and practical features, it helps you maximise the potential of your Mac.

3 issues for £1
then £17.95 every 6 months payable by Direct Debit

WebUser
Web User is packed with fantastic free software, must-visit new websites, PC and web tips, brilliant money-saving tips, easy-to-follow workshops and comprehensive hardware and software reviews.

3 issues for £1
then £19.99 every 13 issues payable by Direct Debit

COMPUTER SHOPPER
Computer Shopper tests more products than any other magazine in the UK. Packed with features, workshops and in-depth advice Computer Shopper will keep you ahead of the latest developments in technology.

3 issues for £1
then £21.99 every 6 months payable by Direct Debit

PC PRO
PC Pro is the UK's number one magazine for IT enthusiasts and professionals. Stay ahead of the latest developments with essential news, reviews and insight.

3 issues for £1
then £19.99 every 6 months payable by Direct Debit

CUSTOM PC
Custom PC is the ultimate magazine for PC enthusiasts with a passion for performance hardware and customisation. Each issue is delivered with wit, style and authority and is a must-read for anyone serious about customisation.

3 issues for £1
then £15.99 every 6 months payable by Direct Debit

If you enjoy your first three issues for £1, your subscription will continue at the low rate quoted above with great savings on the shop price. If you are not completely satisfied, you can write to cancel your subscription within your trial period and pay no more than the £1 already debited.

CALL 0844 844 0053
quote code G1201PMB

CHAPTER 10

IN THIS CHAPTER

Improving your search
  ranking 132

Displaying random photos
  on your site 135

Making a slideshow for
  your website 138

Hosting your own videos 142

Make your site work on
  mobile devices 144

Google charts and graphs 147

Embedding Google Maps
  on your site 150

Hosting with Google
  Apps 153

Advanced projects

Using the information acquired so far, you're well on your way to creating an attractive, well-designed website with gadgets such as those mentioned in chapter 7. In this chapter, we'll show you how to make your site even better using more advanced techniques.

Most of these projects involve programming in JavaScript and PHP. Master these skills and you'll be able to add customised

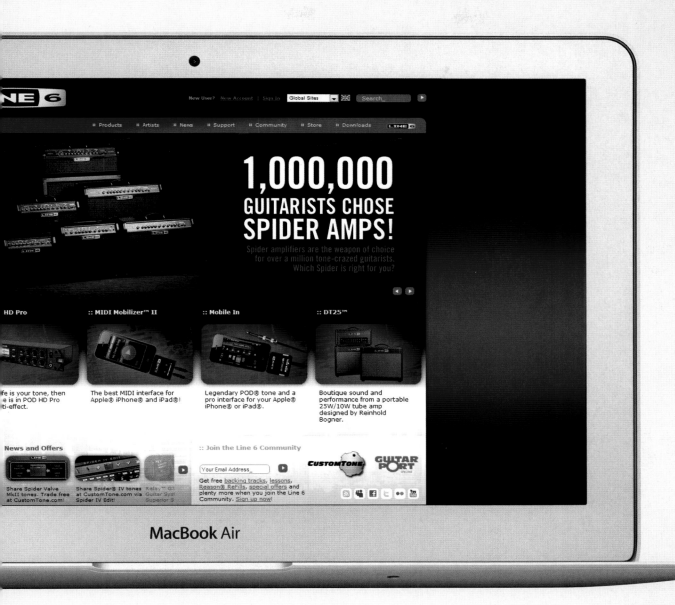

MacBook Air

interactive features such as Google Maps and full-screen slideshows with transitions to your site.

We'll also show you how to make your site display properly on handheld devices such as smartphones, and explain how to optimise your site to improve its ranking in search engines such as Google, thus ensuring you get as many hits as possible.

Improving your search ranking

Make sure your site has prime position in the results pages of search engines such as Google and you're sure to get more visitors

SKILL LEVEL
Beginner
Intermediate
Expert
HOW LONG
2-4 hours

If you want as many people as possible to find your website, you need to do a few extra jobs to ensure your site ranks highly on search results. It's easy to add your site to search engines so friends or people with similar interests can find it. You must have a publicly visible website, such as www.redcotbarn.co.uk, to be able to add it to a search engine, so dedicated web hosting is essential (see chapter 1 for details). If your site is hosted for free and you don't have your own unique domain, you won't be able to do this project.

Web search engines are capable of searching through content from all over the internet almost instantly. Google knows what's on all these web pages, and can search through them so quickly because it holds a huge index of the words and phrases found on all the pages. This index works in much the same way as the index in a book, which lists words alphabetically, so you can quickly find the word you're looking for and, hence, the pages in which the word appears. Search engines all work differently, but there are three main steps used by them all: crawling, indexing and searching.

DISCOVERY CHANNELS

Crawling is the process by which search engines find out about new and updated web pages that need to be added to the index. Billions of pages from all over the internet have to be visited and downloaded. This is usually achieved by an automated computer program that runs on a large number of computers. These programs are called spiders or bots. The crawling process begins with a list of URLs generated from previous crawl processes and new websites submitted by webmasters. As the spider visits each of the web pages in the list, it records the links found and adds them to the list of pages to be visited.

The web pages are downloaded, analysed and broken down into words and phrases, which are stored in the

index. The index also takes note of special content in the web page, such as the title. This content can improve the search accuracy and present excerpts in the search results. The indexing process can extract information from sources other than HTML web pages, such as images and even Flash files.

KEY CONCERNS

Searching involves matching the keywords that are searched for against words and phrases from the index to find relevant web pages. Each search engine has a different method for calculating which are the most relevant results. The factors for what makes one result more relevant than another can be quite complicated and are often a well-kept secret. Since Google is the most popular search engine, we'll concentrate here on how to improve your rankings with Google.

Adding your own website to a search engine for crawling is simply a matter of going to the submission page, such as www.google.com/addurl for Google,

Right: It's quite easy to add your site to Google's web-crawling system

http://search.yahoo.com/info/submit.html for Yahoo! and http://search.msn.com/docs/submit.aspx for Microsoft's Live Search. There's no charge for this, but you'll have to wait a few days for the crawler to visit your website and update the indexes before your site appears in the search results.

Each search engine uses a different set of rules to decide which web pages are most relevant to a search query, so it's difficult to work out how to make your own website rank well. However, you can strategically design or modify web pages so they achieve a good ranking in search results. This is known as search engine optimisation (SEO). As many companies rely on their websites appearing highly in search results, SEO has become a lucrative business.

Search engine providers generally disapprove of people trying to beat the system by artificially improving their search ranking. However, by following some simple guidelines it's easy to ensure that your website can be successfully crawled and indexed.

● Use a descriptive `<title>` tag in each of your web pages. Search engines will use this tag as a source of important information about your page, and will often use it as the basis for the link in their results pages.

● Add a meta description to your pages. This should describe the page in greater detail than the title, and may be used by the search engine to generate an excerpt of the content in the results page. The meta description tag should be added to the `<head>` tag in the HTML page, so for example:

```
<html>
  <head>
    <title>Redcot Barn Holiday Home
    </title>
```

```
<meta name="description" content="
  This is the home page for Redcot
  Barn. View accommodation, facilities,
  location and prices.">
  </head>
</html>
```

● Use `<h1>` and `<h2>` tags as well as bold fonts to pick out headings and emphasise text. Search engines will identify these tags as a source of significant keywords and will increase the relevancy score when searches are made using them. Don't repeat keywords in hidden parts of the page that the user cannot see in a bid to fool the indexer. Search engines can detect this; their reputation is based on the quality of their results. In the worst-case scenario, the search engine will discover what you are up to and remove your website from the index completely.

CALLING OFF THE SEARCH

Sometimes you'll need to prevent search engines crawling and indexing content from certain parts of your website. You might want to do this if certain web pages contain information that you don't want to make searchable, or if you have web pages that link to many gigabytes of data. Search engine crawlers tend to use a lot of bandwidth as they download all the reachable content on your website, so it's easy to exceed the maximum bandwidth limit of a hosted website by having lots of content available. Exceeding your bandwidth limit can make your website become temporarily unavailable or lead to expensive hosting bills.

In these cases, add a special file to the root of your website, called robots.txt. This gives instructions to the search engine crawlers about which parts of your website should not be processed. A simple robots.txt file that

Above left: Adding a meta description tag, which describes the content of a web page, helps to ensure that Google shows your site when people search for the same terms

Above right: Use HTML heading tags to emphasise keywords, since search engines will pick up on these

Right: Google Webmaster Tools will help you select which pages on your site are searchable

Far right: Webmaster Tools will also help you diagnose problems with your site, and provide tips on how to improve your ranking

prevents crawlers processing specific files and directories looks like this:

```
User-agent: *
Disallow: /tmp/
Disallow: /images/
Disallow: /old/index.html
```

The first line allows you to give instructions to a particular crawler. Using * indicates that the rules should be applicable to all crawlers. The following lines are rules that prevent the crawling of specific directories and files. It's easy to drastically alter the content indexed by a search engine by changing this file, sometimes by more than you intended, so be careful with your changes.

MASTER PLAN

Google has a set of free tools called Webmaster Tools, which can help you create a robots.txt file and get more information about which parts of your website are being indexed. Webmaster Tools allow you to find out more about how Google (and hence other search engines) sees your website. They also help diagnose problems that are preventing pages being searchable, and improve your overall search visibility. You just need an active Google account, which is easy to create. Once you have an account, log on to the Webmaster Tools homepage at www.google.com/webmasters/tools. After you've logged in, you can add URLs for the websites that you want to use the tools on, such as www.redcotbarn.co.uk.

You can type in any URL, even those you do not own or control, which is a security problem. Before you can use the tools on a particular website, you have to prove to the tools that you are in charge of it (see box, left).

Once your website is verified, you can access the full set of tools. These are divided into five main sections: Diagnostics, Statistics, Links, Sitemaps and Tools. The first section, Diagnostics, is where you can find out about any errors that Google encountered when crawling your website, such as broken links or pages with missing titles.

You can also see an overview of pages that were excluded by the robots.txt file to ensure that you have it set up correctly. Ideally, you'll want as few errors as possible, so you should check this report often.

The Statistics section provides various reports, including what kinds of searches people are using to find your website and an overview of keywords found in your indexed web pages. You can also see a list of the top phrases used in external links to your site, such as in anchor tags. Google is interested in how other people link to your site and includes this information in its relevancy calculations. The Links section provides much more information about external links to your website.

Sitemaps are meta data files you can add to your website to describe its layout, ensuring that crawlers can find pages they might otherwise miss. This is particularly useful if you have web pages with dynamic content, using JavaScript to create page links, or pages that don't have links to them. The Sitemaps section in the Webmaster Tools allows you to upload and manage sitemaps. For more information and a wizard to get you started, see www.xml-sitemaps.com.

The final section, Tools, has several useful utilities, including a page to create and analyse robots.txt files. Here you can make sure your robots.txt file is up to date and test any changes before uploading a new file. You can use the 'Remove URLs page' option to resolve issues with pages that no longer exist, or those that create problems by being in the Google index.

ONWARDS AND UPWARDS

Although SEO is a complicated subject, you're now armed with the knowledge of how search engines work, so you should be able to lift your site up their rankings. Using utilities such as Google Webmaster Tools, you can create a custom robots.txt file to fine-tune the way the crawling process interacts with your website. You'll find plenty of information online with more tips for targeting specific search engines. Just remember: keep it simple, and let the search engines do the hard work for you.

TIP

To prove you own your website, upload an empty file to it or paste a meta tag into the <head> section of your home page. The information you need will be supplied by Google and looks like:

```
<meta name="verify-
v1" content="2Q7fj
HeYmi=">
```

When you've added it, ask Google to match the details it supplied against the meta tag on your site's home page. This will prove you are the owner of the site.

Displaying random photos on your site

You can display photos to make your site look fresh for returning visitors, even if nothing else has changed since they last looked at it

An important step in making your website look professional is to make it dynamic, which means certain elements are created only when the visitor clicks a link to the page. This is usually achieved using a scripting language and a database. PHP is a popular scripting language that can extract content from a database. It runs on a web server, generating standard HTML pages that are sent to the visitor's web browser, allowing any browser to view a page with PHP scripts. PHP files are normal text files, so you can do all your PHP work using Windows' built-in Notepad. However, these files must end in .php.

Here we'll show you how to write a simple script to show a random photo. You'll need to download the files from our website (see Tip, right) to do this project.

GETTING STARTED

Create a folder called 'scripts' in the server's root and upload the common.php file. Create a folder called randomimage and upload the remaining files and images folder here. Open Notepad and test-page.php, and you'll see a file that looks like normal HTML, except there's a block of code in the middle:

```
<?php
  require "../scripts/common.php";
  $randomImage = getRandomImagePath
    ("./images");
?>
<p><?php
  echo "<img src=\"$randomImage\">";
?></p>
```

The <?php starts a new block of PHP code; the ?> ends it. As you can see, there are two blocks of PHP code. The first block uses 'require' to include another PHP file stored in the scripts folder in the server's root folder. It's this file that contains the function (that is, reusable code that does a specific job) for showing the random image. You should save your PHP functions into separate files, so you can reuse them in other scripts later.

The second line of the script does the work. It uses the getRandomImageInPath() function to search the folder we're using ("./images") for a picture. It stores the file's name in the $randomImage variable. A variable is a virtual storage box for data, and anything starting with a $ is a variable. The second block of code uses the 'echo' command to output an HTML img tag using the contents of our variable as the image source.

INSIDE THE COMMON.PHP FILE

If you open the common.php file, you'll see that it contains many functions. These are all used to display a random function. The first is the getRandomImagePath that we used in the test-page.php file:

```
function getRandomImagePath($aDirectory)
{
  $imagePaths = getImagesInPath
    ($aDirectory);
  $size = count($imagePaths);
  if($size > 0)
  {
    $randomIndex = mt_rand(0, $size
      - 1);
    return $imagePaths[$randomIndex];
  }
  else
  {
    return false;
  }
}
```

SKILL LEVEL

Beginner
Intermediate
Expert

HOW LONG
2 hours

TIP
The examples we have used should work regardless of your web-hosting package. To save you having to type in our examples, all the files are available for download from www. redcotbarn.co.uk/ advancedprojects/ randomimage. Here you will also find the working demonstrations. To try the test files on your web server, you'll need to use the same directory structure as we have.

Random image in HTML

Above: a random image can help to keep your website looking fresh for anyone who visits on a regular basis

This function stores the folder it is passed in the `$aDirectory` variable. The next line calls a function named getImagesInPath with our folder to create an array of all the images found. This is stored in the `$imagePaths` variable. Arrays are indexed lists, where each entry can be accessed through its index number; `$imagePaths[0]` refers to the first item in the list, as arrays are indexed from 0, not 1.

NUMBER CRUNCHING

Next, the `built-in count()` function is used to see how big the list is and store its size in the `$size` variable. It then checks to see if `$size` is greater than 0. If it isn't, the list is empty and false is returned. If it is greater than 0, the script picks a random image from the list. A random number is stored in the `$randomIndex` variable. This uses the built-in `mt_rand()` function, which creates a random image between its two inputs; 0 is the first entry and `$size -1` is the last. The image stored at `$randomIndex` using `$imagePaths[$randomIndex]` is returned to the calling script. To create the list of images, the getImagesInPath function looks like this:

```
function getImagesInPath
  ($aDirectory)
{
  if ($handle = opendir($aDirectory))
  {
    while (($filename = readdir
```

```
    ($handle)) !== false)
  {
    $nextPath = "$aDirectory/
      $filename";

    if(isJpegFile($nextPath))
    {
      $imagePaths[] = $nextPath;
    }
  }

  closedir($handle);
}
  return $imagePaths;
}
```

This function attempts to open the folder in the `$aDirectory` variable using the built-in `opendir()` function. If this folder can't be accessed, false is returned. Otherwise, the script returns a handle, needed to access the files. It's stored in the `$handle` variable. Next, there's a while loop, which operates like this: while a statement is true, every instruction inside the loop is performed. This is used to read through the folder and examine each file. The function `readdir($handle)` reads a file and stores the result in a variable called `$filename`. It returns false when all files have been read, and this is the cue to cancel the loop.

NEXT IN LINE

For each file that is read, the `$nextPath` variable is used to store the folder and filename. The script checks to see if the file stored in `$nextPath` is a JPEG using the `isJpegFile()` function. If it is, the result is stored in an array called `$imagePaths`; the empty square brackets mean 'create a new list entry'. Then, `closedir($handle)` closes access to a file. When the while loop has ended, the list of JPEG files is returned. `IsJpegFile` uses two functions:

```
function isJpegFile($aPath)
  {
    if(is_file($aPath))
    {
      return endsWith(strtolower
        ($aPath), ".jpg");
    }
    else
    {
      return false;
    }
  }

function endsWith($aString, $aSuffix)
  {
    $stringLength = strlen($aString);
```

```
$suffixLength = strlen($aSuffix);
if($stringLength < $suffixLength)
{
  return false;
}

$endOfString = substr($aString,
 $stringLength - $suffixLength);
return $endOfString == $aSuffix;
}
?>
```

The first function takes a path to a file. It checks if there is a file using `is_file()`. If there is, it finds out if it ends with .jpg using the `endWith()` function. Everything is converted to lower-case using `strtolower()`, to avoid complications from upper-case characters. This is important if you use a Linux-based web host; file and folder names are case-sensitive in Linux, but not Windows.

The `endsWith` function works out the length of the string and the length of the suffix that is being searched for. The file's suffix is separated and stored in the `$endOfString` variable. This is done using `substr` (sub-string), which takes two arguments: the string that needs breaking up, and the numerical character position of the start of the break. This returns just the suffix. Next, `$endOfString == $aSuffix` is returned. This returns true if they match and false if they don't.

It's now easy to write a function to look for other file types. If you wanted `isGifFile()` you would create it in the same way, but you would use the line `return`

`endsWith(strtolower($aPath, ".gif")`. However, a neater solution is to have a PHP script that can be integrated into an HTML page. Visit www.redcotbarn. co.uk/advancedprojects/randomimage to see it in action. The code for the page uses `{img src="random-image.php"}`. Random-image.php acts as an image file. If you view its code in Notepad, you'll see it uses the same code and `getRandomImagePath()` function as the first example.

The remaining code makes the PHP file act like an image file. `$handle = fopen($imagepath, 'rb')` opens the physical JPEG file. The 'header' code is used to tell a web browser there's a JPEG coming, where it's stored and how big it is. As a different image is required each time, this code also tells the browser not to store the file in its cache. The `fpassthrough()` line tells PHP to stream the contents of the file to the browser – in other words, to send the JPEG image through.

GOING FURTHER

You now have code that you can use more than once in multiple web pages. You will probably want to modify this project to suit the way your website works. If you're using different folders to us, just update the path to the common.php file. You'll also need to point people towards the directory where you keep your images.

This project can be extended to look for different image types such as GIFs. You could also make your script look for both JPEGs and GIFs. You could use an OR statement to see if a field is a JPEG file or GIF file. If you get stuck, you may well find the help you need by reading the PHP documentation.

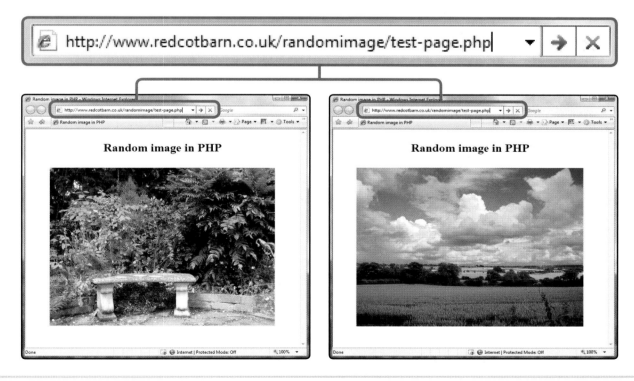

Left: Each time the page is refreshed, a random image will be displayed

Making a slideshow for your website

The right slideshow can bring a touch of class to your website. Here we show you how to create a sophisticated online slideshow using PHP

On page 135 of this chapter, we showed you how to write a PHP script to display random photos on your website. However, sometimes you'll want to show more than just one photo. A slideshow is an efficient and effective way for visitors to see a selection of images. On page 97, we showed you how to create a simple slideshow with Picasa. In this project, we're going to go further and create a customised slideshow using JavaScript.

Using JavaScript, you can create stunning slideshows that work in any web browser without requiring plug-ins or extensions. A few years ago, web-based slideshows were static and dull, or written in Flash. While there's nothing wrong with Flash, it can sometimes limit the accessibility of your website, as users need a browser that supports it and must download a plug-in for it to work. These days, web browsers have excellent CSS support, while the maturity of modern JavaScript libraries means you can create appealing slideshows directly in HTML.

CHOOSING A JAVASCRIPT LIBRARY

There are many JavaScript libraries dedicated to creating slideshows. One of the best is TripTracker, which can be found at http://slideshow.triptracker.net. TripTracker is free to use as long as the script isn't used for profit, so it's perfect for personal home pages. JavaScript is normally stored in separate files and not in the HTML, but the scripts for setting up these slideshows are so simple it is easier to include them directly in a page of HTML using a script tag. It's only worth saving the script as a separate file if you need to reuse the same slideshow on a different page.

The TripTracker library allows you to create a slideshow that displays a series of photos, using pictures stored on your website. Once launched, the slideshow presents each photo using the full size of the web browser window, scaling down the images if necessary.

The slideshow adjusts itself to suit the sizes of the images you use and the size of the monitor on which images are viewed. Bear in mind that this image scaling takes place in the web browser itself. Don't upload photos directly to your website from your digital camera without resizing them first, or else everyone who looks at your website will have to wait while huge photos are downloaded.

To add a slideshow to an HTML page, you first need to add a reference to the TripTracker JavaScript library. Usually, it's a good idea to download the JavaScript library and add it to your own website. However, in this case we recommend adding a reference in your HTML that points to the TripTracker website. This way, you will ensure that you're always using the latest version of the slideshow library; it's periodically updated with new features and bug fixes, such as adding support for the latest web browsers such as Internet Explorer 8.

Add the slideshow library with the following script tag (as we've done in simple.html at www.redcotbarn.co.uk/advancedprojects/slideshows/simple.html):

```
<script type="text/javascript" src="
  http://slideshow.triptracker.net/
  slide.js"></script>
```

Next, you need to set up the slideshow with the images you want shown. This is done as another script block, usually using images that are stored on your site, although you can use images from another site if you prefer. In simple.html you'll see a slideshow that shows a series of JPEG images. The script tag looks like this:

```
<script type="text/javascript">
  var slideshow = new PhotoViewer();
  slideshow.add('images/garden/
    flowers1.jpg');
  slideshow.add('images/garden/
```

```
      flowers2.jpg');
</script>
```

```
<a href="javascript:void(slideshow.
show(0))">View the slideshow</a>
```

Above: The TripTracker slideshow in action on our website

The first line of code (after the `<script>` tag) creates a PhotoViewer object that represents the slideshow and its configuration. Once you have the slideshow object, just add paths to the images you want to show. In our example, the images are stored in a directory called images/garden. It's a good idea to keep all your images in folders with descriptive names, so you'll know where to find things. Once you've added all the photos, you're almost done.

STARTING THE SLIDESHOW

You now need a way to start the slideshow. Usually, you would do this by making visitors click on an HTML link, but you can easily do it by making the slideshow a link from an image or another HTML element. The HTML for starting the slideshow from a link looks like this:

This calls the `show()` function on the slideshow object we created earlier. The 0 in brackets is the parameter that is passed to the show method, and determines where you want the slideshow to start. Usually this will be 0, since you want to start with the first image. The examples at www.redcotbarn.co.uk/advancedprojects/slideshows will show you what the slideshow looks like.

You're not limited to one slideshow per page, either; you can add as many as you like. The trick is to create multiple PhotoViewer objects with different names. In our example, we've called the PhotoViewer object 'slideshow' as defined by the line that starts `var slideshow`. We've put an example of multiple slideshows on a page on our website. Here, you'll see two slideshows in the same HTML page. The benefit of having multiple slideshows on one page is that you

TIP
Follow our examples by visiting www.redcotbarn.co.uk/advancedprojects/slideshows.

TIP
To view the HTML source code of a page you're viewing in Internet Explorer, choose View source from the View menu.

can group photos into albums, without the need to create a separate web page for each slideshow.

CUSTOMISING THE SLIDESHOW

There are several ways to customise your slideshows. One tool lets you add a caption and date to each photo. This appears underneath the image by the navigation controls. Click the 'Slideshow with captions' link on our website for an example.

The only additions to the code are extra parameters for the add() function on PhotoViewer. The caption and date are both optional parameters, so you can add both, or just a caption. The following line does both:

```
slideshow.add('images/garden/flowers
1.jpg', 'Small Yellow Flowers',
'12/10/2008 15:35');
```

Customising the animation of the slideshow is also easy. Just use extra functions after you've defined all the pictures you want to use. These functions are called in

the same way as the add() function, and are in the style '<nameofyourslideshow>.<nameoffunction>'.

The most useful setting is setSlideDuration, which, as it implies, is used to control how long each slide is shown in milliseconds. The default is 4000, which means each photo remains onscreen for four seconds.

The animated effect used as a transition from one slide to the next can be turned off. The slideshow uses a panning and fading effect, which can be turned off by calling disablePanning() and disableFading(). Other options are enableAutoPlay(), which causes the animation to start when the user clicks the link to the slideshow, and enableLoop(), which makes the slideshow loop indefinitely. Look at 'Slideshow with custom animation' on our website see a slideshow playing automatically without any panning and fading effects.

You can also change the background and shade effect colour, by calling setBackgroundColor(colour) and setShadeColor(colour). Colours are defined using standard web hexadecimal numbers, with the default value #000000 (black). (See the page at

Below left and right: One of TripTracker's benefits is full-screen photos

http://en.wikipedia.org/wiki/Web_colors for a list of hexadecimal web colours.) If you don't like the shade effect, remove it by calling `disableShade()`. The default for the image caption is 10 pixels. Change this to 12 or 14 by calling `setFontSize(size)`. Click on 'Slideshow with custom appearance' on our website for an example that uses a different shade of background colour and a larger font.

You can change the toolbar that controls the playback. The 'photo link' and 'email photo link' buttons allow users to view the photo directly or email a link of the photo to a friend with their email client. You can remove these buttons by calling the `disableEmailLink()` and `disablePhotoLink()` functions. Remove the whole toolbar by calling `disableToolbar()`.

You can even configure what the slideshow does when you click on it with the mouse. The default is to close the slideshow. Using `setOnClickEvent(slideshow.startSlideShow)` causes the slideshow to play when you click on it, and `setOnClickEvent(slideshow.permalink)` shows the current photo in a new window. Click on 'Slideshow with custom controls' on our website for an example that removes the toolbar and sets the slideshow to start playing when you click on it.

IMPLEMENTING PHP

Part of the PHP script used on page 135 is able to find all the images in a directory, which you can reuse here to set up a slideshow more quickly. You can use that script, common.php, which is available in the 'Display random images' section of Advanced Projects on our website. The benefit of using PHP to make slideshows is that you can upload new images to your website and have them appear automatically in your slideshow, without having to update the HTML manually.

Create a PHP file with the .php extension containing the following script (see automatic.php, which is included in the sample files for slideshows on our website):

```
<script type="text/javascript">
    var slideshow = new PhotoViewer();
```

Left: You can customise which controls are shown in the toolbar

2/2   Big Yellow Flower

```php
<?php
  require "./scripts/common.php";
  $images = getImagesInPath
   ("images/nature");
  foreach ($images as $image)
  {
    echo "slideshow.add('$image');
     \n";
  }
?>
</script>
```

This PHP script reuses the `getImagesInPath()` function from common.php. Give it the name of a folder, and it returns a list of the paths of all image files found. It's easy to loop through all the image paths, adding each one to the slideshow. When this page is viewed in a browser, the HTML page will look like simple.html, but there's no need to type in all the image paths.

In the PHP version, the images are shown in alphanumerical order according to their filename. To control the sort order, name your images with a numeric prefix such as 01-, 02-, 03-. This way, you can make sure the photos appear in the order you want.

HotScripts **Other free scripts**

There are thousands of other scripts you can use to spice up your website. A great resource can be found at www.hotscripts.com. Scripts are categorised by type, and include Ajax, JavaScript and PHP, among others. Most are free to use, so it's simply a matter of searching through the listings to find what you're after.

For example, if you want text to appear on a page letter by letter, so it looks like someone is typing it, try downloading Typewriter Ticker 2.0. This free piece of JavaScript works on many browsers and operating systems.

Hosting your own videos

Hosting your own videos looks smarter than embedding YouTube's player. Here's how to use the free Flowplayer for a professional look

You can embed clips from free video-sharing services such as YouTube into your web pages, but the results don't look very professional. If your web-hosting account offers unlimited bandwidth you can host your own videos, which means you're free from restrictions on size, length, quality, format and content. You'll also get better-quality video, as services such as YouTube will convert your videos, degrading them in the process.

The Flowplayer app is ideal for hosting your own videos as it's highly customisable, looks good and has detailed documentation online. It's Flash-based and supports two video formats: Flash Video (*.flv) and H.264 (*.mp4). We recommend using the latter, as it's much better quality.

If your videos aren't in a supported format, you'll need to convert them first using Any Video Converter, which is free from www.any-video-converter.com/products/for_video_free. Keep the bitrate as low as possible to keep the file size down. When the videos are in the right format you can upload them to your website via FTP.

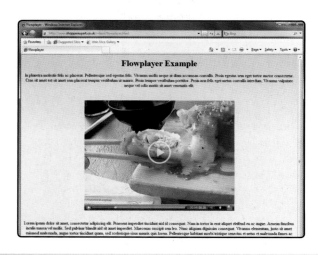

Right: Using Flowplayer means your visitors don't have to put up with adverts

INSTALLATION

To install the player, download the Flowplayer distribution from http://flowplayer.org and upload the files to your website. A sensible place to store the files is in a folder named flowplayer. Now you're ready to create a web page to use them together:

```
<!DOCTYPE html>
<head>
  <script src="flowplayer/flowplayer-3.1.4.
  min.js">
  </script>
</head>
<body>
  <a href="video.mp4" style="display:
  block;width:425px;height:300px;"
  id="player"></a>
  <script>
  flowplayer("player", "flowplayer/
  flowplayer-3.1.5.swf");
  </script>
</body>
</html>
```

In the head of the page, the JavaScript file is called. The <a> tag is used to identify which video to play and where to place it. The href attribute specifies where the video is stored – here, it's in the same folder as the HTML page, but you could store it in a videos folder and call it by using href="videos/video.mp4".

The style attribute uses CSS to define the pixel dimensions of the player that's created. Ideally, this should match the video's size, if you want the best quality. This CSS can also be put into a separate <style> tag or, preferably, a separate .css file.

The script that follows creates the video player and embeds it in the page. The "player" parameter passed to the `flowplayer()` function must match the id attribute of the `<a>` tag so Flowplayer knows which tag to attach itself to in the page. This script must appear in the page after the `<a>` tag to ensure the script runs properly.

Flowplayer lets you create multiple video players in the same web page without any loss of performance. Just add multiple player `<a>` tags and give them a common class attribute instead of a unique id. In the script used to initialise Flowplayer, use the tag and class name (`"a.player"`) and a player will be created for each of the tags. Flowplayer manages system performance by preventing multiple players playing at the same time, automatically stopping videos as others are started.

MAKING A SPLASH

In Flowplayer, the content shown before the video is played is known as the splash. If you configure Flowplayer for a splash, when the web page loads this will be shown rather than the default behaviour, which is to start the video. The splash could be an image or HTML code. You might choose a frame from the video or a large play button and some text that describes the video. You can customise the background of the splash by using the CSS background-image property and giving it an image to display:

```
<style>
 .player {
  width: 425px; height: 300px;
  background-image: url("splash.
   jpg");
 }
</style>

<div href="video.flv" class="player">
 <img src="play-button.jpg"/>
</div>
```

All other content for the splash, such as images and text, can be created by adding HTML to the body of the tag hosting the player, just as with a regular web page.

As well as creating splashes, you can customise the player's appearance, including the control bar, by using HTML, CSS and custom images. This can get complicated, but it's worth investigating if you want to change the default appearance. You'll find details of this advanced 'skinning' technique at the Flowplayer website.

CONFIGURATION

You can configure the video player by passing extra options to the `flowplayer()` function as a third parameter. These can control the appearance and behaviour of the player as well as providing hooks to allow you to integrate it better into your web pages. You can set the clip properties and the features of the video being played, and create playlists:

Left: Flowplayer enables you to put multiple videos on a page

```
<script>
 flowplayer("player", "flowplayer/
 flowplayer-3.1.5.swf", {
  clip: {url:"video.flv", autoPlay:
  false, accelerated: true }
 });
</script>
```

This code would create a player using the video specified in the URL parameter, which is an alternative way of providing the video reference in the `href` attribute of the player tag. This video will not autoplay when the page is loaded, but will use hardware acceleration if it's present.

A playlist is a series of clips that Flowplayer will play in sequence. You can set the properties of each clip in a playlist, but the simplest way to create one is to list the videos you want to show:

```
<script>
 flowplayer("player", "flowplayer/
 flowplayer-3.1.5.swf", {
  clip: { autoPlay:false },
  playlist: [ "video-1.flv",
   "video-2.flv" ]
 });
</script>
```

If you want to customise the player's behaviour further, you will be able to find a number of other configuration properties on the Flowplayer website.

Hosting your own videos isn't for everyone, but it does provide you with total control over the content and quality of the videos, as well as the design and behaviour of the player. It's a lot more work than copying the 'embed' code from YouTube, though. However, the flexibility you gain by hosting videos yourself can often make it worth the extra effort.

Make your site work on mobile devices

These days, you need to ensure your site works on handheld devices as well as desktop computers. Fortunately, CSS and PHP make this easy

If you aren't designing your website for mobile browsers, you're well behind the times. Catering for mobile viewers is no longer an optional extra – it's a must. Fortunately, it's easy to cater to their needs with a little bit of CSS and some snippets of PHP.

If you want your site to feature in your visitors' bookmarks on their mobile devices you should offer a version of your sites that strips down the pages to their fundamentals. We don't mean plain text – just easy-to-read, easily scanned pages that present as much detail as possible at each screen's default zoom level.

Here we'll explain how to make your website work on a mobile device without doubling up content on each page. Google hates duplicate content, and if you want to maintain a good search ranking, you should do all you

can to ensure that the page content features in Google's database just once. Furthermore, if you were to create two versions of every page it would be more work and take up twice the space on the server.

The secret is to use one page, two stylesheets and a few lines of PHP to detect which browser the viewer is using, and then pick the most appropriate stylesheet for the device through which the visitor is browsing.

IDENTITY PARADE
Every browser – mobile or desktop – identifies itself to the server from which it loads pages. Its name is part of the User Agent, which is a string of data containing its name, version and rendering engine. You can test this by creating a new page containing the following code:

```php
<?php
    $browser = $_SERVER['HTTP_USER_AGENT'];
    echo $browser;
?>
```

Save it with a .php extension, upload it to your server and browse to it twice: once in your regular browser, and once in another browser on your machine. Each will display a different line of data identifying the specific browser build. In Internet Explorer, it will include the term 'MSIE'. In Safari, you'll see the word 'WebKit', and if you view it on an iPhone or iPad, it will include the words 'iPhone' or 'iPad'. You'll find a list of common User Agent strings at http://whatsmyuseragent.com/CommonUserAgents.asp.

We can interrogate this information using PHP and a search command that hunts out a specific portion of text. That command is `strpos`, which looks for a string of text (hence the 'str' part of the command) and returns the position at which it appears (the 'pos' part of the command). The result is a number pinpointing how

Right: The PHP code needed to determine which browser is being used is actually quite simple

Far left: Our news.php page as it appears in a regular browser, with a sidebar, a headline and a teaser

Left: The page on an iPhone with stylesheets switched to the mobile edition, which left-aligns the header, reverses its colour and puts the links below the text

many characters into the data the string starts or, if it doesn't appear, it returns a fail. This failure is key to the job in hand.

CODE BREAKERS

We're going to create a page that automatically picks a regular stylesheet for full-size browsers and a mobile stylesheet for iPhones and iPod Touches. We can use the command to search through the User Agent for the terms 'iPhone' and 'iPod' and, if either appears, show just the mobile stylesheet. Create a new file (we've called ours news.php) and enter the code in the screenshot opposite. Pass this file to your server and load it in your browser. The results aren't very inspiring, but they're really just the building blocks: all the information is there on the page, and it just needs styling.

The most important part is the PHP code that appears between the opening `<?php` and the `?>` that precedes the `<title>` tag. This section interrogates the User Agent and serves up the appropriate stylesheet. In this case, we've created one stylesheet for iPhone and iPod Touch users, and another for visitors using a regular browser on a desktop or laptop computer.

Section-by-section, it works like this. The `<?php` is the standard opening for a section of PHP code. It tells the browser not to render the code as part of the page, but to act on any commands it includes. It's balanced by the closing `?>`. There then follows this section:

```
$browser = $_SERVER['HTTP_USER_AGENT'];
$iphone = 'iPhone';
$ipod = 'iPod';
```

Here we define the variables. Every piece of data we want to use has to be stored in a variable. In this case, we've stored the User Agent in the variable `$browser`, and our two search terms in the strings `$iphone` and `$ipod`. We could have defined the search terms

wherever they're used in the code, but by assigning them to a variable we know that they can be changed in just one place and that, if they are used elsewhere on the page, each use will reflect the change.

Once our variables are defined, we can start to use them. Now consider:

```
if(strpos($browser, $iphone)==false)
```

We come to `strpos`. Start with a conditional statement (if), which tests the validity of the bracketed statement that follows. In this line, we tell the browser to act only if the data stored in the variable `$iphone` doesn't appear within the User Agent data, which is stored in the variable `$browser` – in other words, if the result is 'false'.

If it is, it moves on to the next line. If not – if it returns a number indicating the position within `$browser` where the contents of the variable `$iphone` appear – then it ignores the rest of the code until it finds an 'else' statement. Assuming the result is false, we know the user isn't using an iPhone, so we need to check they're not using an iPod Touch:

```
{
    if(strpos($browser, $ipod)==false)
    {
```

This is in effect the same code as above, but this time it checks for the word 'iPod', which you'll remember is stored in the `$ipod` variable. If it doesn't find it – the result is 'false' – it will execute the line that follows. If not, it will do the same as it did with the iPhone search line and jump forward to the line marked 'else'.

COMMAND PERFORMANCE

At this point, we've done all our checking and we know the user isn't using an iPhone or an iPod Touch. We could add further commands to check for Android and

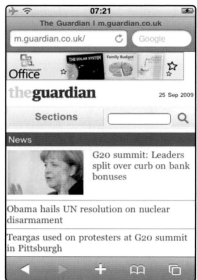

Right: The Guardian's front page as it would appear to anyone visiting from a desktop or laptop computer...

Far right: ... and the same page viewed on an iPhone

mobile versions of Opera, but for the sake of brevity we'll assume we're happy with the results and act on them.

```
print '<link href="notiphone.css"
rel="stylesheet" type="text/css">';
   }
      }
```

Finally, we're going to output some results. Using the 'print' command is like punching a hole through the PHP code section to address the fabric of our page directly and add to it what appears between the single quote marks. In this instance, we're going to write a line of HTML into the header of the page, as it appears within tag braces. It won't appear on the visitor's screen, but will make up a part of the underlying code and replace all the PHP code we're working on.

The line performs just one function: it loads an external stylesheet called 'notiphone.css', which styles up any pages that aren't displayed on an iPhone or iPod Touch and is thus optimised for regular, large displays:

```
else
   {
      print '<link href="iphone.css"
       rel="stylesheet" type="text/
       css">';
         }
?>
```

This section of code tells the browser which stylesheet to use if the result of either 'strpos' test returns anything other than 'false' to indicate that the visitor is using an iPhone or an iPod Touch. It calls in a different stylesheet called 'iphone.css', which is built with the iPhone's tall, narrow display in mind.

STYLING IT UP

Now all we need to do is build the stylesheets for each platform. The files iphone.css and notiphone.css are very similar, but notiphone.css has a lot of positional information, putting the link's sidebar to the right of the main body content and using the 'container' layer to constrict the elements of the page within a 600-pixel layer. The iphone.css file is less fiddly, as it lets the layers fill the full width of the screen to accommodate either horizontal or vertical viewing.

Mobile users are likely to want to browse information more quickly, so we've also applied the visibility tag to any lines styled using '.teaser'. These lines are the short descriptions that explain every headline. By hiding them, we've pulled the headlines closer together on the mobile screen without them crashing into one another. A greater number of links to more information will be displayed within a smaller space, allowing mobile visitors to skim-read the news and quickly find their way to the full stories should they want to read more.

TAKING THINGS FURTHER

You can create an unlimited number of stylesheets for your website and layer as many conditional strpos tests as necessary within the PHP segment to pick the right one. This gives you a great level of control over how your page renders in each particular browser, but it needn't be confined to detecting mobile browsers.

With just a few tweaks, it's an effective means of remaining backwards-compatible with older browsers while also catering for your most up-to-date audience. Furthermore, by using a refresh command within the text you 'print' on to the page, you can open different pages to users of older browsers. Online banks routinely use this tactic to restrict their services to the most modern and secure browsers.

Google charts and graphs

If you want attractive graphs and charts on your web pages, Google Charts is ideal – and it's surprisingly easy to use, too

How would you go about adding a graph to your site? The most obvious way would be to fire up Excel or Photoshop and make it yourself. But this increases your workload, as you'll have to update each graph by hand every time the data changes.

It's far quicker to use an Application Programming Interface (API) – in this case, Google Charts. This is a powerful text-based tool that lets you enter strings of data and have them rendered as full-colour graphics. The results are drawn at Google's end, so it doesn't sap your bandwidth. Better still, it's completely free.

CALLING THE API

To explain the fundamentals, we'll start by creating a simple rainfall pie chart for Lowestoft railway station. The Met Office (http://metoffice.gov.uk) tells us that this station saw rain an average of 115 days each year (31%) between 1961 and 1990. Ignoring leap years, this means that 250 days (69%) were rain-free. To represent this as a pie chart, enter the following URL in your browser:

http://chart.apis.google.com/chart?cht=p&chd=t:69,31&chl=Sunny|Rainy&chs=300x200

The result is a flat, two-tone pie chart. Study this address, and you'll see how it works and how you can tweak it. We'll take each part in turn, starting with:

http://chart.apis.google.com/chart?

This is the call to Google's API, which you have to use every time you want to create a chart or graph. The question mark is a delimiter telling the browser that what follows isn't part of the address itself, but a string of information to be passed to the page it loads. That information is split into four parts, separated by ampersands (&), and denoting the following:

cht   chart type – in this case, a 2D pie chart, denoted by p. Change this to p3 if you want a 3D chart
chd   chart data, with each part separated by a comma
chl   chart labels, with each label separated by a pipe (|)
chs   chart size, measured as width x height

Notice how the chart labels (chl) come in the same order as the data (chd) they describe. Although 69 and 31 are held in a separate descriptor from the labels that describe them, the API knows which relates to which because of the order they follow.

EMBEDDING YOUR CHART

The chart is a graphic, so you could save it to your computer and upload it to your web host's server in the usual way. However, it's more efficient to make a direct call to Google's API from your page and have it handle the embedding on the fly. To do this, wrap it in an <img> image tag as follows:

```
<img src="http://chart.apis.google.com/
  chart?cht=p&amp;chd=t:69,31&amp;chl=
  Sunny|Rainy&amp;chs=300x200">
```

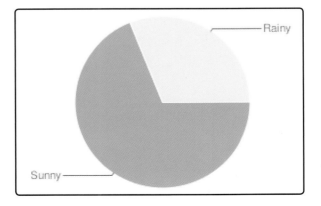

Left: Using Google Charts it's easy to make a quick pie chart using default colours and add more than two segments

Notice how we've changed each '&' to '&' when we've embedded the image. This is so the page renders the ampersand as an ampersand, not as the start of a special character. Enter this as a single line in any text editor, save it as chart.htm and open it in your browser. Your graph is now embedded on an otherwise empty web page (see the screen on the previous page), and you can mould it to meet your exact requirements.

WORKING ON THE APPEARANCE

Certain types of data – such as progress towards a known goal, or data that changes over time – can't be represented by a pie chart. In these instances, you would use a meter, line or bar chart. These charts are selected by changing the option that follows the cht delimiter to one of 10 other chart types, including Venn diagrams, scatter charts and 3D bar codes.

To invoke a meter chart to measure, for example, progress towards a fundraising goal, we'd change the chart type to cht=gom, which stands for Google-O-Meter. This is one of the simplest charts; it shows a single percentage measurement, where 0 per cent is no progress at all and 100 per cent marks completion. If our goal was to raise £5,000 and we had reached £4,000, we'd have raised 80 per cent and could represent it on a meter as follows:

http://chart.apis.google.com/chart?cht=gom&chd=t:80 &chl=£4,000!&chs=250x125

If you wanted to embed it in your page as an image, replace each '&' with '&'. Most web browsers reformat (encode) the URL. Some browsers, including Internet Explorer, don't encode the '£' we've put in our text label, but Chrome and Safari do. To include a pound sign (or any other non-ASCII character that isn't a-z, A-Z or 0-9), it's best to encode it yourself. The '£' becomes %C2%A3, and you can generate this at http://andrewu.co.uk/tools/uriencoder, taking the decoded text from the URL Safe Encoding box.

The default green to red gradient implies some kind of danger level receding as we raise more money, so we'l change it so it runs from light to dark blue. Specify a

start and end colour using hexadecimal codes, in which light blue is CCFFFF and dark blue 0000CC. We'll use the label chco (chart colour) within our URL, as follows:

http://chart.apis.google.com/chart?cht=gom&chd=t:80& chl=£4,000!&chs=250x125&chco=CCFFFF,0000CC

DRAWING A LINE

So far, we have plotted sets of only one or two data items. Let's return to our weather example and use a line chart to plot Cardiff's average temperatures for each month of the year between 1961 and 1990. Again, this data is drawn from the Met Office website. The URL is as follows:

http://chart.apis.google.com/chart?cht=lc&chs=400x200& chdt:7.5,7.6,10.1,13,16.3,19.2,21,20.7,18.2,14.7,10.6,8.5

Here, our chart type is a line chart (cht=lc) that's 400x200 pixels in size (chs=400x200). The long string of data that follows the 'cht=t:' is the mean temperatures for each month of the year, in degrees Celsius. The result is an accurately plotted graph, but not in the least informative:

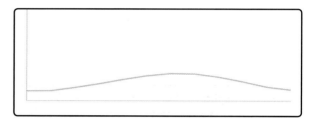

The range of data is so narrow, with the highest and lowest temperatures less than 13 degrees apart. To accentuate the climb and fall, we need to set the highest and lowest points on the scale manually. As the highest recorded temperature is 21 degrees, we'll set the maximum to 25; with the lowest being 7.5, we'll set the bottom of our scale to 5. We'll do this using the label chds to denote the chart data set, as follows:

http://chart.apis.google.com/chart?cht=lc&chs=400x200 &chd=t:7.5,7.6,10.1,13,16.3,19.2,21,20.7,18.2,14.7,10.6, 8.5&chds=5,25

Reload the graph, and you'll see that it's starting to make more sense, but it's still not clear what it shows. We need to add some labels and a scale. This is a two-stage operation: we need to warn the API that some labels are coming its way, and then tell it what those labels are. For the warning, add '&chxt=x,y' to the end of the URL above. This tells the API that we want data on both of our axes. Reload the page and you'll see them appear, although at the moment they bear little resemblance to the actual data we're showing; they simply mark out five divisions on each axis at 20, 40, 60, 80 and 100 per cent.

Right: Changing the colour of the Google-O-Meter removed any notion of danger from this fund-raising progress graph

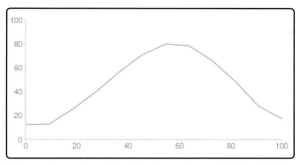

We need to replace the default numbers with data labels, taking each axis in turn. Each axis is assigned a number; the horizontal (x) axis is 0, and the vertical (y) axis is 1. We use these numbers to direct the labels to each axis, by adding the following to the end of our URL:

&chxl=0:|Jan|Feb|Mar|Apr|May|Jun|Jul|Aug|Sep| Oct|Nov|Dec|1:|5|10|15|20|25|

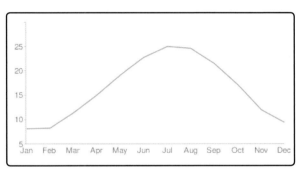

This looks complicated, but it's actually simple. We start with chxl, which is a label that stands for chart axis label. We then specify the words that appear on each axis. The 0 (the x axis) shows the months of the year. Notice that each one is separated by a pipe (|), just like the labels in the pie chart. However, unlike the pie chart example, we also include a pipe at the start and end of the string of labels, because we want to follow it with the data for the y axis (axis 1), which shows the temperatures. These run in five-degree increments between five and 25 degrees.

CLOSE RELATIONS
Now we just need to tie together the labels and the line, which, by the time you get to the middle of the year (when it has moved away from both axes), is difficult to relate to the labels. We'll do this with grid lines.

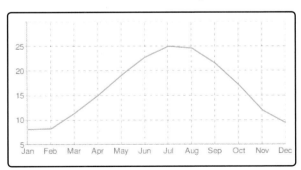

These are defined using the label chg (chart grid). Within this label we can set, among other things, the number of increments on each axis. With January and December on the start and end of our x axis, we need 10 vertical gridlines between them for the months of February to November, and five running horizontally, out from the measurements on the y axis.

When defining a scale, we need to convert our numbers into percentages. With ten divisions between the months for a total of 11 gaps, each one needs to be 9.09 per cent of the size of the total axis. With five temperature notches, each grid line running out of the y axis needs to be separated from its nearest neighbour by 20 per cent of the total axis height. The label and code we need to add to the end of our URL is therefore '&chg=9.09,20'.

PUTTING IT ALL TOGETHER
Finally, we need to give our chart a title. Chart titles are defined by the label chtt, with each word in the title linked by a '+' and legends denoted by the label chdl (chart data legend). They are added directly to the end of the URL, as follows:

&chtt=Avg+temp+in+Cardiff+1961+to+1990&chdl= Celsius

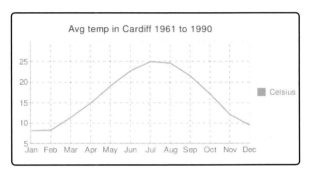

Our graph is now complete; the full URL below gives a line chart tracking the average monthly temperatures over a 30-year period, complete with manually specified limits on the temperature axis, grid lines and labels at each increment:

http://chart.apis.google.com/chart?cht=lc&chs=400x200 &chd=t:7.5,7.6,10.1,13,16.3,19.2,21,20.7,18.2,14.7,10.6,8 .5&chds=5,25&chxt=x,y&chxl=0:|Jan|Feb|Mar|Apr|M ay|Jun|Jul|Aug|Sep|Oct|Nov|Dec|1:|5|10|15|20|2 5|&chg=9.09,20&chtt=Avg+temp+in+Cardiff+1961+to+ 1990&chdl=Celsius

It's taken a while to build, but now it's in place we can copy the formula and tweak it for use in other situations. If the data should change, the results will be updated quickly without us having to re-plot our pixels with a mouse.

Embedding Google Maps on your site

Using Google Maps and some JavaScript, you can add a fully customised interactive map to your site to help your visitors get their bearings

SKILL LEVEL

Beginner
Intermediate
Expert

HOW LONG
2 hours

Google Maps (http://maps.google.co.uk) is more than just a website that shows maps. It's a fully customisable application that you can embed in your own website. By using the Google Maps JavaScript application programming interface (API), you can add maps to any web page, which can then be viewed in a normal web browser without requiring extra plug-ins. Using the Google Maps API, you can easily create annotated maps with information such as the location of your holiday home, travel directions, favourite places to hang out and anything else you can imagine.

JavaScript is a lightweight programming language that can be used to add interactivity to HTML pages. All modern web browsers support it. The JavaScript is stored separately from the HTML in files with a .js extension. This helps to keep your website presentation separate from the JavaScript code, and enables you to use the same functions in multiple HTML files without having to duplicate the code.

JavaScript files can be included in your HTML pages by using the script tag `<script src="test.js" type="text/javascript"></script>`. This should be placed in the `<head>` section of the HTML.

Below: This is all the code needed to show a Google Map on a web page

Alternatively, place the JavaScript code directly inside the `<script>` and `</script>` tags in the `<head>` section, as we've done in this project.

MAP READING

The Google Maps API is divided into four main sections: map objects, events, controls and overlays. Map objects are the JavaScript objects that represent the map and essentials such as the coordinate system. Events enable the map to respond to user interaction from the mouse and keyboard; they allow the map to pan when you click and drag the mouse, for example. Controls refer to the map controls used to pan and zoom, as well as other controls that can alter the type of map being viewed, such as satellite images. Overlays represent things that are shown onscreen, such as the map image itself. The Overlays section covers other things, such as lines, markers and informational windows such as speech bubbles.

The API allows you to fully customise a Google map. Just about everything can be altered, down to the content of the map itself. We can only cover the basics here, but a full reference for the Google Maps API can be found at http://code.google.com/apis/maps/documentation.

WORKING WITH THE API

The following script tag enables you to include the Google Maps API in an HTML web page:

```
<script src="http://maps.google.com/
  maps?file=api&amp;v=2&amp;key=<your
  key>" type="text/javascript"></script>
```

Once this script tag is in your HTML page, you'll have access to the API. The screen on the left shows an example that places a basic map into an HTML page. You can see a function that loads the map in the `<head>`

```
simple[1] - Notepad
File  Edit  Format  View  Help
<!DOCTYPE html PUBLIC "-//W3C//DTD XHTML 1.0 Strict//EN" "http://www.w3.org/TR/xhtml1/DTD/xhtml1-strict.dtd">
<html xmlns="http://www.w3.org/1999/xhtml">
  <head>
    <meta http-equiv="content-type" content="text/html; charset=utf-8"/>
    <title>Simple Map</title>
    <script src="http://maps.google.com/maps?file=api&amp;v=2&amp;key=lzT34RA" type="text/javascript"></script>
    <script type="text/javascript">

    function load()
    {
      if (GBrowserIsCompatible())
      {
        var map = new GMap2(document.getElementById("map"));
        map.setCenter(new GLatLng(51.500789, -0.142264), 13);
      }
    }

    </script>
  </head>
  <body onload="load()" onunload="GUnload()">
    <div id="map" style="width: 500px; height: 300px"></div>
  </body>
</html>
```

section with another set of script tags. First, the `load()` function checks that the current web browser is compatible with the Google Maps API. All modern web browsers are supported, but this ensures that the web page can respond to older web browsers without showing any errors. The second line creates a variable called `map`. This contains a GMap2 object, which is the core object that represents the map.

The map is created by passing a reference to the `div` (a structural HTML element) that will hold it (described in the `<body>` section). The `div` is referenced by using the `document.getElementById()` method, which gets elements in the HTML document by their ID attributes. The final line uses the `setCenter` function on the new map object to set the point at which the map is centred using a latitude and longitude coordinate. Don't worry where the values (51.500789, -0.142264) come from just yet. The parameter to `setCenter` sets the map zoom level from 0 (far out) to 20 (close in).

Next, you'll need to include the load function and create an area in the HTML page where you can place the map; this is shown between the `<body>` tags at the bottom of the screen opposite. The `<body>` tag uses two JavaScript event handlers that are used to manage the map. The `onload` attribute calls the JavaScript function that will create the map and which will be run when the HTML page is loaded. The `onunload` attribute is used to call `GUnload()` – defined by Google – which releases all memory used by the map when either the web browser is closed or a different HTML page is viewed. This is very important; if you don't call `GUnload()` then the resources used by the map won't be released and the web browser will gradually get slower, until it runs out of memory.

The `<div>` tag marks an area of the page that is to be filled by the map. Its ID needs to match the reference used by `document.getElementByID`, which was used earlier. Using CSS you can specify that the map should be 500 pixels high and 300 pixels wide. You can change these values as necessary. You can also use CSS rules to set where the map appears on the page.

If you go to www.redcotbarn.co.uk/advancedprojects/maps/simple.html, you'll see a map that's centred on Buckingham Palace. The map acts just like any other Google map, so you can click the map and drag it around, for example.

ADDING CONTROLS

The full Google Maps service has a scaling and positioning toolbar. This is disabled by default, but can be shown by adding the following line to the `load()` function in the code opposite:

```
map.addControl(new GLargeMapControl())
```

Other controls can also be added, many of which

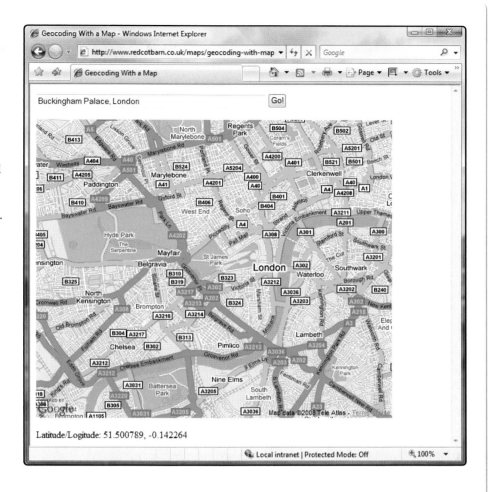

Latitude/Longitude: 51.500789, -0.142264

you'll see if you visit the website at http://maps.google.co.uk. These include `GSmallMapControl`, which creates a smaller control with no zooming slider bar, `GOverviewMapControl`, which adds an overview map to the bottom right-hand corner of the main map, `GSmallZoomControl`, which contains the zoom controls, and `GScaleControl`, which adds a scale legend that updates automatically when you zoom in or out. Furthermore, the scroll wheel on the mouse can be made to control the zoom level of the map using `map.enableScrollWheelZoom()`.

All these controls have default layout positions that are the same as those on Google Maps, but you can override the defaults and put them anywhere you like.

UPDATING LOCATIONS

Once you've got a map that can be controlled, you need to be able to update its starting location. This is done by changing the coordinates in the `GLatLng()` function. To work out the latitude and longitude coordinates of an address, we use a process called geocoding. Google provides a function to do this in its API, and we've implemented a version of it in the example here. It takes an address that you type in and displays a map of the location, along with the latitude

Above: On the Redcot Barn website, click the 'Geocoding with a map' link in the Advanced Projects section to type in a location and see its longitude and latitude

TIP
Before you can use Google Maps on your site, you need to request a key from http://code.google.com/apis/maps/signup.html. This key is registered to a domain name and helps Google to track usage statistics and prevent abuse of the service.

```
geocoding-with-map[1] - Notepad
File  Edit  Format  View  Help
<!DOCTYPE html PUBLIC "-//W3C//DTD XHTML 1.0 Strict//EN" "http://www.w3.org/TR/xhtml1/DTD/xhtml1-strict.dtd">
<html xmlns="http://www.w3.org/1999/xhtml">
  <head>
    <meta http-equiv="content-type" content="text/html; charset=utf-8"/>
    <title>Geocoding with a Map</title>
    <script src="http://maps.google.com/maps?file=api&amp;v=2&amp;key=lzT34RA" type="text/javascript"></script>
    <script type="text/javascript">

      var map = null;
      var geocoder = null;

      function load()
      {
        if (GBrowserIsCompatible())
        {
          map = new GMap2(document.getElementById("map"));
          map.setCenter(new GLatLng(51.500789, -0.142264), 13);

          geocoder = new GClientGeocoder();
        }
      }

      function findAddress(anAddress)
      {
        if (geocoder)
        {
          geocoder.getLatLng(anAddress, function(aPoint)
          {
            if (!aPoint)
            {
              alert("Sorry, can't locate [" + anAddress + "]");
            }
            else
            {
              map.setCenter(aPoint, 13);
              var elem = document.getElementById("latLng");
              elem.innerHTML = aPoint.lat() + ", " + aPoint.lng();
            }
          });
        }
      }

    </script>
  </head>
  <body onload="load()" onunload="GUnload()">
    <form action="#" onsubmit="findAddress(this.address.value); return false">
      <p>
        <input type="text" size="60" name="address" value="Buckingham Palace, London" />
        <input type="submit" value="Go!" />
      </p>
      <div id="map" style="width: 600px; height: 500px"></div>
      <p>Latitude/Logitude: <span id="latLng">51.500789, -0.142264</span></p>
    </form>
  </body>
</html>
```

Above: The code used to display the map in the screenshot on the previous page

and longitude at the bottom. Once you have the coordinates of your chosen location, you can enter these into the `setCenter` function.

CUSTOMISING YOUR MAP

Positioning the map is just the beginning. To make it really useful, you'll want to place markers to highlight specific locations, such as your house. Once you know the latitude and longitude coordinates for all the locations, this task is easy. Just use the following code in the `load()` function after the `setCenter()` line:

```
var latLng = new GLatLng(51.500789,
  -0.142264);
var marker = new GMarker(latLng);
```

```
map.addOverlay(marker);
```

This places a marker on the map, where Buckingham Palace is. You can add as many markers as you like, but you need to use new variable names, such as `latLng2` and `marker2`, `latLang3` and `marker3`.

You can then add information windows to the markers that look like speech bubbles, which are activated when the user clicks on a marker. These windows can contain any HTML you like, including pictures and links to other websites. Here is the important section:

```
var latLng = new GLatLng(51.500789,
  -0.142264);
var marker = new GMarker(latLng);
GEvent.addListener(marker, "click",
  function()
{
  marker.openInfoWindowHtml("<p>
    Buckingham Palace</p></p>London
    </p>");
});
map.addOverlay(marker);
```

`GEvent.addListener` is used to 'listen' for a mouse click on the specified marker. When the user clicks on the marker, the inner function is executed, causing an information window to be opened. You can have only one information window open at a time, but you can provide one information window for each marker.

GOING FURTHER

This has been a quick overview of the Google Maps API, but there's plenty more to explore. As we've said, every part of the API is customisable. You can change the appearance of all the controls and use custom images for the markers. On the simpler side, the GDirections utility provides driving instructions for navigating between two locations; this function is used for the gadget we showed you how to use on page 95. Still, you should now be able to create some impressive additions to your website.

Below: Here we can see the map with its standard controls (left), the thumbnail disabled and the controls repositioned (middle), and the marker and information bubble highlighted (right)

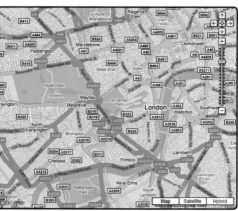
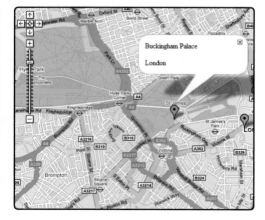

Hosting with Google Apps

Save yourself time, money and hassle by using Google Apps to host your own private versions of Docs, Calendar and Gmail

One of the main benefits of registering your own domain name is that you can get personalised email addresses. Unfortunately, the service you get often isn't as good or as usable as free services such as Google's Gmail client.

Luckily, you don't have to put up with substandard email interfaces any more. Google's Apps service allows you to use Gmail for your own private email addresses (as opposed to the @gmail.com address you get with a Gmail account), complete with 7GB of disk space and excellent web space. You can also have personalised Google Docs and Calendar services for free. Best of all, it's easy to set up and configure. Here, we'll show you how to get the ultimate email – and applications for your domain – for free.

UNDERSTANDING DNS

To arrange for Google to manage your email instead of your web-hosting company, you'll need to edit the DNS settings for your domain name. DNS is the service that converts the 'friendly' names that we see, such as www.redcotbarn.co.uk, into the IP addresses that computers use to communicate over the internet. Think of DNS as a kind of telephone directory for the internet, where you look up the IP address of a service using its name.

One of the most important DNS records is the Mail Exchange (MX) record, which tells incoming email messages where they should go. In order to change your email provider, the MX record for your domain needs to be changed, so that incoming mail will be sent to Google instead. You'll also need to make a second DNS change so that your email and other services are easier to access. By default, Google's services are accessed through a long Google URL, which isn't very helpful or easy to remember. If you'd like to be able to access your email through a more memorable URL using a

subdomain, such as http://webmail.redcotbarn.co.uk, you'll need to create a CName entry for your domain. This is a special DNS entry that tells a connecting web browser to where it should be redirecting.

This may sound like a daunting task, but it's very easy to do. However, you should check with your web-hosting provider to find out whether you can create or modify MX and CName entries for your domain, as not all providers allow this. If you've not yet chosen a web-hosting provider but want Google to handle your email, you should check each service to make sure that it allows the modification of MX and CName entries.

For example, WebFusion (www.webfusion.com) has a web control panel that doesn't support these changes. However, WebFusion's support can make the changes for you if requested by email. This is likely to be the same for other web hosts, too. All you'll have to do is provide the information that we'll be giving you over the next couple of pages.

SKILL LEVEL

Beginner
Intermediate
Expert

HOW LONG
2 days

Below: Type in the name of the domain you want to use for Google Apps, but don't use the leading 'www.'

Right: Updating the MX record tells your web host where to send incoming email

Below: You need to verify ownership of a domain by creating an MX record

In order to show the process more easily, though, we're using a Dreamhost account, as the control panel lets you make all the changes you need; Dreamhost is a US-based web-hosting provider. If you have to change your details by email, it's probably worth getting all the changes done in one go via a single message, using the table of settings opposite.

REGISTERING WITH GOOGLE
Before you start changing any DNS settings, you need to register your domain with Google. Go to www.google.com/a and click on the 'See details and sign up' button. The next page will try to get you to sign up for the premium service, which costs $50 (around £31) per email user per year, and gives you more disk space, a guaranteed level of service and no adverts. You can upgrade to this later, but for now just stick with the free version. Click on the Standard Edition link below the large blue button and then click Get Started.

Select 'Administrator: I own or control this domain' and type your domain name into the box, remembering not to add the leading 'www.', then click Get Started. Fill out your contact details, type in a valid email address, and click Continue. Choose a username that will be used to manage this account. This will also be the primary email address (in the style 'username@yourdomain.com'). Enter a password and click 'I accept. Continue with setup'.

Next, you'll be asked to verify that you own the domain. There are two ways of doing this in Google: you

TIP
Manage your domain by going to www.google.com/a and selecting 'Returning user, sign in here'. You'll be able to create new users and add new applications.

Custom MX Records
Advanced users only. This can easily break your email!

MX Record: required	ASPMX.L.GOOGLE.COM
MX Record:	
MX Record:	
MX Record:	
MX Record:	
MX Record:	
MX Record:	
MX Record:	

(Your mail will be delivered to these mail servers rather than DreamHost.)

I will still check my email at DreamHost. ☐
Check this **only** if you're using the MX of an outside spam filtering service like Postini that still

either have to upload a file to your web-hosting account that Google provides, or create a new CName DNS record. The second option is good if you don't have any web hosting and use your account only for email. For either method, follow the onscreen instructions and then click the Verify button.

ACTIVATING EMAIL
Once you've verified your account, Google will let you configure the services it offers – we'll start with email. First, make sure that you've downloaded all your messages from your current service provider to your computer. We'll show you how to upload these messages to your new account shortly.

On the configuration page, click the Activate email link. On the next page, you'll be given instructions on how to edit your account's DNS settings to update your MX record. This tells your web host where to send any incoming mail. Open a new browser window, log on to your web-hosting package, edit your DNS settings and go to the MX settings page. Delete every entry in there and make the first entry 'ASPMX.L.GOOGLE.COM.' – don't forget to include the '.' at the end of the 'COM'. Save the changes. Go back to the Google Apps page and click 'I have completed these steps'.

Google will now check that your MX record has been updated, which can take up to 48 hours to complete. Until this step is finished, you can't edit any more settings, so keep checking your account for changes. You may log on to find that Google is updating its servers, which could take up to an hour to complete. This is simply Google creating disk space and setting up email hosting for your account. You can't do anything until this process has finished.

SELECTING A CUSTOM URL
Once your email has been activated, you'll be able to receive email at the address you specified when you registered for Google Apps. To access this email account, Google gives you a very long URL, which is hard to

(optional)

Nameserver 4:
(optional)

Set these nameservers for davidludlo

Add a custom DNS record to davidludlow.com:

Name: ogle6bbccd006b3ec10a.davidludlow.com
(leave blank for just 'davidludlow.com')

Type: CNAME ▾
(Want MX? Go here!)

Value: google.com

Comment: Domain Verification

Add Record Now!

Non-editable DreamHost DNS records for davidludlow.com:

Record (davidludlow.com zone)		Type	Value
		A	208.113.193.227
		NS	ns1.dreamhost.com.
		NS	ns2.dreamhost.com.
		NS	ns3.dreamhost.com.
	ftp	A	208.113.193.227
	www	A	208.113.193.227

remember. Fortunately, you can change this for a custom URL, such as mail.yourdomain.com.

To do this, click on the Email link in the Google Apps Dashboard and then click Change URL. After that, click on the second Radio button and type in the custom URL you want. Google defaults to mail.yourdomain.com, but you can choose anything followed by '.yourdomain.com'. Click Continue. To finish configuration, open a new window, access your web host control panel, create a new CName record with the URL you just created for your email, and point it at ghs.google.com. Once this is done, click 'I've completed these steps'. It takes up to a couple of hours after the DNS records have been updated before you can access your email using the new URL.

UPLOADING YOUR OLD EMAIL

With your email working, you can upload your old email to your new account using Google's Email Uploader (http://code.google.com/p/google-email-uploader). This free utility can upload email from Outlook, Outlook Express and Thunderbird email clients to your Google account. Unfortunately, Windows Mail isn't currently supported.

Download the application to your computer and install it. Don't worry if you get 'Error 2' when installing it under Windows – the application will still have installed successfully. Run Email Uploader and type in your username and password for your Google account, then click Sign In. The application will list any compatible email applications that you have installed. Use the tree structure to select the folders and contacts you want to upload, click Next and then click Upload to transfer your messages to your new account.

GETTING BETTER ACCESS

If you're used to accessing your email via a desktop application, you may not want to use your new email's web interface all the time. Fortunately, you don't have to, as you can use IMAP access. Unlike POP email access, IMAP stores your email on a server, and changes made by your desktop client are reflected in the web client – and vice versa. To enable IMAP access, log on to your email and click the Settings link at the top of the page. Click on Forwarding and POP/IMAP, and click Enable

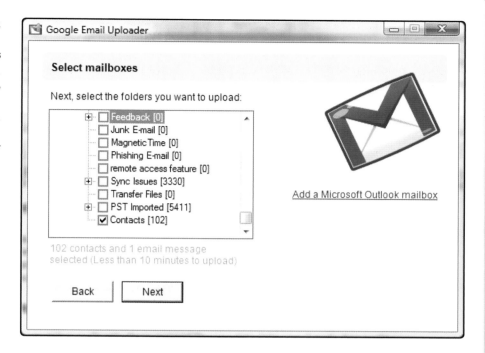

Add a Microsoft Outlook mailbox

Above: Google's free utility allows you to upload all your old emails to your new account

IMAP. Then click Save Changes. How you get your email client working depends on the application you're using, but Google provides detailed instructions for all the common applications at http://tinyurl.com/yvzozd.

GOING BEYOND EMAIL

If you log on to the Dashboard for your domain, you'll see that several services have already been activated. These include Calendar for organising appointments, Docs for creating and sharing office documents online, and Sites, which lets you create your own website easily. These are all private versions of the services that Google already offers to all web users.

Each of the services will be set so it can be accessed only by a long Google URL. This is easy to change. Click on the name of the service you want to set and click on the Change URL link. Click the second radio button and type in the subdomain you want to use, such as calendar.yourdomain.com. As with the URL you changed for your email access, you need a CName record that points at ghs.google.com for each URL you created.

Table of settings

Service	Suggested URL	DNS Type	DNS Record
Email	N/A	MX	ASPMX.L.GOOGLE.COM.
Email	mail.yourdomain.com	CName	ghs.google.com
Docs	docs.yourdomain.com	CName	ghs.google.com
Calendar	calendar.yourdomain.com	CName	ghs.google.com

Glossary

AJAX Asynchronous JavaScript and XML. Used to create interactive web page elements, Ajax enables web apps to exchange data with a web server in the background and update parts of a web page without reloading it.

Alt tags Text included in an HTML `<img>` tag to be displayed in place of an image when it can't be displayed, or when the mouse is hovered over it.

Android A mobile phone operating system owned by Google.

API Application Programming Interface. This is an interface for letting web browsers or web servers communicate with other programs.

Bandwidth The amount of data that can be transferred in a specified amount of time. With websites, this tends to refer to the amount of data that can be uploaded and downloaded per month.

Body Everything within the `<body>` section of an HTML page is displayed in a web browser.

Bookmark A link to a particular website, saved for future use so the visitor can easily return to the same page without searching for it, or typing in a URL.

Blog Short for web log, a blog is a regularly updated website that usually contains diary entries or news stories.

Broken link A link that, when clicked on, leads to an error message because the destination page doesn't exist.

Browser An application used to view web pages. The most popular is Microsoft's Internet Explorer, but Firefox, Chrome and Safari are significant others.

Compression Storing data in a format that uses less disk space and bandwidth. Image files are typically compressed to make them around a tenth of their original size.

CSS Cascading Style Sheets provide more control over a layout than HTML. When you use CSS, you can make a single change that automatically updates every web page on your site.

CSS3 The latest version of CSS. It allows you to create effects such as shadows and rounded corners without resorting to using a graphics program or complex programming.

Directory See Folder.

Domain name A unique address for a website that includes everything up to the .com or other extension; for example, in www.redcotbarn.co.uk the domain name is *redcotbarn*.

Download Transfer of a file from a website to your computer's hard disk.

Dynamic Refers to any interactive parts of a website, such as a Google Map or a YouTube video, where visitors can control the object's behaviour.

Flash A vector-based multimedia format developed by Adobe for use on the web. It's commonly used for videos, games and animations.

Folder A named container on your hard disk that stores a collection of files.

FTP File Transfer Protocol. An FTP application allows you to upload your website from your hard disk to your web-hosting provider's server.

GIF Graphics interchange format. An image format similar to PNG that is well suited to logos, icons or images with only a small number of colours.

Head The top section of an HTML page, which gives the web browser information about how the page

should be displayed, along with links to related CSS files. This can also contain meta tags.

Hits The number of times a web page is visited, measured by tools such as Google Analytics.

Host see Web-hosting provider.

HTML The language web browsers use to interpret how pages are displayed.

HTML5 The latest version of HTML. It isn't yet an official standard, but most modern web browsers support it to some extent. HTML5 simplifies the code needed for a web page.

HTTP HyperText Transfer Protocol. A set of rules that are used to transfer files from web servers to web browsers.

Hyperlink see Link.

JavaScript A programming language that provides a way to produce dynamic content on a web pages.

JPG or **JPEG** Joint Photographic Experts Group Format. The most common image format used on the internet, usually used for photos.

Keywords Search terms entered into a search engine to locate relevant websites. These words should be used as meta tags on web pages to improve search rankings.

Link A page element that, when clicked on, takes the visitor to another page in your site or an external website.

Menu See Navigation bar.

Meta tag A keyword that describes the content of a web page, stored in the `<head>` section of each HTML file. Meta tags can be used by search engines as part of the ranking process, which determines how relevant a website is to a user's search.

MP3 One of the most common audio formats used on the internet, and compatible with virtually all computers and audio players.

MySQL An open-source database management system that uses the SQL programming language to add, remove and modify information in the database.

Navigation bar A set of links that help visitors navigate to the main sections of your website. Navigation bars are commonly placed across the top of the page, vertically on the left-hand side and across the bottom of a web page.

Open source Any program for which the source code – the collection of human-readable files that are converted into a computer-executable format – is made publicly available for use or modification.

Page impressions Also known as page hits, this is the number of times a web page has been visited.

PHP Recursive acronym that stands for PHP hypertext preprocessor. PHP is a web-scripting language which is typically used to produce HTML web pages, but can also produce images.

PNG Portable Network Graphic. An image format originally designed as an alternative to GIF. Unlike GIF, animation is not supported, but like GIF, PNG files don't lose any data when compressed.

Podcast An audio version of a blog. Podcasts are usually relatively short radio-style clips that contain spoken information or entertainment, which can include music.

Resolution The resolution of a monitor, measured in pixels, indicates how much information can fit onscreen. A typical resolution is 1,024x768, which refers to the number of horizontal and vertical pixels respectively.

RSS feeds Standing for Really Simple Syndication, an RSS feed is a regularly updated information source that tells RSS reader programs about new blog posts, news stories or podcasts that are available on a certain website.

Scripts Short pieces of programming code that perform actions on a web page. Scripts can include code written in programming languages including Java, PHP, Perl, CGI, ASP and others.

Search engine optimisation Usually referred to as SEO, this is the technique or techniques used to increase a website's ranking on a search engine.

Server space The storage for websites provided by web-hosting companies.

Site map An ordered set of text links that lists all the pages on a website in one convenient place.

SSL Secure sockets layer. An encryption technology used for ensuring the security of data sent across the internet.

Streaming Content such as video or audio that is viewed by a user while it is being delivered to them over an internet or network connection.

Subdomain Some web hosts allow you to create several separate websites using similar domain names to your main website. For example, a subdomain of www.eppingkarate.co.uk could be www.members.eppingkarate.co.uk.

Tag Notifications or commands in an HTML document which define how it looks and works.

Thumbnail A small image or photograph, which can usually be clicked on to see a larger version.

TLD Top-level domain. This is the final part of a website's URL. Examples include .com, .co.uk, .org, .gov.uk, .net and many others.

Traffic The number of visitors to a website.

Uniques When analysing visitors to a website, the number of uniques is the number of different users viewing it. This figure is often more useful than knowing the total number of page impressions or hits.

Upload The process of copying your website files from your hard disk to your web host's servers.

URL Uniform resource locator. This is the unique address of every page on the web. For example, www.bbc.co.uk is unique to the BBC's homepage, while www.redcotbarn.co.uk/ directions/index.html will take you straight to Redcot Barn's Driving Directions page.

Visitor Someone arriving at a page on your website either by typing its URL into their web browser or clicking on a link from another website or a search engine. Used interchangeably with 'user' and 'reader'.

Web Short for World Wide Web. Invented in 1990 by Sir Tim Berners-Lee.

Web-hosting provider A service provider that stores your website on its servers to make it constantly available to visitors. Other services, such as email, can also be included.

Web page An HTML document that forms part of a website.

Web-safe colours Not all web browsers can display all colours, but most support a standardised selection of 256 colours. Using only web-safe colours ensures your website will be correctly displayed since, if a browser cannot display any of the colours you chose, it will display alternatives.

Web server A computer that runs the necessary software and has the networking capabilities to deliver web pages over HTTP. The software used is typically Apache or IIS.

Website builder A software application or an online program that can be used to create a website.

WYSIWYG What you see is what you get. A WYSIWYG editor is one that allows you to create web pages in a graphical form, much like desktop publishing software. It automatically converts the pages you create into the required HTML code.

XML Xtensible Markup Language. Similar to HTML but, instead of describing the content of a web page, XML describes the content in terms of what data is being described.

BUILD A BETTER WEBSITE 2013

EDITORIAL
Editor
David Ludlow
Production Editor
Steve Haines
Art Editor
Colin Mackleworth
Digital Production Manager
Nicky Baker
Cover illustration
Ian Naylor

CONTRIBUTORS
Gareth Beach, Emily Hodges,
James Lumgair, David McKinnon,
Mike Mosedale, Matt Preston,
Julian Prokaza, Nik Rawlinson,
Matthew Sparkes, Dave Stevenson

PHOTOGRAPHY
Danny Bird, Jan Cihak

ADVERTISING
Account Manager Katie Wood

MANAGEMENT
MagBooks Publisher
Dharmesh Mistry
Operations Director
Robin Ryan
MD Advertising
Julian Lloyd-Evans
Newstrade Director
David Barker
Commercial & Retail Director
Martin Belson
Chief Operating Officer
Brett Reynolds
Group Finance Director
Ian Leggett
Chief Executive
James Tye
Chairman
Felix Dennis

MAG**BOOK**

The 'MagBook' brand is a
trademark of Dennis Publishing Ltd,
30 Cleveland St, London W1T 4JD.
Company registered in England.
All material © Dennis Publishing Ltd,
licensed by Felden 2012, and may
not be reproduced in whole or part
without the consent of the publishers.

LICENSING & SYNDICATION
To license this product, please
contact Carlotta Serantoni on
+44 20 7907 6550, email
carlotta_serantoni@dennis.co.uk.
For syndication queries, please
contact Anj Dosaj-Halai on +44 20
7907 6132, email anj_dosaj-halai@
dennis.co.uk.

LIABILITY
While every care was taken during
the production of this MagBook, the
publishers cannot be held responsible
for the accuracy of the information
or any consequence arising from
it. Dennis Publishing takes no
responsibility for the companies
advertising in this MagBook.

Printed by BGP, Bicester, Oxon.

The paper used within this MagBook
is produced from sustainable fibre,
manufactured by mills with a valid
chain of custody.

ISBN 1-78106-043-6

When you have finished with
this magazine please recycle it.